# Asset Management

# Asset Management

**Edited by**
Joseph Lowell

Willford Press
www.willfordpress.com

Published by Willford Press,
118-35 Queens Blvd., Suite 400,
Forest Hills, NY 11375, USA



ISBN: 978-1-68285-456-3

**Cataloging-in-Publication Data**

Asset management / edited by Joseph Lowell.
p. cm.
Includes bibliographical references and index.
ISBN 978-1-68285-456-3
1. Assets (Accounting)--Management. 2. Management. I. Lowell, Joseph.
HF5681.A8 A87 2018
657.7--dc23

For information on all Willford Press publications
visit our website at www.willfordpress.com

WILLFORD PRESS

Printed in China.

# Contents

# Preface

Asset management refers to the practice of controlling, managing, and maintaining any type of assets, both tangible and intangible. Assets are generally concerned with things which have a financial value to a company or a firm like stocks, land, buildings, production plants, machinery, pension fund, etc. The different sub-fields of asset management include, enterprise management, financial asset management, public asset management, etc. Most of the topics introduced in this text cover new techniques and the applications of asset management. In this book, constant effort has been made to make the understanding of the difficult concepts of asset management as easy and informative as possible, for the readers. The textbook is appropriate for those seeking detailed information in this area.

A detailed account of the significant topics covered in this book is provided below:

Chapter 1- Assets are resources that can produce value owned by individuals and organizations. Current asset, financial asset, intangible asset, stranded asset, net operating assets, hard asset and capital asset are some types of assets. This is an introductory chapter which will introduce briefly all the significant aspects of asset management.

Chapter 2- Asset management is the management of the value of an entity. Infrastructure asset management, IT asset management, fixed assets management, asset health management and digital asset management are some topics related to asset management which play a key role in the process. This chapter is an overview of the subject matter incorporating all the major aspects of asset management.

Chapter 3- Fixed asset is the property that cannot be converted into cash. They can be of two types: freehold assets and leasehold assets. Fixed asset register and fixed-asset turnover are important topics in regard with the subject matter. This chapter has been carefully written to provide an easy understanding of the varied facets of fixed asset.

Chapter 4- Liquid assets are assets that can be bought and sold without much effect to the price of the asset. The most liquid asset is cash. Liquidation is the process of exchanging a less liquid asset to a more liquid asset. The topics elaborated in this chapter will help in gaining a better perspective about liquid assets.

Chapter 5- Investment is done with the intention of some benefit in the future. Investment management, P2P asset management, investment strategy, assets under management, global assets under management and separately managed account have been explained. This chapter is an overview of the subject matter incorporating all the major aspects of investment and investment management.

Chapter 6- Depreciation is the decrease in the value of any asset. Some of the methods of depreciation are straight-line depreciation, annuity depreciation, doubling declining balance method, group depreciation method and composite depreciation method. The chapter on depreciation offers an insightful focus, keeping in mind the complex subject matter.

Chapter 7- Turnkey asset management program is used to outsource the client's assets whereas mobile enterprise asset management is the maintenance of public assets, building and grounds. Mobile asset management and asset integrity management systems are other topics included in this section. The topics discussed in the chapter are of great importance to broaden the existing knowledge of asset management.

Chapter 8- Assets need to be maintained in order to protect them from wear and tear. Effective maintenance involves systematic checking and assessment of fixed assets through scheduled maintenance and preventive maintenance. Asset management is best understood in confluence with the major topics listed in the following chapter.

Chapter 9- The software used in asset management are software asset management, asset recovery software, ManageEngine AssetExplorer, AMS device manager, rational asset manager and computerized maintenance management system. Software asset management is the practice of managing the maintenance and deployment of the software application of any institution. The major software used in asset management are discussed in this chapter.

It gives me an immense pleasure to thank our entire team for their efforts. Finally in the end, I would like to thank my family and colleagues who have been a great source of inspiration and support.

**Editor**

1

# An Overview of Assets and its Types

Assets are resources that can produce value owned by individuals and organizations. Current asset, financial asset, intangible asset, stranded asset, net operating assets, hard asset and capital asset are some types of assets. This is an introductory chapter which will introduce briefly all the significant aspects of asset management.

## Asset

An asset is an economic resource. Anything tangible or intangible that can be owned or controlled to produce value and that is held by a company to produce positive economic value is an asset. Simply stated, assets represent value of ownership that can be converted into cash (although cash itself is also considered an asset).

The balance sheet of a firm records the monetary value of the assets owned by that firm. It covers money and other valuables belonging to an individual or to a business. One can classify assets into two major asset classes: tangible assets and intangible assets. Tangible assets contain various subclasses, including current assets and fixed assets. Current assets include inventory, while fixed assets include such items as buildings and equipment.

Intangible assets are nonphysical resources and rights that have a value to the firm because they give the firm some kind of advantage in the marketplace. Examples of intangible assets include goodwill, copyrights, trademarks, patents and computer programs, and financial assets, including such items as accounts receivable, bonds and stocks.

## Formal Definition

An asset is a resource controlled by the entity as a result of past events and from which future economic benefits are expected to flow to the entity (Framework Par 49a).

## Characteristics

One of the most widely accepted accounting definitions of asset is the one used by the International Accounting Standards Board. The following is a quotation from the IFRS Framework: "An asset is a resource controlled by the enterprise as a result of past events and from which future economic benefits are expected to flow to the enterprise."

This means that:

- The probable present benefit involve a capacity, singly or in combination with other assets, in the case of profit oriented enterprises, to contribute directly or indirectly to future net cash flows, and, in the case of nonprofit organizations, to provide services;
- The entity can control access to the benefit;
- The transaction or event giving rise to the entity's right to, or control of, the benefit has already occurred.

Employees are not considered assets like machinery is, even though they can generate future economic benefits. This is because an entity does not have sufficient control over its employees to satisfy the Framework's definition of an asset. Resources that are expected to yield benefits only for a short time can also be considered not to be assets, for example in the USA the 12 month rule excludes items with a useful life of less than a year.

Similarly, in economics an asset is any form in which wealth can be held.

## Accounting

In the financial accounting sense of the term, it is not necessary to be able to legally enforce the asset's benefit for qualifying a resource as being an asset, provided the entity can control its use by other means.

The accounting equation is the mathematical structure of the balance sheet. It relates assets, liabilities, and owner's equity:

Assets = Liabilities + Capital (where capital for a corporation equals owner's equity)
Liabilities = Assets – Capital
Equity = Assets – Liabilities

Assets are listed on the balance sheet. On a company's balance sheet certain divisions are required by generally accepted accounting principles (GAAP), which vary from country to country. Assets can be divided into e.g. current assets and fixed assets, often with further subdivisions such as cash, receivables and inventory.

Assets are formally controlled and managed within larger organizations via the use of asset tracking tools. These monitor the purchasing, upgrading, servicing, licensing, disposal etc., of both physical and non-physical assets.

## Current Assets

Current assets are cash and other assets expected to be converted to cash or consumed either in a year or in the operating cycle (whichever is longer), without disturbing the normal operations of a business. These assets are continually turned over in the course of a business during normal business activity. There are 5 major items included into current assets:

1. Cash and cash equivalents – it is the most liquid asset, which includes currency, deposit accounts, and negotiable instruments (e.g., money orders, cheque, bank drafts).

2. Short-term investments – include securities bought and held for sale in the near future to generate income on short-term price differences (trading securities).

3. Receivables – usually reported as net of allowance for non-collectable accounts.

4. Inventory – trading these assets is a normal business of a company. The inventory value reported on the balance sheet is usually the historical cost or fair market value, whichever is lower. This is known as the "lower of cost or market" rule.

5. Prepaid expenses – these are expenses paid in cash and recorded as assets before they are used or consumed (common examples are insurance or office supplies).

Marketable securities: Securities that can be converted into cash quickly at a reasonable price.

The phrase *net current assets* (also called *working capital*) is often used and refers to the total of current assets less the total of current liabilities.

## Long-term Investments

Often referred to simply as "investments". Long-term investments are to be held for many years and are not intended to be disposed of in the near future. This group usually consists of three types of investments:

1. Investments in securities such as bonds, common stock, or long-term notes.

2. Investments in fixed assets not used in operations (e.g., land held for sale).

3. Investments in special funds (e.g. sinking funds or pension funds).

Different forms of insurance may also be treated as long term investments.

## Fixed Assets

Also referred to as PPE (property, plant, and equipment), these are purchased for continued and long-term use in earning profit in a business. This group includes as an asset land, buildings, machinery, furniture, tools, IT equipment, e.g., laptops, and certain wasting resources e.g., timberland and minerals. They are written off against profits over their anticipated life by charging depreciation expenses (with exception of land assets). Accumulated depreciation is shown in the face of the balance sheet or in the notes. An asset is an important factor in a balance sheet.

These are also called capital assets in management accounting.

## Intangible Assets

Intangible assets lack of physical substance and usually are very hard to evaluate. They include patents, copyrights, franchises, goodwill, trademarks, trade names, etc. These assets are (according to US GAAP) amortized to expense over 5 to 40 years with the exception of goodwill.

Websites are treated differently in different countries and may fall under either tangible or intangible assets.

## Tangible Assets

Tangible assets are those that have a physical substance, such as currencies, buildings, real estate, vehicles, inventories, equipment, art collections, and precious metals.

Depreciation is applied to tangible assets when those assets have an anticipated lifespan of more than one year. This process of depreciation is used instead of allocating the entire expense to one year.

Tangible assets such as art, furniture, stamps, gold, wine, toys and books have become recognized as an asset class in their own right and many high-net-worth individuals will seek to include these tangible assets as part of their overall asset portfolio. This has created a need for tangible asset managers.

## Comparison: Current Assets, Liquid Assets and Absolute Liquid Assets

| Current assets | Liquid assets | Absolute liquid assets |
|---|---|---|
| Stocks | | |
| Prepaid expenses | | |
| Bills receivable | Bills receivable | |
| Cash in hand | Cash in hand | Cash in hand |
| Cash at bank | Cash at bank | Cash at bank |
| Accrued incomes | Accrued incomes | Accrued incomes |
| Loans and advances (short term) | Loans and advances (short term) | Loans and advances (short term) |
| Trade investments (short term) | Trade investments (short term) | Trade investments (short term) |

## Asset (Economics)

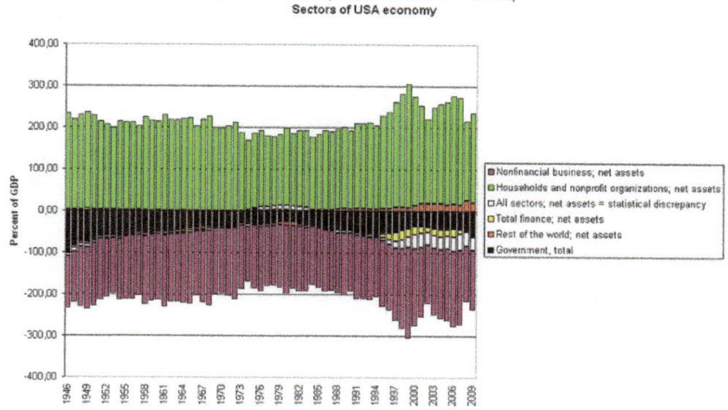


Net financial assets of sectors of USA economy, 1945-2009

An asset in economic theory is an output good which can only be partially consumed (like a portable music player) or input as a factor of production (like a cement mixer) which can only be partially used up in production. The necessary quality for an asset is that value remains after the period of analysis so it can be used as a store of value. As such, financial instruments like corporate bonds and common stocks are assets because they store value for the next period. If the good or factor is used up before the next period, there would be nothing upon which to place a value.

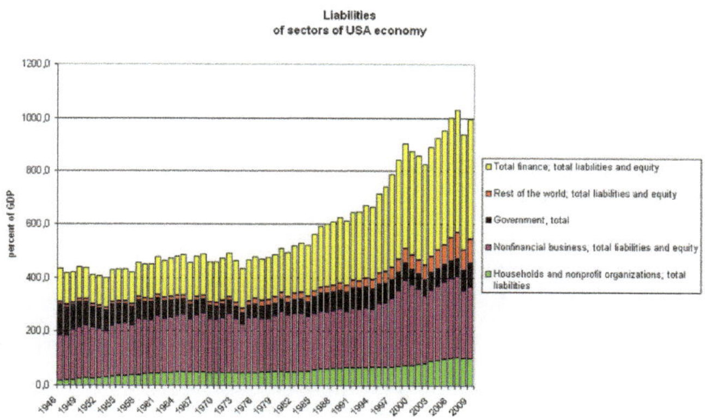


Liabilites of sectors of USA economy, 1945-2009, based on flow of funds statistics of the Federal Reserve System.

As a result of this definition, assets only have positive futures prices. This is analogous to the distinction between consumer durables and non-durables. Durables last more than one year. A classic durable is an automobile. A classic non-durable is an apple, which is eaten and lasts less than one year. Assets are that category of output which economic theory places prices upon. In a simple Walrasian equilibrium model, there is but a single period and all items have prices. In a multi-period equilibrium model, while all items have prices in the current period. Only assets can survive into the next period and thus only assets can store value and as a result, only assets have a price today for delivery tomorrow. Items which depreciate 100% by tomorrow have no price for delivery tomorrow because by tomorrow it ceases to exist.

The subfield of asset pricing (or valuation) is the financial evaluation of the value of such assets; the primary method used by today's financial analysts is the discounted cash flow method (DDM). Under the DDM, an asset's future cash flows are either assumed to be known with certainty (as in a Treasury Bond which is risk free) or estimated. These future cash flows are discounting used present values.

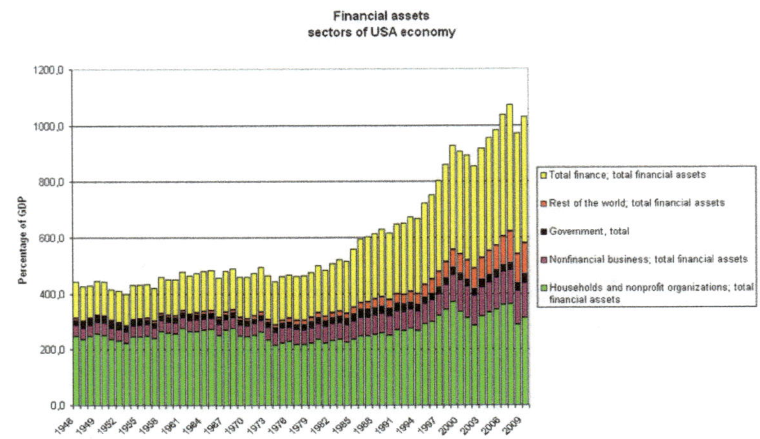


Financial assets of sectors of USA economy, 1945-2009, based on flow of funds statistics of the Federal Reserve System.

The Flow of Funds tables from the Federal Reserve System provide data about assets, which are tangible assets and financial assets, and liabilities. The difference, assets minus liabilites, is net worth.

## Current Asset

In accounting, a current asset is any asset which can reasonably be expected to be sold, consumed, or exhausted through the normal operations of a business within the current fiscal year or operating cycle (whichever period is longer). Typical current assets include cash, cash equivalents, short-term investments (marketable securities), accounts receivable, stock inventory, supplies, and the portion of prepaid liabilities, sometimes referred to as prepaid expenses, which will be paid within a year.

On a balance sheet, assets will typically be classified into current assets and long-term assets.

The current ratio is calculated by dividing total current assets by total current liabilities. It is frequently used as an indicator of a company's liquidity, its ability to meet short-term obligations.

The quick ratio, or acid-test, measures the ability of a company to use its *near cash* or quick assets to extinguish or retire its current liabilities immediately. Quick assets are those that can be quickly turned into cash if necessary.

## Related Accounting Topics

Associated accounting issues include recognizing accounts receivable, valuing accounts receivable, and disposing of accounts receivable.

In the UK, most companies have a credit control department.

Other types of accounting transactions include accounts payable, payroll, and trial balance.

## Intangible Asset

An intangible asset is an asset that lacks physical substance (unlike physical assets such as machinery and buildings) and usually is very hard to evaluate. It includes patents, copyrights, franchises, goodwill, trademarks, trade names, the general interpretation also includes software and other intangible computer based assets. Contrary to other assets, they generally—though not necessarily—suffer from typical market failures of non-rivalry and non-excludability.

## Definition

Intangible assets have been argued to be one possible contributor to the disparity between company value as per their accounting records, and company value as per their market capitalization. Considering this argument, it is important to understand what an intangible asset truly is in the eyes of an accountant. A number of attempts have been made to define intangible assets:

- Prior to 2005 the Australian Accounting Standards Board issued the Statement of Accounting Concepts number 4 (SAC 4). This statement did not provide a formal definition of an intangible asset but did provide that tangibility was not an essential characteristic of asset.
- International Accounting Standards Board standard 38 (IAS 38) defines an intangible asset as: "an identifiable non-monetary asset without physical substance." This definition is in addition to the standard definition of an asset which requires a *past event* that has given rise to a resource that the entity *controls* and from which *future economic benefits* are expected to flow. Thus, the extra requirement for an intangible asset under IAS 38 is *identifiability*. This criterion requires that an intangible asset is separable from the entity or that it arises from a contractual or legal right.
- The Financial Accounting Standards Board Accounting Standard Codification 350 (ASC 350) defines an intangible asset as an asset, other than a financial asset, that lacks physical substance.

The lack of physical substance would therefore seem to be a defining characteristic of an intangible asset. Both the IASB and FASB definitions specifically preclude monetary assets in their definition of an intangible asset. This is necessary in order to avoid the classification of items such as accounts receivable, derivatives and cash in the bank as an intangible asset. IAS 38 contains examples of intangible assets, including: computer software, copyright and patents.

## Research and Development

R&D is considered as one among several other intangible assets (e.g., about 16 percent of all intangible assets in the US ), even if most countries treat R&D as current expenses for both legal and tax purposes. While most countries report some intangibles in their National Income and Product Accounts (NIPA), no country has included a comprehensive measure of intangible assets. Yet, economists recognize the growing contribution of intangible assets in long-term GDP growth.

IAS 38 requires any project that results in the generation of a resource to the entity be classified into two phases: a research phase, and a development phase.

Research is defined as "the original and planned investigation undertaken with the prospect of gaining new scientific or technical knowledge and understanding. For example, a company can carry a research on one of its products which it will use in the entity of which results in future economic income.

Development is defined as "the application of research findings to a plan or design for the production of new or substantially improved materials, devices, products, processes, systems, or services, before the start of commercial production or use."

The accounting treatment of such expenses depends on whether it is classified as research or development. Where the distinction cannot be made, IAS 38 requires that the entire project be treated as research and expensed through the Statement of Comprehensive Income.

As research expenditure is highly speculative, there is no certainty that future economic benefits will flow to the entity. As such, prudence dictates that research expenditure be expensed through the Statement of Comprehensive Income. Development expenditure, however, is less speculative and it becomes possible to predict the future economic benefits that will flow to the entity. The matching concept dictates that development expenditure be capitalised as the expenditure will generate future economic benefit to the entity.

The classification of research and development expenditure can be highly subjective, and it is important to note that organisations may have an ulterior motive in its classification of research and development expenditure. Less scrupulous directors may manipulate financial statements through their classification of research and development expenditure.

## Financial Accounting

### General Standards

The International Accounting Standards Board (IASB) offers some guidance (IAS 38) as to how intangible assets should be accounted for in financial statements. In general, legal intangibles that are developed internally are not recognized and legal intangibles that are purchased from third parties are recognized. Wordings are similar to IAS 9.

Under US GAAP, intangible assets are classified into: Purchased vs. internally created intangibles, and Limited-life vs. indefinite-life intangibles.

### Expense Allocation

Intangible assets are typically expensed according to their respective life expectancy. Intangible assets have either an identifiable or indefinite useful life. Intangible assets with identifiable useful lives are amortized on a straight-line basis over their economic or legal life, whichever is shorter. Examples of intangible assets with identifiable useful lives include copyrights and patents. Intangible assets with indefinite useful lives are reassessed each year for impairment. If an impairment has occurred, then a loss must be recognized. An impairment loss is determined by subtracting the asset's fair value from the asset's book/carrying value. Trademarks and goodwill are examples of intangible assets with indefinite useful lives. Goodwill has to be tested for impairment rather than amortized. If impaired, goodwill is reduced and loss is recognized in the Income statement.

### Taxation

For personal income tax purposes, some costs with respect to intangible assets must be capitalized rather than treated as deductible expenses. Treasury regulations generally require capitalization of costs associated with acquiring, creating, or enhancing intangible assets. For example, an amount paid to obtain a trademark must be capitalized. Certain amounts paid to facilitate these transactions are also capitalized. Some types of intangible assets are categorized based on whether the asset is acquired from another party or created by the taxpayer. The regulations contain many provisions intended to make it easier to determine when capitalization is required.

Given the growing importance of intangible assets as a source of economic growth and tax revenue, as well as the fact that their non-physical nature makes it easier for taxpayers to engage in tax strategies such as income-shifting or transfer pricing, tax authorities and internation organizations have been designing ways to link intangible assets to the place where they were created, hence defining nexus. Intangibles for corporations are amortized over a 15 year period, equivalent to 180 months.

Definition of "intangibles" differs from standard accounting, in some US state governments. These governments may refer to stocks and bonds as "intangibles."

## Intangible Asset Finance

Intangible Asset Finance is the branch of finance that deals with intangible assets such as patents (legal intangible) and reputation (competitive intangible). Like other areas of finance, intangible asset finance is concerned with the interdependence of value, risk, and time.

## Basic Principles

In 2003, one estimate put the economic equilibrium of intangible assets in the U.S. economy at $5 trillion, which represented over one-third or more of the value of U.S. domestic corporations in the first quarter of 2001.

One of the goals of people working in this field is to unlock the "hidden value" found in intangible assets through the techniques of finance. Another goal is to measure how firm performance correlates with intangible asset management.

Intangible assets include business processes, Intellectual Property (IP) such as patents, trademarks, reputations for ethics and integrity, quality, safety, sustainability, security, and resilience. Today, these intangibles drive cash flow and are the primary sources of risk. Intangible asset information, management, risk forecasting and risk transfer are growing services as the economic base divests itself of physical assets. Rights to tangible and intangible assets are intangible, and can be traded globally.

## Business Models

A number of intangible asset business models have evolved over the years.

- Patent Licensing & Enforcement Companies ("P-LECs"): These are firms that acquire patents for the sole purpose of securing licenses and/or damages awards from infringing parties. Perhaps the most famous P-LEC is NTP, Inc., which has successfully asserted patents related to email push technology. Another name for a P-LEC is "patent troll," although this is viewed as a pejorative reference. Recently, hedge funds have raised capital for the specific purpose of investing in patent litigation. One such hedge fund is Altitude Capital Partners, which is based in New York City.

- Royalty stream securitizers: These are firms that are engaged in the buying and selling of what are essentially specialized asset-backed securities. The assets that are securitized are typically intellectual properties, such as patents, that have been bearing royalties for a period of time. Royalty Pharma is a well known firm that uses this business model, and which has done by far the largest and most high-profile deals in this space. Royalty Pharma handled what many consider to be the first pharmaceutical patent-backed securitization to be rated by

Standard and Poors, which involved a patent on the HIV drug Zerit. The other parties involved in the Zerit transaction were Yale (the owner of the patent) and Bristol Myers Squibb.

- Reinsurers: These are firms that use the techniques of reinsurance to mitigate intangible asset risks. In the same way that some firms issue cat bonds to mitigate the risks associated with extreme weather, earthquakes, or other natural disasters, firms exposed to substantial intangible risk can issue "intangible asset risk-linked securities" that transfer intangible risk to hedge funds and other players in the capital markets with a sufficient appetite for risk. Steel City Re, which is based in Pittsburgh, is a thought leader regarding the use of risk transfer techniques to protect and recover intangible asset value.
- Market makers: Firms that are working to provide more liquidity to the market for intellectual property. Early market makers offered on-line intellectual property exchanges where buyers and sellers could exchange rights in licensed intellectual property, usually patents. On April 22, 2008, Ocean Tomo reported that it had transacted approximately $70 million in its IP auctions across Europe and the United States. In 2009, The Intellectual Property Exchange International (IPXI), headquartered in Chicago, will begin operations as the world's first stock exchange with an intellectual property focus.
- Investment Research Firms: Companies that provide specific advice to investors on intellectual property issues. Recently, hedge fund managers have been hiring patent attorneys to follow and handicap outcomes in high-stakes patent cases.

## Significant Transactions

- 1997: David Bowie securitizes the future royalty revenues earned from his pre-1990 music catalogue by issuing Bowie Bonds.
- 2000: BioPharma Royalty Trust completes the $115 million securitization of a single Yale patent with claims covering Stavudine, which is a reverse transcriptase inhibitor and the active ingredient in the drug Zerit. This was the first publicly rated patent securitization in the U.S. At the time of the deal, Bristol Myers Squibb had the exclusive rights to distribute Zerit in the U.S. Not long after closing slow sales of Zerit along with an accounting scandal at Bristol Myers Squibb triggered the accelerated and premature amortization of the transaction. Many observers believe that this deal was ultimately unsuccessful because of a lack of diversification as it involved a single patent and a single licensee.
- 2005: UCC Capital Corporation securitization of BCBG Max Azria's royalty receivables generated from worldwide intellectual property rights worth $53 million. This transaction is recognized as the first "whole company securitization" involving primarily intangible assets. UCC Capital Corporation was

founded by Robert W. D'Loren, and was acquired by NexCen Brands, Inc. in 2006. NexCen sold substantially all of its assets to Levine Leichtman Capital Partners in 2010.

- 2005: Ocean Tomo holds its first live IP auction. Although proceeds from the first auction were unremarkable, the relative success of the Ocean Tomo auctions that followed showed that the live auction is a reasonably viable business model for monetizing intellectual property.
- 2006: Marvel Entertainment's film rights securitization in conjunction with Ambac Financial Group to provide a triple-A financial guarantee on a credit facility for Marvel backed by a slate of 10 films to be produced by Marvel Studios and intellectual property related to some of Marvel's most popular comic book characters.

## Government, Societies, Think Tanks, and Other Non-profits

On June 23, 2008, the United States National Academies hosted a one-day conference in Washington, D.C. entitled "Intangible Assets: Measuring and Enhancing Their Contribution to Corporate Value and Economic Growth."

The Intangible Asset Finance Society provides a forum for finance, innovation, legal and management professionals to discover better ways to create, capture and preserve the value of intangible assets.

The Athena Alliance is a non-profit organization dedicated to public education and research on the emerging global information economy. On April 16, 2008 it published a widely circulated working paper on the topic of intangible asset finance.

## Financial Asset

A financial asset is a non-physical asset whose value is derived from a contractual claim, such as bank deposits, bonds, and stocks. Financial assets are usually more liquid than other tangible assets, such as commodities or real estate, and may be traded on financial markets.

## Types

According to the International Financial Reporting Standards (IFRS), a financial asset can be:

- Cash or cash equivalent,
- Equity instruments of another entity,
- Contractual right to receive cash or another financial asset from another entity or to exchange financial assets or financial liabilities with another entity under conditions that are potentially favourable to the entity,

- A contract that will or may be settled in the entity's own equity instruments and is either a non-derivative for which the entity is or may be obliged to receive a variable number of the entity's own equity instruments, or a derivative that will or may be settled other than by exchange of a fixed amount of cash or another financial asset for a fixed number of the entity's own equity instruments.

## Treatment of Financial Assets under IFRS

Under IFRS, financial assets are classified into four broad categories which determine the way in which they are measured and reported:

- Financial assets "held for trading" — i.e., which were acquired or incurred principally for the purpose of selling, or are part of a portfolio with evidence of short-term profit-taking, or are derivatives — are measured at fair value through profit or loss.
- Financial assets with fixed or with determinable payments and fixed maturity which the company has to be willing and able to hold till maturity are classified as "held-to-maturity" investments. Held-to-maturity investments are either measured at fair value through profit or loss by designation, or determined to be financial assets available for sale by designation.
- Financial assets with fixed or determinable payments which are not listed in an active market are considered to be "loans and receivables". Loans and receivables are also either measured at fair value through profit or loss by designation or determined to be financial assets available for sale by designation.
- All other financial assets are categorized as financial assets "available for sale" and are measured at fair value through profit or loss by designation.

For financial assets to be measured at fair value through profit or loss *by designation*, designation is only possible at the amount the asset was initially recognized at. Moreover, designation is not possible for equity instruments which are not traded in an active market *and* the fair value of which cannot be reliably determined. Further (alternative) requirements for designation are e.g. at least a clear diminution of a "mismatch" with other financial assets or liabilities, an internal valuation and reporting and steering at fair value, or a combined contract with an embedded derivative which is not immaterial and which may be separated. Regarding financial assets available for sale *by designation*, designation is only possible at the amount the asset was initially recognized at as well. However, there are no further restrictions or requirements.

## Security (Finance)

A security is a tradable financial asset. The term commonly refers to any form of financial instrument, but its legal definition varies by jurisdiction. In some jurisdictions the term specifically excludes financial instruments other than equities and fixed income instruments. In some jurisdictions it includes some instruments that are close to equities and fixed income, e.g. equity warrants. In some countries and languages the term "security" is commonly used in day-to-day parlance to mean any form of financial instrument, even though the underlying legal and regulatory regime may not have such a broad definition.

In the United Kingdom, the national competent authority for financial markets regulation is the Financial Conduct Authority; the definition in its Handbook of the term "security" applies only to equities, debentures, alternative debentures, government and public securities, warrants, certificates representing certain securities, units, stakeholder pension schemes, personal pension schemes, rights to or interests in investments, and anything that may be admitted to the Official List.

In the United States, a security is a tradable financial asset of any kind. Securities are broadly categorized into:

- debt securities (e.g., banknotes, bonds and debentures)
- equity securities (e.g., common stocks)
- derivatives (e.g., forwards, futures, options and swaps).

The company or other entity issuing the security is called the issuer. A country's regulatory structure determines what qualifies as a security. For example, private investment pools may have some features of securities, but they may not be registered or regulated as such if they meet various restrictions.

Securities may be represented by a certificate or, more typically, "non-certificated", that is in electronic (dematerialized) or "book entry" only form. Certificates may be *bearer*, meaning they entitle the holder to rights under the security merely by holding the security, or *registered*, meaning they entitle the holder to rights only if he or she appears on a security register maintained by the issuer or an intermediary. They include shares of corporate stock or mutual funds, bonds issued by corporations or governmental agencies, stock options or other options, limited partnership units, and various other formal investment instruments that are negotiable and fungible.

## Classification

Securities may be classified according to many categories or classification systems:

- Currency of denomination
- Ownership rights
- Terms to maturity
- Degree of liquidity

- Income payments
- Tax treatment
- Credit rating
- Industrial sector or "industry". ("Sector" often refers to a higher level or broader category, such as *Consumer Discretionary*, whereas "industry" often refers to a lower level classification, such as *Consumer Appliances*.)
- Region or country (such as country of incorporation, country of principal sales/ market of its products or services, or country in which the principal securities exchange where it trades is located)
- Market capitalization
- State (typically for municipal or "tax-free" bonds in the US)

## New Capital

Securities are the traditional way that commercial enterprises raise new capital. These may be an attractive alternative to bank loans depending on their pricing and market demand for particular characteristics. Another disadvantage of bank loans as a source of financing is that the bank may seek a measure of protection against default by the borrower via extensive financial covenants. Through securities, capital is provided by investors who purchase the securities upon their initial issuance. In a similar way, a government may issue securities too when it needs to increase government debt.

## Type of Holder

Investors in securities may be retail, i.e. members of the public investing other than by way of business. The greatest part of investment, in terms of volume, is wholesale, i.e. by financial institutions acting on their own account, or on behalf of clients. Important institutional investors include investment banks, insurance companies, pension funds and other managed funds.

## Investment

The traditional economic function of the purchase of securities is investment, with the view to receiving income or achieving capital gain. Debt securities generally offer a higher rate of interest than bank deposits, and equities may offer the prospect of capital growth. Equity investment may also offer control of the business of the issuer. Debt holdings may also offer some measure of control to the investor if the company is a fledgling start-up or an old giant undergoing 'restructuring'. In these cases, if interest payments are missed, the creditors may take control of the company and liquidate it to recover some of their investment.

## Collateral

The last decade has seen an enormous growth in the use of securities as collateral. Purchasing securities with borrowed money secured by other securities or cash itself is called "buying on margin". Where A is owed a debt or other obligation by B, A may require B to deliver property rights in securities to A, either at inception (transfer of title) or only in default (non-transfer-of-title institutional). For institutional loans, property rights are not transferred but nevertheless enable A to satisfy its claims in the event that B fails to make good on its obligations to A or otherwise becomes insolvent. Collateral arrangements are divided into two broad categories, namely security interests and outright collateral transfers. Commonly, commercial banks, investment banks, government agencies and other institutional investors such as mutual funds are significant collateral takers as well as providers. In addition, private parties may utilize stocks or other securities as collateral for portfolio loans in securities lending scenarios.

On the consumer level, loans against securities have grown into three distinct groups over the last decade: 1) *Standard Institutional Loans,* generally offering low loan-to-value with very strict call and coverage regimens, akin to standard margin loans; 2) *Transfer-of-Title (ToT) Loans,* typically provided by private parties where borrower ownership is completely extinguished save for the rights provided in the loan contract; and 3) Non-Transfer-of-Title Credit Line facilities where shares are not sold and they serve as assets in a standard lien-type line of cash credit. Of the three, transfer-of-title loans have fallen into the very high-risk category as the number of providers has dwindled as regulators have launched an industry-wide crackdown on transfer-of-title structures where the private lender may sell or sell short the securities to fund the loan. Institutionally managed consumer securities-based loans, on the other hand, draw loan funds from the financial resources of the lending institution, not from the sale of the securities.

Collateral and sources of collateral are changing, in 2012 gold became a more acceptable form of collateral. However more recently Exchange-traded funds (ETFs) seen by many as the ugly ducklings of the collateral world have started to become more readily available and acceptable. But in a world where collateral is becoming scarce and efficiency is everything, many of these mallards are proving themselves to be not so ugly after all—many more are veritable swans. The problem, until now, for collateral managers has been deciphering the bad eggs from the good, which proves to be a time consuming and inefficient task.

## Debt and Equity

Securities are traditionally divided into debt securities and equities.

## Debt

Debt securities may be called debentures, bonds, deposits, notes or commercial paper depending on their maturity, collateral and other characteristics. The holder of a debt security is typically entitled to the payment of principal and interest, together with other contractual rights under the terms of the issue, such as the right to receive certain information. Debt securities are generally issued for a fixed term and redeemable by the issuer at the end of that term. Debt securities may be protected by collateral or may be unsecured, and, if they are unsecured, may be contractually "senior" to other unsecured debt meaning their holders would have a priority in a bankruptcy of the issuer. Debt that is not senior is "subordinated".

Corporate bonds represent the debt of commercial or industrial entities. Debentures have a long maturity, typically at least ten years, whereas notes have a shorter maturity. Commercial paper is a simple form of debt security that essentially represents a post-dated cheque with a maturity of not more than 270 days.

Money market instruments are short term debt instruments that may have characteristics of deposit accounts, such as certificates of deposit, Accelerated Return Notes (ARN), and certain bills of exchange. They are highly liquid and are sometimes referred to as "near cash". Commercial paper is also often highly liquid.

Euro debt securities are securities issued internationally outside their domestic market in a denomination different from that of the issuer's domicile. They include eurobonds and euronotes. Eurobonds are characteristically underwritten, and not secured, and interest is paid gross. A euronote may take the form of euro-commercial paper (ECP) or euro-certificates of deposit.

Government bonds are medium or long term debt securities issued by sovereign governments or their agencies. Typically they carry a lower rate of interest than corporate bonds, and serve as a source of finance for governments. U.S. federal government bonds are called *treasuries*. Because of their liquidity and perceived low risk, treasuries are used to manage the money supply in the open market operations of non-US central banks.

Sub-sovereign government bonds, known in the U.S. as municipal bonds, represent the debt of state, provincial, territorial, municipal or other governmental units other than sovereign governments.

Supranational bonds represent the debt of international organizations such as the World Bank, the International Monetary Fund, regional multilateral development banks and others.

## Equity

An equity security is a share of equity interest in an entity such as the capital stock of a company, trust or partnership. The most common form of equity interest is common stock, although preferred equity is also a form of capital stock. The holder of an equity is a shareholder, owning a share, or fractional part of the issuer. Unlike debt securities, which typically require regular payments (interest) to the holder, equity securities are not entitled to any payment. In bankruptcy, they share only in the residual interest of the issuer after all obligations have been paid out to creditors. However, equity generally entitles the holder to a pro rata portion of control of the company, meaning that a holder of a majority of the equity is usually entitled to control the issuer. Equity also enjoys the right to profits and capital gain, whereas holders of debt securities receive only interest and repayment of principal regardless of how well the issuer performs financially. Furthermore, debt securities do not have voting rights outside of bankruptcy. In other words, equity holders are entitled to the "upside" of the business and to control the business.

## Hybrid

Hybrid securities combine some of the characteristics of both debt and equity securities.

Preference shares form an intermediate class of security between equities and debt. If the issuer is liquidated, they carry the right to receive interest or a return of capital in priority to ordinary shareholders. However, from a legal perspective, they are capital stock and therefore may entitle holders to some degree of control depending on whether they contain voting rights.

Convertibles are bonds or preferred stock that can be converted, at the election of the holder of the convertibles, into the common stock of the issuing company. The convertibility, however, may be forced if the convertible is a callable bond, and the issuer calls the bond. The bondholder has about 1 month to convert it, or the company will call the bond by giving the holder the call price, which may be less than the value of the converted stock. This is referred to as a forced conversion.

Equity warrants are options issued by the company that allow the holder of the warrant to purchase a specific number of shares at a specified price within a specified time. They are often issued together with bonds or existing equities, and are, sometimes, detachable from them and separately tradeable. When the holder of the warrant exercises it, he pays the money directly to the company, and the company issues new shares to the holder.

Warrants, like other convertible securities, increases the number of shares outstanding, and are always accounted for in financial reports as fully diluted earnings per share, which assumes that all warrants and convertibles will be exercised.

## Markets

### Primary and Secondary Market

Public securities markets are either primary or secondary markets. In the primary market, the money for the securities is received by the issuer of the securities from investors, typically in an initial public offering (IPO). In the secondary market, the securities are simply assets held by one investor selling them to another investor, with the money going from one investor to the other.

An initial public offering is when a company issues public stock newly to investors, called an "IPO" for short. A company can later issue more new shares, or issue shares that have been previously registered in a shelf registration. These later new issues are also sold in the primary market, but they are not considered to be an IPO but are often called a "secondary offering". Issuers usually retain investment banks to assist them in administering the IPO, obtaining SEC (or other regulatory body) approval of the offering filing, and selling the new issue. When the investment bank buys the entire new issue from the issuer at a discount to resell it at a markup, it is called a firm commitment underwriting. However, if the investment bank considers the risk too great for an underwriting, it may only assent to a best effort agreement, where the investment bank will simply do its best to sell the new issue.

For the primary market to thrive, there must be a secondary market, or aftermarket that provides liquidity for the investment security—where holders of securities can sell them to other investors for cash. Otherwise, few people would purchase primary issues, and, thus, companies and governments would be restricted in raising equity capital (money) for their operations. Organized exchanges constitute the main secondary markets. Many smaller issues and most debt securities trade in the decentralized, dealer-based over-the-counter markets.

In Europe, the principal trade organization for securities dealers is the International Capital Market Association. In the U.S., the principal trade organization for securities dealers is the Securities Industry and Financial Markets Association, which is the result of the merger of the Securities Industry Association and the Bond Market Association. The Financial Information Services Division of the Software and Information Industry Association (FISD/SIIA) represents a round-table of market data industry firms, referring to them as Consumers, Exchanges, and Vendors. In India the equivalent organisation is the securities exchange board of India (SEBI).

## Public Offer and Private Placement

In the primary markets, securities may be offered to the public in a public offer. Alternatively, they may be offered privately to a limited number of qualified persons in a private placement. Sometimes a combination of the two is used. The distinction between the two is important to securities regulation and company law. Privately placed securities are not publicly tradable and may only be bought and sold by sophisticated qualified investors. As a result, the secondary market is not nearly as liquid as it is for public (registered) securities.

Another category, sovereign bonds, is generally sold by auction to a specialized class of dealers.

## Listing and Over-the-counter Dealing

Securities are often listed in a stock exchange, an organized and officially recognized market on which securities can be bought and sold. Issuers may seek listings for their securities to attract investors, by ensuring there is a liquid and regulated market that investors can buy and sell securities in.

Growth in informal electronic trading systems has challenged the traditional business of stock exchanges. Large volumes of securities are also bought and sold "over the counter" (OTC). OTC dealing involves buyers and sellers dealing with each other by telephone or electronically on the basis of prices that are displayed electronically, usually by financial data vendors such as SuperDerivatives, Reuters, Investing.com and Bloomberg.

There are also eurosecurities, which are securities that are issued outside their domestic market into more than one jurisdiction. They are generally listed on the Luxembourg Stock Exchange or admitted to listing in London. The reasons for listing eurobonds include regulatory and tax considerations, as well as the investment restrictions.

## Market

London is the centre of the eurosecurities markets. There was a huge rise in the eurosecurities market in London in the early 1980s. Settlement of trades in eurosecurities is currently effected through two European computerized clearing/depositories called Euroclear (in Belgium) and Clearstream (formerly Cedelbank) in Luxembourg.

The main market for Eurobonds is the EuroMTS, owned by Borsa Italiana and Euronext. There are ramp up market in Emergent countries, but it is growing slowly.

## Physical Nature

## Certificated Securities

Securities that are represented in paper (physical) form are called certificated securities. They may be *bearer* or *registered.*

## DRS Securities

Securities may also be held in the Direct Registration System (DRS), which is a method of recording shares of stock in book-entry form. Book-entry means the company's transfer agent maintains the shares on the owner's behalf without the need for physical share certificates. Shares held in un-certificated book-entry form have the same rights and privileges as shares held in certificated form.

## Bearer Securities

Bearer securities are completely negotiable and entitle the holder to the rights under the security (e.g. to payment if it is a debt security, and voting if it is an equity security). They are transferred by delivering the instrument from person to person. In some cases, transfer is by endorsement, or signing the back of the instrument, and delivery.

Regulatory and fiscal authorities sometimes regard bearer securities negatively, as they may be used to facilitate the evasion of regulatory restrictions and tax. In the United Kingdom, for example, the issue of bearer securities was heavily restricted firstly by the *Exchange Control Act* 1947 until 1953. Bearer securities are very rare in the United States because of the negative tax implications they may have to the issuer and holder.

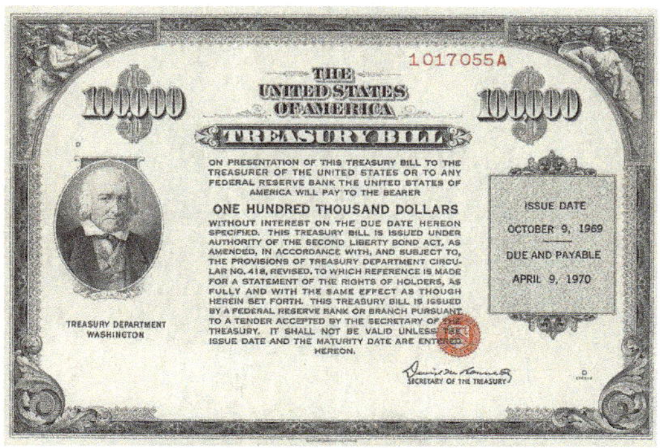


1969 $100,000 Treasury Bill

In Luxembourg, the law of 28 July 2014 concerning the compulsory deposit and immobilisation of shares and units in bearer form adopts the compulsory deposit and immobilisation of bearer shares and units with a depositary allowing identification of the hoders thereof.

## Registered Securities

1981 $10,000 15.875% Registered Note

In the case of registered securities, certificates bearing the name of the holder are issued, but these merely represent the securities. A person does not automatically acquire legal ownership by having possession of the certificate. Instead, the issuer (or its appointed agent) maintains a register in which details of the holder of the securities are entered and updated as appropriate. A transfer of registered securities is effected by amending the register.

## Non-certificated Securities and Global Certificates

Modern practice has developed to eliminate both the need for certificates and maintenance of a complete security register by the issuer. There are two general ways this has been accomplished.

## Non-certificated securities

In some jurisdictions, such as France, it is possible for issuers of that jurisdiction to maintain a legal record of their securities electronically.

In the United States, the current "official" version of Article 8 of the Uniform Commercial Code permits non-certificated securities. However, the "official" UCC is a mere draft that must be enacted individually by each U.S. state. Though all 50 states (as well as the District of Columbia and the U.S. Virgin Islands) have enacted some form of Article 8, many of them still appear to use older versions of Article 8, including some that did not permit non-certificated securities.

## Global Certificates, Book Entry Interests, Depositories

To facilitate the electronic transfer of interests in securities without dealing with inconsistent versions of Article 8, a system has developed whereby issuers deposit a single global certificate representing all the outstanding securities of a class or series with a universal depository. This depository is called The Depository Trust Company, or DTC. DTC's parent, Depository Trust & Clearing Corporation (DTCC), is a non-profit cooperative owned by approximately thirty of the largest Wall Street players that typically act as brokers or dealers in securities. These thirty banks are called the DTC participants. DTC, through a legal nominee, owns each of the global securities on behalf of all the DTC participants.

All securities traded through DTC are in fact held, in electronic form, on the books of various intermediaries between the ultimate owner, e.g. a retail investor, and the DTC participants. For example, Mr. Smith may hold 100 shares of Coca-Cola, Inc. in his brokerage account at local broker Jones & Co. brokers. In turn, Jones & Co. may hold 1000 shares of Coca-Cola on behalf of Mr. Smith and nine other customers. These 1000 shares are held by Jones & Co. in an account with Goldman Sachs, a DTC participant, or in an account at another DTC participant. Goldman Sachs in turn may hold millions of Coca-Cola shares on its books on behalf of hundreds of brokers similar to Jones & Co.

Each day, the DTC participants settle their accounts with the other DTC participants and adjust the number of shares held on their books for the benefit of customers like Jones & Co. Ownership of securities in this fashion is called beneficial ownership. Each intermediary holds on behalf of someone beneath him in the chain. The ultimate owner is called the beneficial owner. This is also referred to as owning in "Street name".

Among brokerages and mutual fund companies, a large amount of mutual fund share transactions take place among intermediaries as opposed to shares being sold and redeemed directly with the transfer agent of the fund. Most of these intermediaries such as brokerage firms clear the shares electronically through the National Securities Clearing Corp. or "NSCC", a subsidiary of DTCC.

## Other Depositories

Besides DTC, two other large securities depositories exist, both in Europe: Euroclear and Clearstream.

## Divided and Undivided Security

The terms "divided" and "undivided" relate to the proprietary nature of a security.

Each divided security constitutes a separate asset, which is legally distinct from each other security in the same issue. Pre-electronic bearer securities were divided. Each instrument constitutes the separate covenant of the issuer and is a separate debt.

With undivided securities, the entire issue makes up one single asset, with each of the securities being a fractional part of this undivided whole. Shares in the secondary markets are always undivided. The issuer owes only one set of obligations to shareholders under its memorandum, articles of association and company law. A share represents an undivided fractional part of the issuing company. Registered debt securities also have this undivided nature.

## Fungible and Non-fungible Security

The terms "fungible" and "non-fungible" are a feature of assets.

If an asset is fungible, this means that if such an asset is lent, or placed with a custodian, it is customary for the borrower or custodian to be obliged at the end of the loan or custody arrangement to return assets equivalent to the original asset, rather than the specific identical asset. In other words, the redelivery of fungibles is equivalent and not *in specie*. For example, if an owner of 100 shares of IBM transfers custody of those shares to another party to hold for a purpose, at the end of the arrangement, the holder need simply provide the owner with 100 shares of IBM identical to those received. Cash is also an example of a fungible asset. The exact currency notes received need not be segregated and returned to the owner.

Undivided securities are always fungible by logical necessity. Divided securities may or may not be fungible, depending on market practice. The clear trend is towards fungible arrangements.

## Regulation

In the US, the public offer and sale of securities must be either registered pursuant to a registration statement that is filed with the U.S. Securities and Exchange Commission (SEC) or are offered and sold pursuant to an exemption therefrom. Dealing in securities is regulated by both federal authorities (SEC) and state securities departments. In addition, the brokerage industry is supposedly self policed by Self Regulatory Organizations (SROs), such as the Financial Industry Regulatory Authority (FINRA), formerly the National Association of Securities Dealers (or NASD) or the MSRB.

With respect to investment schemes that do not fall within the traditional categories of securities listed in the definition of a security (Sec. 2(a)(1) of the 33 act and Sec. 3(a)(10) of the 34 act) the US Courts have developed a broad definition for securities that must then be registered with the SEC. When determining if there is an "investment contract" that must be registered the courts look for an investment of money, a common enterprise and expectation of profits to come primarily from the efforts of others.

## Toxic Asset

Toxic asset is a popular term for certain financial assets whose value has fallen significantly and for which there is no longer a functioning market, so that such assets cannot be sold at a price satisfactory to the holder. Because assets are offset against liabilities and frequently leveraged, this decline in price may be quite dangerous to the holder. The term became common during the financial crisis of 2007-2008, in which they played a major role.

When the market for toxic assets ceases to function, it is described as "frozen". Markets for some toxic assets froze in 2007, and the problem grew much worse in the second half of 2008. Several factors contributed to the freezing of toxic asset markets. The value of the assets were very sensitive to economic conditions, and increased uncertainty in these conditions made it difficult to estimate the value of the assets. Banks and other major financial institutions were unwilling to sell the assets at significantly reduced prices, since lower prices would force them to reduce significantly their stated assets, making them, at least on paper, insolvent.

## Origin

The term was in limited use at least as early as 2006, and may have been coined by or popularized by Angelo Mozilo, founder of Countrywide Financial, who used the term "toxic" to describe certain mortgage products in emails in spring of 2006, as revealed in SEC filings:

> "The 100% loan-to-value subprime loan is the most dangerous product in existence and there can be nothing more toxic" (March 28, 2006)

Regarding Countrywide's subprime 80/20 loans:

> "In all my years in the business I have never seen a more toxic prduct [sic]. It's not only subordinated to the first, but the first is subprime. In addition, the FICOs are below 600, below 500 and some below 400. With real estate values coming down the product will become increasingly worse." (April 17, 2006)

## Market Freeze

When the supply and demand of a good equal each other, so buyers and sellers are matched, one says that the "market clears".

Classical economics and neoclassical economics posit that market clearing happens by the price adjusting—upwards if demand exceeds supply and downwards if supply exceeds demand. Therefore, it reaches equilibrium at a price that both buyers and sellers will accept, and, in the absence of outside interference (in a free market), this will happen.

This has not happened for many types of financial assets during the financial crisis that began in 2007, hence one speaks of "the market breaking down".

One can explain this alternately as the price not adjusting down—the price is too high, with supply being too high, or alternatively demand being too low, or by the theory of an equilibrium price not holding—the price at which sellers will sell is higher than the price at which buyers will buy.

Prior to the crisis, banks and other financial institutions had invested significant amounts of money in complicated financial assets, such as collateralized debt obligations and credit default swaps. The value of these assets was very sensitive to economic factors, such as housing prices, default rates, and financial-market liquidity. Prior to the crisis, the value of these assets had been estimated, using the prevailing economic data.

When it became clear that such conditions would not continue, it was no longer clear how much revenue the assets were likely to generate and, hence, how much the assets were worth. Since the assets were typically very sensitive to economic conditions, even relatively small uncertainties in the economic conditions could lead to large uncertainties in the value of the assets, which made it difficult for buyers and sellers in the market to agree on prices.

Furthermore, banks and other large financial institutions were reluctant to accept lower prices for these assets, since lower prices would force them to recalculate the total value of their assets, and, if the loss was sufficiently large, force them to declare a negative total value. Several banks in the autumn of 2008 were forced to accept buy-outs or mergers because it was believed that they were in this situation. This re-evaluation of total assets based on prevailing market prices is known as mark-to-market pricing. The term *zombie bank* was introduced to describe banks, which would have become bankrupt if their assets had been revalued at realistic levels. Toxic assets, by increasing the variance of banks' assets, can turn otherwise healthy institutions into zombies. Potentially solvent banks will make too few good loans. This is the debt overhang problem. Alternatively, potentially insolvent banks with toxic assets will seek out very risky speculative loans to shift risk onto their depositors and other creditors.

Further, insolvent banks with toxic assets are unwilling to accept significant reductions in the price of the toxic assets, but potential buyers were unwilling to pay prices anywhere near the loans's face value. With potential sellers and buyers unable to agree on prices, the markets froze with no transactions occurring. In some cases, markets remained frozen for several months.

## Geithner Attempt at Bail-out

On March 23, 2009, U.S. Treasury Secretary Timothy Geithner announced a Public-Private Investment Partnership (PPIP) to buy toxic assets from banks. The major stock market indexes in the United States rallied on the day of the announcement, rising by over six percent with the shares of bank stocks leading the way. PPIP has two primary programs. The Legacy Loans Program will attempt to buy residential loans from bank's balance sheets. The Federal Deposit Insurance Corporation (FDIC)] will provide non-recourse loan guarantees for up to 85 percent of the purchase price of legacy loans. Private sector asset managers and the U.S. Treasury will provide the remaining assets. The second program is called the legacy securities program, which will buy mortgage backed securities (RMBS) that were originally rated AAA and commercial mortgage-backed securities (CMBS) and asset-backed securities (ABS) which are rated AAA. The funds will come in many instances in equal parts from the U.S. Treasury's Troubled Asset Relief Program (TARP) monies, private investors, and from loans from the Federal Reserve's Term Asset Lending Facility (TALF). The initial size of the Public Private Investment Partnership is projected to be $500 billion. Economist and Nobel Prize winner Paul Krugman has been very critical of this program, arguing that the non-recourse loans lead to a hidden subsidy that will be split by asset managers, bank shareholders, and creditors. Banking analyst Meridith Whitney argues that banks will not sell bad assets at fair market values because they are reluctant to take asset write downs. Removing toxic assets would also reduce the upward volatility of banks' stock prices. Because stock is a call option on a firm's assets, this lost volatility will hurt the stock price of distressed banks. Therefore, such banks will only sell toxic assets at above market prices.

However, that argument ignores the possibility of simultaneously adjusting bank liabilities by legislation or regulation, as requested in the September, 2009, $24 billion plan proposed by FDIC chair Sheila Bair, which would have shielded shareholders but could have led to non-astronomical management bonuses. Bair's plan was never implemented. Because the number of commercial bankruptcy filings continues to increase, there is evidence for negative feedback pressure indicating that toxic assets still need to be addressed.

## Types of Assets

An example of a market which froze is the Canadian ABCP ("asset-backed credit paper") market. The term "toxic asset" is generally associated with financial instruments like CDOs ("collatoralized debt obligations", assets generated from the resale of portions of a bank's mortgages), CDS ("credit default swaps"), and the subprime mortgage market -particular the lower tranches-, but the term does not have a precise definition.

## Related Terms

Before the financial crisis started, the term "toxic waste" was used to describe the lowest tranch of the subprime mortgage market. "Legacy assets" is a euphemism coined by Robert Gibbs as an attempted re-branding of toxic assets.

Toxic security is the name applied during the aftermath of the subprime meltdown to financial instruments which cannot be readily identified as an asset or a liability. According to George Soros, "the toxic securities in question are not homogeneous". One example would be a credit default swap that entitles the holder to a regular stream of small payments but obliges the holder to make a large payment if a specified event occurs. John Gapper describes one such instrument, a "tail risk" swap:

*Structured finance gave banks and others more chances to take on "tail risk". This is an insurance-like trading strategy: one institution writes swaps or options that provide it with regular payments in exchange for taking another's risk of default. In most cases, this produces profits, but occasionally it is disastrous.*

The right to receive a stream of payments is accounted for as an asset. The obligation to make a payment is accounted for as a liability. In the case of a credit default swap, the number and amount of payments in and out is subject to an undetermined risk.

The net value of the expected cash flows is calculable by reference to a model, but the calculations require a degree of confidence in the probabilities of the named event occurring which may be unwarranted. "There is no doubt there could be disagreement on what the fair value for these securities is," said Lawrence Levine, director at RSM McGladrey.

## Net Operating Assets

Net operating assets (NOA) are a business's operating assets minus its operating liabilities. NOA is calculated by reformatting the balance sheet so that operating activities are separated from financing activities. This is done so that the operating performance of the business can be isolated and valued independently of the financing performance. Financing activities do not create value unless the company is in the finance industry, therefore reformatting the balance sheet allows investors to value just the operating activities and hence get a more accurate valuation of the company.

## Calculation

- NOA = operating assets – operating liabilities

To calculate NOA the balance sheet must be reformatted to separate operating activities from financing activities. Operating activities are anything that involves the day-to-day running of the business such as accounts receivable, inventory, etc.; and financing activities are any accounts that are “interest-bearing” or have financial characteristics and are not related to the regular operations such as debt and equity investments. The reformatted balance sheet should look like this:

```
Balance sheet of XYZ, Ltd. as of ...

OPERATING ACTIVITIES :

Current assets

  - Current liabilities

  = Net current assets

  + Non-current assets

  - Non-current liabilities

  = NET OPERATING ASSETS (NOA)

FINANCING ACTIVITIES

Net financing obligations

Equity
```

The basic equation is:

- Operating assets = total assets – cash
- Operating liabilities = total liabilities – short-term notes – long-term notes

## Application

Calculating NOA is necessary for applying the *Discounted Abnormal Operating Earnings valuation model.* DAOE is one of the most widely accepted valuation models because it is considered the least sensitive to forecast errors. NOA can also be used in the calculation of Free cash flow (FCF) and therefore the Discounted cash flow model. However it is not necessary to calculate FCF.

- $$\text{DAOE} = \frac{\text{NOPAT}(t) - \text{WACC} \times \text{NOA}(t-1)}{\text{WACC}} + \text{NOA} - \text{BVD}$$

- $$\text{FCF} = \text{NOPAT} - \text{Change in NOA}$$

- $$\text{DCF} = \frac{\text{FCF}}{\text{WACC}} - \text{BVD}$$

## Stranded Asset

Stranded assets are "assets that have suffered from unanticipated or premature write-downs, devaluations or conversion to liabilities". Stranded assets can be caused by a variety of factors and are a phenomenon inherent in the 'creative destruction' of economic growth, transformation and innovation, as such they pose risks to individuals and firms and may have systemic implications. Coal and other hydrocarbon resources may have the potential to become stranded as the world engages in a fossil fuel phase out.

The term is important to financial risk management in order to avoid economic loss after an asset has been converted to a liability. Accountants have measures to deal with the impairment of assets (e.g. IAS 16) which seek to ensure that an entity's assets are not carried at more than their recoverable amount. In this context, stranded assets are also defined as an asset that has become obsolete or non-performing, but must be recorded on the balance sheet as a loss of profit.

## In the Context of the Environment

The term *stranded assets* has gained significant prominence in environmental and climate change discourses, where the focus has been on how environment-related factors (such as climate change policy) could strand assets in different sectors. According to the Stranded Assets Programme at the University of Oxford's Smith School of Enterprise and the Environment, some of the environment-related risk factors that could result in stranded assets are:

- environmental challenges (e.g. climate change, natural capital degradation)
- changing resource landscapes including resource depletion (e.g. shale-gas abundance, phosphate scarcity)
- new government regulations (e.g. carbon pricing, air pollution regulation, carbon bubble)
- falling clean-technology costs (e.g. solar PV, onshore wind, electric vehicles)
- evolving social norms (e.g. fossil fuel divestment campaign) and consumer behaviour (e.g. certification schemes)

- litigation (e.g. carbon liability) and changing statutory interpretations (e.g. fiduciary duty, disclosure requirements)

In the context of upstream energy production, the IEA defines stranded assets as "those investments which are made but which, at some time prior to the end of their economic life (as assumed at the investment decision point), are no longer able to earn an economic return, as a result of changes in the market and regulatory environment."

The carbon bubble is one popular example of how an environment-related risk factor could create stranded assets.

In discussions of electric power generation deregulation, the related term stranded costs represents the existing investments in infrastructure for the incumbent utility that may become redundant in a competitive environment.

## Hard Asset

Hard Assets are investments with intrinsic value such as oil, natural gas, gold, silver, farmland, natural colored diamonds and commercial real estate. Typically hard assets are an excellent inflation hedge. In general, commodities/hard assets are negatively correlated to both stocks and bonds. In other words, when stocks and bonds decline, commodities tend to appreciate. In addition, during periods of high inflation/negative real interest rates equities and bonds do poorly (see 20% total return over 11 years from 1970 to 1981 for the S&P 500 v. 1,100% increase in oil prices and 550% increase in western Canada farmland prices during same period) while commodity/hard assets appreciate in value.

## Capital Asset

A capital asset is defined to include property of any kind held by an assessee, whether connected with their business or profession or not connected with their business or profession. It includes all kinds of property, movable or immovable, tangible or intangible, fixed or circuWg. Thus, land and building, plant and machinery, motorcar, furniture, jewellery, route permits, goodwill, tenancy rights, patents, trademarks, shares, debentures, securities, units, mutual funds, zero-coupon bonds etc. are capital assets.

## Excluded from the Definition of Capital Assets

1. Any stock in trade, consumable stores, or raw materials held for the purpose of business or profession have been excluded from the definition of capital assets.
2. Any movable property (excluding jewellery made out of gold, silver, precious stones, and drawing, paintings, sculptures, archeological collections, Dinosaur bones, etc.) used for personal use by the assessee or any member (dependent) of assessee's family is not treated as capital assets. *For example*, wearing apparel,

furniture, car or scooter, TV, refrigerator, musical instruments, gun, revolver, generator, etc. is the examples of personal effects.

3. Agricultural land situated in rural area.
4. 6.5% gold bonds or 7% gold bonds 1980, national defense gold bond 1980, issued by the central government.
5. Special bearded bonds, 1991
6. Gold deposit bonds issued under gold deposit scheme, 1999.

## Specific Common Definitions

- In financial economics, capital refers to any asset used to make money, as opposed to assets used for personal enjoyment or consumption. This is an important distinction because two people can disagree sharply about the value of personal assets, one person might think a sports car is more valuable than a pickup truck, another person might have the opposite taste. But if an asset is held for the purpose of making money, taste has nothing to do with it, only differences of opinion about how much money the asset will produce. With the further assumption that people agree on the probability distribution of future cash flows, it is possible to have an objective Capital asset pricing model. Even without the assumption of agreement, it is possible to set rational limits on capital asset value.
- In governmental accounting, or with reference to public capital or infrastructure usually managed by government, a capital asset is defined as any asset used in operations with an initial useful life extending beyond one reporting period. Generally, government managers have a "stewardship" duty to maintain capital assets under their control. *Triple bottom line is widely used public sector accounting methods in which natural capital and social capital are characterized not as intangibles or externalities but as actual capital assets.*
- In some income tax systems (for example, in the United States), gains and losses from capital assets are treated differently than other income. Sale of non-capital assets, such as inventory or stock of goods held for sale, generally is taxed in the same manner as other income. Capital assets generally include those assets outside the daily scope of business operations, such as investment or personal assets. The United States system defines a capital asset by exclusion. Capital assets include all assets *except* inventory of supplies or property held for sale (including subdivided real estate), depreciable property used in a business, accounts or notes receivable, certain commodities derivatives and hedging items, and certain copyrights and similar property held by the creator of the property. The United Kingdom has an even broader definition.

## US Tax Definition Versus Broader Economic Definition

A well-known financial accounting textbook advises that the term be avoided except in tax accounting because it is used in so many different senses, not all of them well-defined. For example it is often used as a synonym for fixed assets or for investments in securities.

However this advice is questionable beyond the US private context. Several public sector standards in global use, notably triple bottom line accounting as defined by ICLEI for world cities, require that employees or the environment or something else be treated as a capital asset. In this context it means something managers have a responsibility to maintain, and to report changes in value as gains or losses.

Capital assets should not be confused with the capital a financial institution is required to hold. This capital is computed from the right-hand side of the balance sheet while assets are found on the left-hand side. *Basel III for a summary of how such requirements are proposed to be calculated.*

## References


- HM Revenue & Customs. "Company Taxation Manual". Archived from the original on 2009-04-18. Retrieved 2008-11-01
- "SAC 4: Definition and Recognition of the Elements of Financial Statements" (PDF). Australian Accounting Standards Board. Retrieved 19 December 2012
- Lev, Baruch; Daum, Juergen (2004). "The dominance of intangible assets: consequences for enterprise management and corporate reporting" (PDF). Measuring Business Excellence. 8 (1): 6–17. doi:10.1108/13683040410524694
- Andrews, Edmund L.; Dash, Eric (March 24, 2009). "U.S. Expands Plan to Buy Banks' Troubled Assets". New York Times. Retrieved February 12, 2009
- "Stranded Assets Programme". Smith School of Enterprise and the Environment. 25 March 2014. Retrieved 11 April 2014

2

# Understanding Asset Management

Asset management is the management of the value of an entity. Infrastructure asset management, IT asset management, fixed assets management, asset health management and digital asset management are some topics related to asset management which play a key role in the process. This chapter is an overview of the subject matter incorporating all the major aspects of asset management.

## Asset Management

Asset management, broadly defined, refers to any system that monitors and maintains things of value to an entity or group. It may apply to both tangible assets (such as buildings) and to intangible assets such as human capital, intellectual property, goodwill and/or financial assets). Asset management is a systematic process of deploying, operating, maintaining, upgrading, and disposing of assets cost-effectively.

The term is most commonly used in the financial sector to describe people and companies that manage investments on behalf of others. These include, for example, investment managers that manage the assets of a pension fund.

Alternative views of asset management in the engineering environment are: the practice of managing assets to achieve the greatest return (particularly useful for productive assets such as plant and equipment), and the process of monitoring and maintaining facilities systems, with the objective of providing the best possible service to users in all dimensions (appropriate for public infrastructure assets).

### By Industry

### Financial Asset Management

The most common usage of the term "asset manager" refers to investment management, the sector of the financial services industry that manages investment funds and segregated client accounts. Asset management is part of a financial company which employs experts who manage money and handle the investments of clients. From studying the client's assets to planning and looking after the investments, all things are looked after by the asset managers and recommendations are provided based on the financial health of each client.

# Infrastructure Asset Management

Infrastructure asset management is the combination of management, financial, economic, engineering, and other practices applied to physical assets with the objective of providing the required level of service in the most cost-effective manner. It includes the management of the entire lifecycle—including design, construction, commissioning, operating, maintaining, repairing, modifying, replacing and decommissioning/disposal—of physical and infrastructure assets. Operation and maintenance of assets in a constrained budget environment require a prioritization scheme. As a way of illustration, the recent development of renewable energy has seen the rise of effective asset managers involved in the management of solar systems (solar park, rooftops and windmills). These teams are actually more and more teaming-up with financial asset managers in order to offer turnkey solutions to investors. Infrastructure asset management became very important in most of the developed countries in the 21st century, since their infrastructure network was almost completed in the 20th century and they have to manage to operate and maintain them cost-effectively. Software asset management is one kind of infrastructure asset management.

## Enterprise Asset Management

Enterprise asset management is the business of processing and enabling information systems that support management of an organization's assets, both physical assets, called "tangible", and non-physical, "intangible" assets.

- Physical asset management: the practice of managing the entire lifecycle (design, construction, commissioning, operating, maintaining, repairing, modifying, replacing and decommissioning/disposal) of physical and infrastructure assets such as structures, production and service plant, power, water and waste treatment facilities, distribution networks, transport systems, buildings and other physical assets. It is related to asset health management

- Infrastructure asset management expands on this theme in relation primarily to public sector, utilities, property and transport systems. Additionally, Asset Management can refer to shaping the future interfaces amongst the human, built, and natural environments through collaborative and evidence-based decision processes

- Fixed assets management: an accounting process that seeks to track fixed assets for the purposes of financial accounting

- IT asset management: the set of business practices that join financial, contractual and inventory functions to support life cycle management and strategic decision making for the IT environment. This is also one of the processes defined within IT service management

- Digital asset management: a form of electronic media content management that includes digital assets

## Public Asset Management

Public asset management, also called corporate asset management, expands the definition of enterprise asset management (EAM) by incorporating the management of all things of value to a municipal jurisdiction and its citizens' expectations. An example in which public asset management is used is land-use development and planning.

An EAM requires an asset registry (inventory of assets and their attributes) combined with a computerized maintenance management system (CMMS). All public assets are interconnected and share proximity, possible through the use of geographic information systems (GIS).

A GIS-centric public asset management standardizes data and allows interoperability, providing users the capability to reuse, coordinate, and share information in an efficient and effective manner by making the GIS geo-database the asset registry. A GIS platform combined with information of both the "hard" and "soft" assets helps to remove the traditional silos of structured municipal functions. While the hard assets are the typical physical assets or infrastructure assets, the soft assets of a municipality includes permits, license, code enforcement, right-of-ways and other land-focused work activities.

The GIS platform is only an assisting tool; asset managers need to make informed decisions about their assets in order to fulfill their organizational goals. While geospatially displayed information can assist in decision-making, the deep understanding of markets, engineering systems, and human interaction enabled by analysis and synthesis of information not found in GIS systems is also present.

## Infrastructure Asset Management

Infrastructure asset management is the integrated, multidisciplinary set of strategies in sustaining public infrastructure assets such as water treatment facilities, sewer lines, roads, utility grids, bridges, and railways. Generally, the process focuses on the later stages of a facility's life cycle specifically maintenance, rehabilitation, and replacement. Asset management specifically uses software tools to organize and implement these strategies with the fundamental goal to preserve and extend the service life of long-term infrastructure assets which are vital underlying components in maintaining the quality of life in society and efficiency in the economy.

## Term

Infrastructure asset management is a specific term of asset management focusing on *physical*, rather than *financial* assets. Sometimes the term infrastructure management is used to mean the same thing, most notably in title of *The International Infrastructure Management Manual* (2000, first edition). Where there is no problem of confusion, the term asset management is more widely used, as in the professional societies: the Asset Management Council in Australia, and the Institute of Asset Management in the UK. In this context, infrastructure is a wide term denoting road and rail, water, power, etc. assets.

The first published use of the term asset management to refer to physical assets is not known for sure. The earliest adopter known for certain is Dr Penny Burns in 1984. The New Zealand Infrastructure Asset Management Manual published in 1996 is an early use of the specific term infrastructure asset management . The term "asset management" was first used in a document published in 1983 by the United States Department of Transportation, Federal Highway Administration entitled: Transportation Resource Management Strategies for Elected Officials of Rural Municipalities and Counties. That document consisted of seven chapters of resource management strategies for each of two types of transportation infrastructure - roads & bridges and public transportation. Each of these two parts of the document focused on the following seven categories: Planning, Prioritization, Contracting Out, Innovative Finance, Human Resource Management, Asset Management and Performance Measurement & Reporting.

## Current Situation

After decades of capital investment in United States's infrastructure such as the Interstate Highway System, local water treatment facilities, electric transmission and utility lines, the need to sustain such infrastructure experiences mounting challenges. The current duress includes tight state and local budgets, deferral of needed maintenance funding, and political pressures to cut public spending. Today, shrinking federal appropriations, progressively aging capital stock, and parochial statuses and interest groups have inhibited flexible procurement strategies. And with the rise of design firms, professional societies, licensures, construction and industry associations, and related specialties the management of the infrastructure system has dramatically altered. As a result, the life cycle of a facility, including Planning, Design, Construction, Operations, Maintenance, Upgrading, and Replacement, has become bifurcated between agencies and firms where Design and Construction becomes contracted separately from Operations and Maintenance. The push for more dual-track strategies and not segmented ones such as Design-Build and Build-Operate-Transfer helps in maintaining public facilities. Yet, over time, the government apparatus focused more on start-up capital expenses for constructing public assets without focused monies on maintenance.

After World War II, with the policies of the Roosevelt Administration, economic boom of the 1950s, and rise in Federalism, public projects became financed through direct government funding. Additionally, the federal government began setting criteria and procedures for architects and engineers to comply on federal construction and related projects. State and local statutes soon followed suit. Over the years, a large bureaucratic machine began administering infrastructure projects through Design-Bid-Build and debt financing methods. This led to hyper-competition of federal, states, and localities over scant federal resources and overall fostered a limited approach in life-cycle attention (namely, no account of operation and maintenance). Asset management attempts to fill in the gaps of such fragmentation for better performance in infrastructure assets.

In Canada, the majority of municipal assets were built between 1960s to 1970s. The average age of municipal infrastructure has increased since the end of the late 1970s, because investment has been insufficient to replace deteriorating assets. This deficit could be the result a shift in financing policy at the end of 1970s, which made the local governments responsible to fund the municipal assets. Recently, in Ontario municipalities are required to develop an asset management plan to receive provincial fund.

## Processes and Activities

The basic premise of infrastructure asset management is to intervene at strategic points in an asset's normal life cycle to extend the expected service life, and thereby maintain its performance. Typically, a long-life-cycle asset requires multiple intervention points including a combination of repair and maintenance activities and even overall rehabilitation. Costs decrease with planned maintenance rather than unplanned maintenance. Yet, excessive planned maintenance increases costs. Thus, a balance between the two must be recognized. While each improvement raises an asset's condition curve, each rehabilitation resets an asset's condition curve, and complete replacement returns condition curve to new level or upgraded level. Therefore, strategically timing these interventions will aid in extending an asset's life cycle. A simple working definition of asset management would be: first, assess what you have; then, assess what condition it is in; and lastly, assess the financial burden to maintain it at a targeted condition.

Essential processes and activities for infrastructure asset management include the following:

- Maintaining a systematic record of individual assets (an inventory)—e.g., acquisition cost, original service life, remaining useful life, physical condition, repair and maintenance consistency
- Developing a defined program for sustaining the aggregate body of assets through planned maintenance, repair, and replacement
- Implementing and managing information systems in support of these systems—e.g., Geographic Information Systems

These processes and activities are interrelated and interdependent aspects that usually cross organizational boundaries including finance, engineering, and operations. Hence, asset management is a comprehensive approach in handling an immense portfolio of public and private capital stock. As example, in 2009, the IBM Maximo software was adopted to manage the maintenance of rolling stock and facilities for three railway systems: the Long Island Rail Road, San Francisco BART system, Washington metrorail. Also, recently, wireless sensors, totaling 663, have been installed on South Korea's Jindo Bridge to detect structural cracks and corrosion. Though in a testing phase among three universities in South Korea, United States, and Japan, the use of wireless technology to may lend itself to future, cost-efficient asset management.

## Work Practices

Politically, many legal and governmental initiatives have emphasized proactive asset management given the current state of an aging infrastructure and fiscal challenges. Recent developments include the Governmental Accounting Standards Board Statement No. 34 that required state and local entities to report in their accounting *all* infrastructure assets not only the privately financed ones such as water supply and utilities paid by user fees. This helps to determine an agency's overall infrastructure asset inventory, timely assessment of physical condition, and annual projection of financial requirements. Additionally, the United States Environmental Protection Agency's Capacity, Management, Operation, and Maintenance (CMOM) initiative works to move away from the compliance-mandate enforcement to proactive partnership with public managers to self-audit their infrastructure systems in assessing capacity, management, and operations/maintenance.

Still other proponents for proactive management include judicial consent decrees for facility managers to resolve noncompliance with environmental standards set by EPA or state environmental protection departments (i.e., laws against sewer overflows); post-9/11 security vulnerability analyses; funding legislation that specifies asset management as qualifying condition to receive/keep award; and professional organizations that are moving the industry to asset management through education, research, and workshops.

Despite the current challenges of the time's financial constraints, one advantage is the growing availability of methodology and technology to employ asset management. But while municipalities have made significant investments and use of software tools in the last 20 years, they are mostly stand-alone systems with limited to no capability for sharing or exchanging information with other tools. Consequently, they operate in isolated silos of information across municipal departments. Data has to be re-interpreted, transformed, and reentered into different software tools several times leading to time-consuming, prone-to-error inefficiencies. Many in academia and industry recognize the need for integrated, multidisciplinary asset management that involves:

- Systemization and coordination of work processes
- Development of centralized share data repositories
- Organization of distributed software tools into modular, extensive-wide software environments

## IIAM Approach

The Institute of Infrastructure Asset Management (IIAM), a U.S.-based transportation consultancy, works to promote the same issues and collaborates with other organizations, such as in the INFRAASSETS2010 conference in Malaysia, in management of public assets.

The IIAM approach to infrastructure asset management is based upon the definition of a Standard of Service (SoS) that describes how an asset will perform in objective and measurable terms. The SoS includes the definition of a "minimum condition grade", which is established by considering the consequences of a failure of the infrastructure asset.

The key components of "Infrastructure Asset Management" are:

- Definition of a Standard of Service
    - Establishment of measurable specifications of how the asset should perform
    - Establishment of a minimum condition grade
- Establishment of a whole-life cost approach to managing the asset
- Elaboration of an Asset Management Plan

## GIS System

Public asset management expands the definition of Enterprise Asset Management (EAM) by incorporating the management of all things which are of value to a municipal jurisdiction and its citizen's expectations. Public Asset Management is the term that considers the importance that public assets affect other public assets and work activities which are important sources of revenue for municipal governments and has various points of citizen interaction. The versatility and functionality of a GIS system allow for the control and management of all assets and land-focused activities. All public assets are interconnected and share proximity, and this connectivity is possible through the use of GIS. GIS-centric public asset management standardizes data and allows interoperability, providing users the capability to reuse, coordinate, and share information in an efficient and effective manner.

Among the GISs in use for infrastructure management in the USA are GE [[Smallworld] and ESRI. An ESRI GIS platform combined with the overall public asset management umbrella of both physical *hard* assets and *soft* assets helps remove the traditional silos of structured municipal functions which serves the citizens. While the hard assets are the typical physical assets or infrastructure assets, the soft assets of a municipality includes permits, license, code enforcement, right-of-ways and other land-focused work activities.

### Capacity Building

An executive education program in infrastructure asset management (Certificate of Advanced Studies Managing Infrastructure Assets, CASMIA, 16ECTS) has been developed since 2012, launched in 2014 and funded by Swiss federal Agency of Energy (SFOE). It is the only individual and organizational learning program worldwide that operates by changing university institute hosts. This ensures that the emerging MIA profession can cope with cross-disciplinary content critically and universities review curriculum. Former university institutes include ETH Zurich (IBI) and University of St. Gallen (HSG-ACA). This program also ensures the highest possible accreditation for an emerging profession, since individuals in this field still outperform institutions in terms of quality of content.

## Fixed Assets Management

Fixed assets management is an accounting process that seeks to track fixed assets for the purposes of financial accounting, preventive maintenance, and theft deterrence.

Organizations face a significant challenge to track the location, quantity, condition, maintenance and depreciation status of their fixed assets. A popular approach to tracking fixed assets uses serial numbered asset tags, which are labels often with bar codes for easy and accurate reading. The owner of the assets can take inventory with a mobile bar code reader and then produce a report.

Off-the-shelf software packages for fixed asset management are marketed to businesses small and large. Some enterprise resource planning systems are available with fixed assets modules.

Some tracking methods automate the process, such as by using fixed scanners to read bar codes on railway freight cars or by attaching a radio-frequency identification (RFID) tag to an asset.

### Fixed Asset Tracking Software

Tracking assets is an important concern of every company, regardless of size. Fixed assets are defined as any 'permanent' object that a business uses internally including but not limited to computers, tools, software, or office equipment. While employees may use a specific tool or tools, the asset ultimately belongs to the company and must be returned. And therefore without an accurate method of keeping track of these assets it would be very easy for a company to lose control of them.

With advancements in technology, asset tracking software is now available that will help any size business track valuable assets such as equipment and supplies. According to a study issued in December, 2005 by the ARC Advisory Group, the worldwide market for enterprise asset management (EAM) was then at an estimated $2.2 billion and was expected to grow at about 5.0 percent per year reaching $2.8 billion in 2010.

Fixed Asset Tracking across multiple locations

Asset tracking software allows companies to track what assets it owns, where each is located, who has it, when it was checked out, when it is due for return, when it is scheduled for maintenance, and the cost and depreciation of each asset.

The reporting option that is built into most asset tracking solutions provides pre-built reports, including assets by category and department, check-in/check-out, net book value of assets, assets past due, audit history, and transactions.

All of this information is captured in one program and can be used on PCs as well as mobile devices. As a result, companies reduce expenses through loss prevention and improved equipment maintenance. They reduce new and unnecessary equipment purchases, and they can more accurately calculate taxes based on depreciation schedules.

The most commonly tracked assets are:

- Plant and equipment
- Buildings
- Fixtures and fittings
- Long term investment
- Machinery
- Vehicles and heavy equipments

## IT Asset Management

IT asset management (ITAM) is the set of business practices that join financial, contractual and inventory functions to support life cycle management and strategic decision making for the IT environment. Assets include all elements of software and hardware that are found in the business environment.

IT asset management (also called IT inventory management) is an important part of an organization's strategy. It usually involves gathering detailed hardware and software inventory information which is then used to make decisions about hardware and software purchases and redistribution. IT inventory management helps organizations manage their systems more effectively and saves time and money by avoiding unnecessary asset purchases and promoting the harvesting of existing resources. Organizations that develop and maintain an effective IT asset management program further minimize the incremental risks and related costs of advancing IT portfolio infrastructure projects based on old, incomplete and/or less accurate information.

## Hardware Asset Management

Hardware asset management entails the management of the physical components of computers and computer networks, from acquisition through disposal. Common business practices include request and approval process, procurement management, life cycle management, redeployment and disposal management. A key component is capturing the financial information about the hardware life cycle which aids the organization in making business decisions based on meaningful and measurable financial objectives.

Software Asset Management is a similar process, focusing on software assets, including licenses, versions and installed endpoints.

## Role of IT Asset Management in an Organization

The IT Asset Management function is the primary point of accountability for the life-cycle management of information technology assets throughout the organization.

Included in this responsibility are development and maintenance of policies, standards, processes, systems and measurements that enable the organization to manage the IT Asset Portfolio with respect to risk, cost, control, IT Governance, compliance and business performance objectives as established by the business.

IT Asset Management uses integrated software solutions that work with all departments that are involved in the procurement, deployment, management and expense reporting of IT assets.

## IT Asset Disposition

When assets need to be removed from the enterprise, they move through various disposition processes. Commonly they are handed over to an IT Asset Disposition vendor to be recycled or destroyed. Assets should be managed properly after going offline to ensure they do not get lost prior to reaching the vendor. The vendor of choice should then have secure procedures for tracking assets during the entire time of their possession. After proper disposal, the vendor provides a certificate of destruction with the serial numbers of assets they destroyed and recycled. The company should then verify the serial numbers on their certificate of destruction with the assets they know they handed over to the vendor. Tracking assets that are offline, prior to disposal, should be approached with the same efficiency and security as when those same assets are online. A good method for choosing a destruction vendor is to find a NAID certified company. They have a corporate responsibility to dispose of e-waste properly to ensure a healthy environment. Look into donation programs in your area.

## ISO

The International Standards Organization (ISO) has a family of standards for IT Asset Management. The ISO 19770 family consists of 4 major parts,

- 19770-1 is a process related standard which outlines best practices for IT Asset Management in an organization. The latest revision dates to 2012 and breaks ITAM processes down into 4 tiers in a maturity matrix.
- 19770-2 is a standard for machine encapsulation (in the form of an XML file known as a SWID tag) of inventory data – allowing users to easily identify what software is deployed on a given device. Initially published in 2009, this standard is currently under redevelopment and is likely to be republished in 2015.
- 19770-3 is a standard which provides a schema for machine encapsulation of entitlements and rights associated with software licenses. The records (known as ENT's) will describe all entitlements and rights attendant to a piece of software and the method for measurement of license/entitlement consumption. This standard is due for submission as a Draft International Standard in 2014 with a view to publication in 2015.
- 19770-4 allows for standardized reporting of utilization of resources. This is crucial when considering complex datacentre license types and for management of cloud based software and hardware (SaaS and IaaS). 19770-4 was proposed in 2012 and should be published in 2015.

These standards help organizations better understand IT Asset Management best practices and collect and manage the data required in IT Asset Management processes.

## Process

ITAM business practices are process-driven and matured through iterative and focused improvements. Most successful ITAM programs are invasive to the organization, involving everyone at some level, such as end users (educating on compliance), budget managers (redeployment as a choice), IT service departments (providing information on warranties), and finance (invoice reconciliation, updates for fixed asset inventories).

IT asset management generally uses automation, including the use small "passive"

RFID tags designed to fit all types of IT assets and smart software designed to track the RFID-tagged asset locations automatically, to manage the discovery of assets, so inventory can be compared to ownership information. Full business management of IT assets requires a repository of multiple types of information about the asset, as well as integration with other systems such as supply chain, help desk, procurement and HR systems and ITSM.

For small and medium-sized businesses, a solution might not have to be so robust as to influence many departments. However, IT assets still need to be tracked for risk management, accurate resource and budget allocation, and accountability of assets' whereabouts. A good solution for small businesses will enable them to search for assets they currently own, manage online and offline assets, and plan accurately for the future. These tasks, however, should be simple, secure and efficient because a small business IT professional's time is very valuable.

## Digital Asset Management

Digital asset management (DAM) consists of management tasks and decisions surrounding the ingestion, annotation, cataloguing, storage, retrieval and distribution of digital assets.

Digital photographs, animations, videos and music exemplify the target areas. Digital asset management systems (DAMS) include computer software and hardware systems that aid in the process of digital asset management.

The term "digital asset management" (DAM) also refers to the protocol for downloading, renaming, backing up, rating, grouping, archiving, optimizing, maintaining, thinning, and exporting files or other binary data.

The efficiency of above mentioned protocols could be ensured through a structured taxonomy.

The "media asset management" (MAM) sub-category of digital asset management mainly addresses audio, video and other media content. The more recent concept of enterprise content management (ECM) often deals with solutions which address similar features but in a wider range of industries or applications.

Smaller DAM systems are easier to categorize as to content and usage since they normally operate in a particular operational context. This would hold true for systems attached to audio or video production systems. The key differentiators here are the type of decoders and I/O (input/output) used for the asset ingest, use and outgest. Since metadata describes the essence (and proxy copies), the metadata can serve as a guide to the playout decoders, transcoders, and channels as well as an input to access control rules. This means that the essence can be treated as a non-described storage object except when being accessed for viewing or editing. There is relevance to this when considering the overall design and use of larger implementations. The closer the asset is to the ingest/edit/playout tool, the greater the technical architecture needs to accommodate delivery requirements such as bandwidth, latency, capacity, access control, availability of resources, etc. The further the asset moves into a general storage architecture (e.g. hierarchical storage management [HSM]) the more it can be treated as a general blob (binary large object) that is typically held in the filesystem, not the database. The impact of this set of needs means that it is possible and reasonable to design larger systems using smaller, more expensive performance-systems at the edge of the network where the essence is being used in its intended form and less expensive systems further back for storage and archival. This type of design exemplifies Infrastructure Convergence Architecture, where the line-of-business operations technology and IT technologies depend on one another for functional and performance (non-functional) requirements.

## Assets

Generally the "asset" being managed is collected and stored in a digital format. There is usually a target version – referred to as "essence" – generally the highest-resolution and highest-fidelity representation. The asset is detailed by its metadata. Metadata is the description of the asset and the description depth can vary depending on the needs of the system, designer, or user. Metadata can describe, but is not limited to, the description of: asset content (what is in the package?); the means of encoding/decoding (e.g. JPEG, tar, MPEG 2); provenance (history to point of capture); ownership; rights of access; as well as many others. There exist some predefined standards and template for metadata such as Dublin Core and PBCore. In cases of systems that contain large-size asset essences, such as MPEG 2 and JPEG2000 for the cases of images and video, there are usually related "proxy" copies of the essence. A proxy copy is a lower-resolution representation of the essence that can be used as a reference in order to reduce the overall bandwidth requirements of the DAM system infrastructure. It can be generated and retained at the time of ingestion of the asset simultaneous or subsequent to the essence, or it can be generated on the fly using transcoders.

## Types of Systems

The following broad categories of digital asset management systems may be distinguished as:

- Brand asset management systems, with a focus on facilitation of content re-use within large organizations. Here the content is largely marketing- or sales-related, for example, product imagery, logos, marketing collateral or fonts, to give a few examples.

- Library asset management systems, with a focus on storage and retrieval of large amounts of infrequently changing media assets, for example in video or photo archiving.
- Production asset management systems focus on managing assets as they are being created for a digital media production (video game, 3D feature film, animation, visual-effects shots, etc.) They usually include work-flow and project-management features coupled with the storage, organization and revision control of frequently changing digital assets.
- Cloud-based digital asset management systems have recently begun to emerge to complement on-premises systems.

DAM software may be open source or proprietary.

# Asset Health Management

Asset health management or (AHM) is the field of study which looks at how to manage the "health" of an asset or assets. This often includes methods to establish asset health and effort to decide the appropriate actions to be taken to manage the assets' health. This also includes the discussion of health at end of life to ensure the asset's full life is used efficiently.

Asset health management includes many different methods which can sometime overlap in their intended scope and methods. Asset health management has become a difficult field to discuss due to the use of the same acronym to describe multiple different approaches and the use of the same approach with different names.

Asset health management can be considered a subset of Asset management.

## Asset Health Management Taxonomy

Asset health management consists of multiple strategies and parts but a rough description is given as follows:

- Asset health diagnostics

  Methods used to establish the current health of the asset
- Asset health prognostics

  Methods used to predict how the health of the asset will change in the future
- Asset health maintenance

  including maintenance, repair, and operations (better referred to as maintenance, repair,and overhaul) These methods are used to keep an asset health, restore health to an asset or through major work restore usable life to an asset.

- Asset end of life decisions
- Asset disposal

### Management of Multiple Assets

There is often also a consideration of additional work done to manage the health of multiple assets within the same framework. Sometimes referred to as Fleet health management and falling within the study of Fleet management It should be noted that while it is common to need to manage the health of multiple assets they are not always vehicles and frequently of mixed type.

When resources are constrained it is a fascinating management problem to consider how best to manage the health of assets. It is rare that assets can be managed in an unconstrained way as resources are always limited by a need to make efficient use of them.

### Asset Health Management Relevant Standards

A collection of some standards which are often use to manage the health of assets. This is not intended to be an exhaustive list and will organically improve.

- Open O&M
- MSG-3

### Asset Health Management Examples

A short list is provided to illustrate the many methods that are some sort of asset health management method or philosophy.

- IVHM
- Built-in_self-test
- Built-in_test_equipment
- HUMS

## Facility Management

Facility management (or facilities management or FM) is a professional management discipline focused upon the efficient and effective delivery of support services for the organizations that it serves. It serves to ensure the integration of people, systems, place, process, and technology.

## Definitions and Scope

Professional FM as an interdisciplinary business function has the objective to coordinate demand and supply of facilities and services within public and private organizations. The term "Facility" (pl. facilities) means something that is built, installed or established to serve a purpose, which, in general, is every "Tangible asset that supports an organization." Examples are real estate property, buildings, technical infrastructure, (HVAC), lighting, transportation, IT-services, furniture, Custodial, grounds, and other user-specific equipment and appliances.

The European standard for facilities management defines it as "the integration of processes within an organization to maintain and develop the agreed services which support and improve the effectiveness of its primary activities."

The International Organization for Standardization will publish the first two international standards relating to facilities management in 2017.

## Scope

FM covers these two main areas: 'Space & Infrastructure' (such as planning, design, workplace, construction, lease, occupancy, maintenance, furniture and cleaning) and 'People & Organization' (such as catering, ICT, HR, accounting, marketing, hospitality). The first refers to the physical built environment with focus on (work-) space and (building-) infrastructure. The second covers the people and the organization and is related to work psychology and occupational physiology. According to the International Facility Management Association (IFMA): "FM is the practice of coordinating the physical workplace with the people and work of the organization. It integrates the principles of business administration, architecture and the behavioral and engineering sciences." In a 2009 Global Job Task Analysis, IFMA identified the core competencies of facility management as:

- communication
- emergency preparedness and business continuity
- environmental stewardship and sustainability
- finance and business
- Hospitality Management
- human factors
- leadership and strategy

- operations and maintenance
- project management
- quality
- real estate and property management
- technology.

The British Institute of Facilities Management adopts the European definition and through its accredited qualification framework offers career path curriculum ranging from school leaver level through to masters degree level that is aligned with the European Qualifications framework.

FM may also cover activities other than business services; these are referred to as non-core functions, and vary from one business sector to another. FM is also subject to continuous innovation and development, under pressure to reduce costs and to add value to the core business of public or private sector client organisations.

Facility management is supported with training and professional qualifications often co-ordinated by FM institutes or associations, and formal degree programmes exist at undergraduate and graduate levels.

## As a Defined Academic Discipline

Facility Management has been recognized as an academic discipline since the 1990s. Initial FM research work in Europe started in universities in the UK, the Netherlands, and the Nordic countries, where academies funded research centres and started to establish courses at Bachelors, Masters and PhD levels. Early European FM research centres include: the Centre for Facilities Management (CFM) founded in Glasgow in 1990, the Centre for People and buildings at Delft University of Technology, and metamorphose at the Norwegian University of Science and Technology. In 2010 Professor Antje Junghans (Chairman EUROFM Research group 2010–2012) conducted a survey with active involvement of researchers and professors from 9 countries and 17 universities on behalf of the European Facility Management research group (Junghans, 2012). Today 50 universities and research institutions are represented in EUROFM. The German Facility Management Association (GEFMA) has certified 16 FM study programs and courses at universities and universities of applied sciences in Germany. University of Moratuwa, Sri Lanka is leading the Facilities Management academic background in Asian region by providing B.Sc. (Hons) Facilities Management since 2006.

## Role of the Facilities Manager

Facilities managers (FMs) operate across business functions.

The number one priority of an FM is keeping people alive and safe.

Facility managers have to operate at two levels:

- Strategically-tactically: helping clients, customers and end-users understand the potential impact of their decisions on the provision of space, services, cost and business risk.
- Operationally: ensuring corporate and cost effective environment for the occupants to function.

This is accomplished by managing:

## EHS: Environment, Health and Safety

The FM department in an organization is required to control and manage many environment and safety related issues. Failure to do so may lead to unhealthy conditions leading to employees falling sick, injury, loss of business, prosecution and insurance claims. The confidence of customers and investors in the business may also be affected by adverse publicity from safety lapses.

## Fire Safety

The threat from fire carries one of the highest risk to loss of life, and the potential to damage or shut down a business. The facilities management department will have in place maintenance, inspection and testing for all of the fire safety equipment and systems, keeping records and certificates of compliance.

## Security

Protection of employees and the business often comes under the control of the facilities management department, in particular the maintenance of security hardware. Manned guarding may be under the control of a separate department.

## Maintenance, Testing and Inspections

Maintenance, testing and inspection schedules are required to ensure that the facility is operating safely and efficiently, to maximize the life of equipment and reduce the risk of failure. Statutory obligations must also be met. The work is planned, often using a computer-aided facility management system.

## Building Maintenance

Building maintenance comprises all preventative, remedial and upgrade works required for the upkeep and improvement of buildings & their components. This works may include disciplines such as painting and decorating, carpentry, plumbing, glazing, plastering, plastering and tiling.

## Cleaning

Cleaning operations are often undertaken out of business hours, but provision may be made during times of occupations for the cleaning of toilets, replenishing consumables (such as toilet rolls, soap) plus litter picking and reactive response. Cleaning is scheduled as a series of periodic (daily, weekly, monthly) tasks.

## Operational

The facilities management department has responsibilities for the day-to-day running of the building, these tasks may be outsourced or carried out by directly employed staff. This is a policy issue, but due to the immediacy of the response required in many of the activities involved the facilities manager will often require daily reports or an escalation procedure.

Some issues require more than just periodic maintenance, for example those that can stop or hamper the productivity of the business or that have safety implications. Many of these are managed by the facilities management "help desk" that staff are able to be contacted either by telephone or email. The response to help desk calls are prioritized but may be as simple as too hot or too cold, lights not working, photocopier jammed, coffee spills, or vending machine problems.

Help desks may be used to book meeting rooms, car parking spaces and many other services, but this often depends on how the facilities department is organized. Facilities may be split into two sections, often referred to as "soft" services such as reception and post room, and "hard" services, such as the mechanical, fire and electrical services.

## Business Continuity Planning

All organizations should have a continuity plan so that in the event of a fire or major failure the business can recover quickly. In large organizations it may be that the staff move to another site that has been set up to model the existing operation. The facilities management department would be one of the key players should it be necessary to move the business to a recovery site.

## Space Allocation and Changes

In many organizations, office layouts are subject to frequent changes. This process is referred to as churn, and the percentage of the staff moved during a year is known as the churn rate. These moves are normally planned by the facilities management department using computer-aided design. In addition to meeting the needs of the business, compliance with statutory requirements related to office layouts include:

- the minimum amount of space to be provided per staff member
- fire safety arrangements

- lighting levels
- signage
- ventilation
- temperature control
- welfare arrangements such as toilets and drinking water

Consideration may also be given to vending, catering or a place where staff can make a drink and take a break from their desk.

## Asset and Liability Management

Initially pioneered by financial institutions during the 1970s as interest rates became increasingly volatile, asset and liability management (often abbreviated ALM) is the practice of managing risks that arise due to mismatches between the assets and liabilities.

The process is at the crossroads between risk management and strategic planning. It is not just about offering solutions to mitigate or hedge the risks arising from the interaction of assets and liabilities but is focused on a long-term perspective: success in the process of maximising assets to meet complex liabilities may increase profitability.

Thus modern ALM includes the allocation and management of assets, equity, interest rate and credit risk management including risk overlays, and the calibration of firm-wide tools within these risk frameworks for optimisation and management in the local regulatory and capital environment.

Often an ALM approach passively matches assets against liabilities (fully hedged) and leaves surplus to be actively managed.

### ALM Objectives and Scope

The exact roles and perimeter around ALM can vary significantly from one bank (or other financial institutions) to another depending on the business model adopted and can encompass a broad area of risks.

The traditional ALM programs focus on interest rate risk and liquidity risk because they represent the most prominent risks affecting the organization balance-sheet (as they require coordination between assets and liabilities).

But ALM also now seeks to broaden assignments such as foreign exchange risk and capital management. According to the Balance sheet management benchmark survey conducted in 2009 by the audit and consulting company PricewaterhouseCoopers (PwC), 51% of the 43 leading financial institutions participants look at capital management in their ALM unit.

The scope of the ALM function to a larger extent covers the following processes:

1. Liquidity risk: the current and prospective risk arising when the bank is unable to meet its obligations as they come due without adversely affecting the bank's financial conditions. From an ALM perspective, the focus is on the funding liquidity risk of the bank, meaning its ability to meet its current and future cash-flow obligations and collateral needs, both expected and unexpected. This mission thus includes the bank liquidity's benchmark price in the market.

2. Interest rate risk: The risk of losses resulting from movements in interest rates and their impact on future cash-flows. Generally because a bank may have a disproportionate amount of fixed or variable rates instruments on either side of the balance-sheet. One of the primary causes are mismatches in terms of bank deposits and loans.

3. Capital markets risk: The risk from movements in equity and/or credit on the balance sheet. An insurer may wish to harvest either risk or fee premia. Risk is then mitigated by options, futures, derivative overlays which may incorporate tactical or strategic views.

4. Currency risk management: The risk of losses resulting from movements in exchanges rates. To the extent that cash-flow assets and liabilities are denominated in different currencies.

5. Funding and capital management: As all the mechanism to ensure the maintenance of adequate capital on a continuous basis. It is a dynamic and ongoing process considering both short- and longer-term capital needs and is coordinated with a bank's overall strategy and planning cycles (usually a prospective time-horizon of 2 years).

6. Profit planning and growth.

7. In addition, ALM deals with aspects related to credit risk as this function is also to manage the impact of the entire credit portfolio (including cash, investments, and loans) on the balance sheet. The credit risk, specifically in the loan portfolio, is handled by a separate risk management function and represents one of the main data contributors to the ALM team.

The ALM function scope covers both a prudential component (management of all possible risks and rules and regulation) and an optimization role (management of funding costs, generating results on balance sheet position), within the limits of compliance (implementation and monitoring with internal rules and regulatory set of rules). ALM intervenes in these issues of current business activities but is also consulted to organic development and external acquisition to analyse and validate the funding terms options, conditions of the projects and any risks (i.e., funding issues in local currencies).

Today, ALM techniques and processes have been extended and adopted by corporations other than financial institutions; e.g., insurance.

## Treasury and ALM

For simplification treasury management can be covered and depicted from a corporate perspective looking at the management of liquidity, funding, and financial risk. On the other hand, ALM is a discipline relevant to banks and financial institutions whose balance sheets present different challenges and who must meet regulatory standards.

For banking institutions, treasury and ALM are strictly interrelated with each other and collaborate in managing both liquidity, interest rate, and currency risk at solo and group level: Where ALM focuses more on risk analysis and medium- and long-term financing needs, treasury manages short-term funding (mainly up to one year) including intra-day liquidity management and cash clearing, crisis liquidity monitoring.

## ALM Governance

The responsibility for ALM is often divided between the treasury and Chief Financial Officer (CFO). In smaller organizations, the ALM process can be addressed by one or two key persons (Chief Executive Officer, such as the CFO or treasurer).

The vast majority of banks operate a centralised ALM model which enables oversight of the consolidated balance-sheet with lower-level ALM units focusing on business units or legal entities.

To assist and supervise the ALM unit an Asset Liability Committee (ALCO), whether at the board or management level, is established. It has the central purpose of attaining goals defined by the short- and long-term strategic plans:

- To ensure adequate liquidity while managing the bank's spread between the interest income and interest expense
- To approve a contingency plan
- To review and approve the liquidity and funds management policy at least annually
- To link the funding policy with needs and sources via mix of liabilities or sale of assets (fixed vs. floating rate funds, wholesale vs. retail deposit, money market vs. capital market funding, domestic vs. foreign currency funding...)

## Legislative Summary

Relevant ALM legislation deals mainly with the management of interest rate risk and liquidity risk:

- Most global banks have benchmarked their ALM framework to the Basel Committee on Banking Supervision (BCBS) guidance 'Principles for the management and supervision of interest rate risk'. Issued in July 2004, this paper has the objective to support the Pillar 2 approach to interest rate risk in the banking book within the Basel II capital framework.
- In January 2013, the Basel Committee has issued the full text of the revised Liquidity Coverage Ratio (LCR) as one of the key component of the Basel III capital framework. This new coming ratio will ensure that banks will have sufficient adequacy transformation level between their stock of unencumbered high-quality assets (HQLA) and their conversion into cash to meet their liquidity requirements for a 30-calendar-day liquidity stress scenario (and thus hoping to cure shortcoming from Basel II that was not addressing liquidity management).

## ALM Concepts

## Building an ALM Policy

As in all operational areas, ALM must be guided by a formal policy and must address:

- Limits on the maximum size of major asset/ liability categories
- Balance sheet mix : in order to follow the old adage 'Don't put all your eggs in one basket'
    - Limits on the mix of balance sheet assets (loans by credit category, financial instruments...) considering levels of risk and return and thus guided by annual planning targets, lending licence constraints and regulatory restrictions on investments.
    - Limits on the mix of balance sheet liabilities such as deposits and other types of funding (all sources of funding are expressed as a % of total assets with the objective to offer comparability and correlate by term and pricing to the mix of assets held) considering the differential costs and volatility of these types of funds
    - Policy limits have to be realistic :based on historical trend analysis and comparable to the peers or the market
- Correlating maturities and terms
- Controlling liquidity position and set limits in terms of ratios and projected net

cash-flows, analyse and test alternative sources of liquidity

- Controlling interest rate risk and establishing interest rate risk measurement techniques
- Controlling currency risk
- Controlling the use of derivatives as well as defining management analysis and expert contribution for derivative transactions
- Frequency and content for board reporting
- But also practical decision such as :
  - Who is responsible for monitoring the ALM position of the bank
  - What tools to use to monitor the ALM framework

| **Policy limits for balance sheet mix on the size of asset/liabilities categories** | |
|---|---|
| **Assets** | **Policy limits as a % of Total Assets** |
| Loans and leases | **70%** |
| Residential mortgage | 30% |
| Commercial loans | 20% |
| Personal loans | 15% |
| Finance leases | 5% |
| Financial investments | 15% |
| Other investments | 5% |
| Inventories | 1% |
| Intangible assets | 3% |
| Cash and cash equivalent | 4% |
| Trade an dother receivables | 2% |
| | **100%** |
| **Liabilities** | |
| Domestic interest bearing deposits | **75%** |
| Term deposit | 42% |
| Demand deposit | 25% |
| Brokered deposits | 8% |
| Short-term borrowings | 4% |
| Long-term debt | 12% |
| Non-interest bearing liabilities | 5% |
| Deferred revenue | 2% |
| Trade and other payable | 2% |
| | **100%** |

Illustrative example of a balance sheet mix limits mechanism

Note that the ALM policy has not the objective to skip out the institution from elaborating a liquidity policy. In any case, the ALM and liquidity policies need to be correlated as decision on lending, investment, liabilities, equity are all interrelated.

## ALM Core Functions

### Managing Gaps

The objective is to measure the direction and extent of asset-liability mismatch through the funding or maturity gap. This aspect of ALM stresses the importance of balancing maturities as well as cash-flows or interest rates for a particular set time horizon.

For the management of interest rate risk it may take the form of matching the maturities and interest rates of loans and investments with the maturities and interest rates of deposit, equity and external credit in order to maintain adequate profitability. In other words, it is the management of the spread between interest rate sensitive assets and interest rate sensitive liabilities..

## Static/Dynamic Gap Measurement Techniques

Gap analysis suffers from only covering future gap direction of current existing exposures and exercise of options (i.e.: prepayments) at different point in time. Dynamic gap analysis enlarges the perimeter for a specific asset by including 'what if' scenarios on making assumptions on new volumes, (changes in the business activity, future path of interest rate, changes in pricing, shape of yield curve, new prepayments transactions, what its forecast gap positions will look like if entering into a hedge transaction.)

## Liquidity Risk Management

The role of the bank in the context of the maturity transformation that occurs in the banking book (as traditional activity of the bank is to borrow short and lend long) lets inherently the institution vulnerable to liquidity risk and can even conduct to the so-call risk of 'run of the bank' as depositors, investors or insurance policy holders can withdraw their funds/ seek for cash in their financial claims and thus impacting current and future cash-flow and collateral needs of the bank (risk appeared if the bank is unable to meet in good conditions these obligations as they come due). This aspect of liquidity risk is named funding liquidity risk and arises because of liquidity mismatch of assets and liabilities (unbalance in the maturity term creating liquidity gap). Even if market liquidity risk is not covered into the conventional techniques of ALM (market liquidity risk as the risk to not easily offset or eliminate a position at the prevailing market price because of inadequate market depth or market disruption), these 2 liquidity risk types are closely interconnected. In fact, reasons for banking cash inflows are :

- when counterparties repay their debts (loan repayments): indirect connect due to the borrower's dependence to market liquidity to obtain the funds
- when clients put deposit: indirect connect due to the depositor's dependence to market liquidity to obtain the funds
- when the bank purchases assets hold: direct connect with market liquidity (security's market liquidity as the ease at trading it and thus potential sharp in price)
- when the bank sells debts it has primary bought: direct connect

# Liquidity Gap Analysis

| Liquidity gap report | | | | | | | |
|---|---|---|---|---|---|---|---|
| Time interval | 1 to 14 days | 15 to 28 days | 29 days up to 3 months | Over 3 months and up to 6 months | Over 6 months and up to 12 months | Over 1 year | Total |
| **Assets (Inflows)** | | | | | | | |
| Overnight Investments | 15 456 | 0 | 0 | 0 | 0 | 0 | 15 456 |
| Investments | 18 890 | 16 678 | 15 034 | 43 278 | 27 413 | 18 996 | 140 289 |
| Loans | 54 234 | 48 098 | 42 896 | 111 567 | 65 447 | 50 320 | 372 562 |
| Other assets | 0 | 0 | 0 | 0 | 0 | 0 | 0 |
| **Total assets** | 88 580 | 64 776 | 57 930 | 154 845 | 92 860 | 69 316 | 528 307 |
| **Liabilities (Outflows)** | | | | | | | |
| Non maturity deposits | 956 | 4 003 | 3 045 | 10 519 | 9 459 | 9 774 | 37 756 |
| Time deposits | 39 671 | 38 004 | 42 590 | 90 488 | 74 933 | 32 309 | 317 995 |
| Total deposits | 40 627 | 42 007 | 45 635 | 101 007 | 84 392 | 42 083 | 355 751 |
| Overnight borrowings | 0 | 0 | 0 | 0 | 0 | 0 | 0 |
| Borrowings | 96 551 | 23 599 | 1 678 | 7 990 | 29 045 | 5 332 | 164 195 |
| Other liabilities | 0 | 0 | 0 | 0 | 0 | 0 | 0 |
| **Total liabilities** | 137 178 | 65 606 | 47 313 | 108 997 | 113 437 | 47 415 | 519 946 |
| | | | | | | | **Cumulative** |
| **Periodic net cash-flow** | -48 598 | -830 | 10 617 | 45 848 | -20 577 | 21 901 | 8 361 |
| **Marginal gap** | | 47 768 | 11 447 | 35 231 | -66 425 | 42 478 | 70 499 |
| Internal limits as gap cannot exceed % of cash outflows | | | | | | | |
| **Scenario analysis** | | | | | | | |
| Retained 75% of time deposit | 29 753 | 28 503 | 31 943 | 67 866 | 56 200 | 24 232 | 238 496 |
| **Projected Net Cash flow** | -18 845 | 27 673 | 42 560 | 113 714 | 35 623 | 46 133 | 246 857 |

Liq gap report2

Measuring liquidity position via liquidity gap analysis is still one of the most common tool used and represents the foundation for scenario analysis and stress-testing.

| Maturity liquidity profile | |
|---|---|
| **Accounts** | **Time interval classification** |
| **Assets (Inflows)** | |
| Cash | 1-14 days time interval |
| Balances with other banks | |
| Current account | Non-withdrawable portion over 1 year period. |
| Money at call and short notice, term | Effective maturity period |
| Investments | |
| Approved securities | Effective maturity period |
| Corporate debentures and bonds, | Effective maturity period |
| Shares/ units of open ended mutual | Over 5 years |
| Investments in subsidiaries/joint | Over 5 years |
| Advances | |
| Bills purchased and discounted | Effective maturity period |
| Cash credit/ overdraft | Base on internal model on client's behavior |
| Term loans | Interim cash flows may be shown under |
| Non performing assets | Over 1 year |
| Fixed assets | Over 5 years |
| Other assets | Effective maturity period |
| **Liabilities (Outflows)** | |
| Capital, reserve and surplus | Over 5 years |
| Current and saving bank deposit | Classified into 2 parts<br>-volatile parts : 1-14 days time interval<br>-Core balance : over 1 year |
| Term deposit | Effective maturity period |
| Certificate of deposit, borrowings | 1-14 days time interval |
| Other liabilities and provisions | |
| Bills payable | 1-14 days time interval |
| Provisions for NPAs | Over 1 year |
| Provisions for depreciation in | Over 5 years |
| Provisions for NPA in investments | Over 1 year |
| Other provisions | Depending on the purpose |
| Other liabilities | Effective maturity period |

| Off-balance sheet position, contingent liabilities/ credit committed/ available - other inflow outflow | |
|---|---|
| Lines of credit committed to institutions (outflow) | 1-14 days time interval |
| Unavailed portion of cash credit/ overdraft (outflow) | Based on internal models |
| Letters of credit/ Guarantees (outflow) | Based on internal models and among various |
| Repos/ bills rediscounted/ swaps, forex, forward...(outflow /inflow) | Effective maturity period |
| Interest payable recivable (inflow/ outflow) | Effective maturity period |

Indicative maturity liquidity profile

To do so, ALM team is projecting future funding needs by tracking through maturity and cash-flow mismatches gap risk exposure (or matching schedule). In that situation, the risk depends not only on the maturity of asset-liabilities but also on the maturity of each intermediate cash-flow, including prepayments of loans or unforeseen usage of credit lines.

## Actions to Perform

- Determining the number and length of each relevant time interval (time bucket)

- Defining the relevant maturities of the assets and liabilities where a maturing liability will be a cash outflow while a maturing asset will be a cash inflow (based on effective maturities or the 'liquidity duration': estimated time to dispose of the instruments in a crisis situation such as withdrawal from the business). For non maturity assets (such as overdrafts, credit card balances, drawn and undrawn lines of credit or any other off-balance sheet commitments), their movements as well as volume can be predict by making assumptions derived from examining historic data on client's behaviour.
- Slotting every asset, liability and off-balance sheet items into corresponding time bucket based on effective or liquidity duration maturity

In dealing with the liquidity gap, the bank main concern is to deal with a surplus of long-term assets over short-term liabilities and thus continuously to finance the assets with the risk that required funds will not be available or into prohibitive level.

Before any remediation actions, the bank will ensure first to :

1. Spread the liability maturity profile across many time intervals to avoid concentration of most of the funding in overnight to few days time buckets (standard prudent practices admit that no more than 20% of the total funding should be in the overnight to one-week period)
2. Plan any large size funding operation in advance
3. Hold a significant productions of high liquid assets (favorable conversion rate into cash in case distressed liquidity conditions)
4. Put limits for each time bucket and monitor to stay within a comfortable level around these limits (mainly expressed as a ratio where mismatch may not exceed X% of the total cash outflows for a given time interval)

## Non-maturing Liabilities Specificity

As these instruments do not have a contractual maturity, the bank needs to dispose of a clear understanding of their duration level within the banking books. This analysis for non-maturing liabilities such as non interest-bearing deposits (savings accounts and deposits) consists of assessing the account holders behavior to determine the turnover level of the accounts or decay rate of deposits.

Calculation to define (example):

- Average opening of the accounts : a retail deposit portfolio has been open for an average of 8,3 years
- Retention rate : the given retention rate is 74,3%

- Duration level : translation into a duration of 6,2 years

Various assessment approaches may be used:

1. To place these funds in the longest-dated time bucket as deposits remain historically stable over time due to large numbers of depositors.
2. To divide the total volume into 2 parts: a stable part (core balance) and a floating part (seen as volatile with a very short maturity)
3. To assign maturities and re-pricing dates to the non-maturing liabilities by creating a portfolio of fixed income instruments that imitates the cash-flows of the liabilities positions.

The 2007 crisis however has evidence fiercely that the withdrawal of client deposits is driven by two major factors (level of sophistication of the counterparty: high-net-worth clients withdraw their funds quicker than retail ones, the absolute deposit size: large corporate clients are leaving faster than SMEs) enhancing simplification in the new deposit run-off models.

## Remediation Actions

- A surplus of assets creates a funding requirement, i.e. a negative mismatch that can be financed
    - By long-term borrowings (typically costlier) : long-term debt, preferred stock, equity or demand deposit
    - By short-term borrowings (cheaper but with higher uncertainty level in term of availability and cost): collateralized borrowings (repo), money market
    - By asset sales : distressed sales (at loss) but sales induce drastic changes in the bank's strategy
- A surplus of liabilities over assets creates the need to find efficient uses for those funds, i.e. a positive mismatch that is not a wrong signal (generally a rare scenario in a bank as the bank always has a target return on capital to achieve and so requires funds to be put to work by acquiring assets) but only means that the bank is sacrificing profits unnecessarily to achieve a liquidity position that is too liquid. This excess of liquidity can be deployed in money market instruments or risk-free assets such as government T-bills or bank certificate of deposit (CDs) if this liability excess belongs to bank's capital (the ALM desk will not take the risk of putting capital in a credit-risk investment).

## Measuring Liquidity Risk

The liquidity measurement process consists of evaluating :

- Liquidity consumption (as the bank is consumed by illiquid assets and volatile liabilities)
- Liquidity provision (as the bank is provided by stable funds and by liquid assets)

2 essential factors are to take into account :

- Speed: the speed of market deterioration in 2008 fosters the need to daily measurement of liquidity figures and quick data availability
- Integrity

But daily completeness of data for an internationally operating bank should not represent the forefront of its procupation as the seek for daily consolidation is a lengthy process that may put away the vital concern of quick availability of liquidity figures. So the main focus will be on material entities and business as well as off-balance sheet position (commitments given, movements of collateral posted)

For the purposes of quantitative analysis, since no single indicator can define adequate liquidity, several financial ratios can assist in assessing the level of liquidity risk. Due to the large number of areas within the bank's business giving rise to liquidity risk, these ratios present the simpler measures covering the major institution concern. In order to cover short-term to long-term liquidity risk they are divided into 3 categories :

1. Indicators of operating cash-flows
2. Ratios of liquidity
3. Financial strength (leverage)

| Liquidity risk oriented ratios | | | |
|---|---|---|---|
| **Category** | **Ratio name** | **Objective and significance** | **Formula** |
| Cash-flow ratio | Cash and short term investment to total assets ratio | Indication of how much available cash the bank has to meet share withdrawals or additional loan demand | Cash + short term investment / total assets Short term investment : part of the current assets section of investment that will expire within the year (most part as stocks and bonds that can be liquidated quickly) |
| Cash-flow ratio | Operating cash flow ratio | Help to gauge the bank's liquidity in the short-term as how well current liabilities are covered by the cash-flow generated by the bank (thus shows its ability to meet near future expenses without to sell assets) | Cash-flow from operations / current liabilities |

| | | | |
|---|---|---|---|
| Ratio of liquidity | Current ratio | Estimation of whether the business can pay debts due within one year out of the current assets:<br>• 1.7 to 2 : the business has enough cash to pay its debts<br>• 1 to 1.5: potential problem to pay debts and raise extra finance | Current assets/ current liabilities<br>• Current assets: cash, accounts receivable, inventory, marketable securities, prepaid expenses<br>• Current liabilities : debt or obligation due within the year, short-term debt, account payable, accrued liabilities and other assets |
| Ratio of liquidity | Quick ratio (acid test ratio) | Adjustement of the current ratio to eliminate no-cash equivalent assets (inventory) and indicate the size of the buffer of cash | Current assets (-stock) / current liabilities |
| Ratio of liquidity | Non core funding dependence ratio | Measure of the bank's current position of how much long term earning assets (more than one year) are funded with non core funds (net short term funds: repo,CDs, foreign deposits and other borrowings maturing within one-year) net of short term investments. The lower the ratio the better | Non core liabilities (-Short term investments) / Long term assets |
| Ratio of liquidity | Core deposits to total assets | Measurement of the extent to which assets are funded through stable deposit base. Correct level : 55% | Core deposit : deposit accounts, withdrawals accounts, savings, money market accounts, retail certificates of deposits |
| Financial strength | Loans to deposit ratio | Simplified indication on the extent to which a bank is funding liquid assets by stable liabilities. A level of 85 to 95% indicating correct level. | Loans + advances to customer net of allowance for impairment losses (-reverse repo) / customer deposit (-repo) |
| Financial strength | Loans to asset ratio | Indication that the bank can effectively meet the loan demand as well as other liquidity needs. Correct level : 70 to 80% | |

## Setting Limits

Setting risk limits still remain a key control tool in managing liquidity as they provide :

- A clear and easily understandable communication tool for risk managers to top management of the adequacy of the level of liquidity to the bank's current exposure but also a good alert system to enhance conditions where the liquidity demands may disrupt the normal course of business
- One of the easiest control framework to implement

## Funding Management

As an echo to the deficit of funds resulting from gaps between assets and liabilities the bank has also to address its funding requirement through an effective, robust and stable funding model.

## Constraints to Take into Account

1. Obtaining funds at reasonable costs
2. Fostering funding diversification in the sources and tenor of funding in the short, medium to long-term (funding mix process)
3. Adapting the maturities of liabilities cash-flow in order to match with funds uses
4. Gaining cushion of high liquid assets (refers to the bank's management of its asset funding sources)

Today, banking institutions within industrialized countries are facing structural challenges and remain still vulnerable to new market shocks or setbacks:

- New regulations from Basel III requirements on new capital buffers and liquidity ratios are increasing the pressure on bank's balance sheet
- Prolonged period of low rates has compressed margins and creates incentives to expand the assets hold in order to cover yields and thus growing exposures (rise in credit and liquidity risks)
- Long-term secured funding has fallen half since 2007 with decrease of the average maturity from 10 to 7 years
- Unsecured funding markets are no longer available for many banks (mostly banks located in southern European countries) with cut access to cheap funding
- Client deposits as the reliable source of stable funding is no more under a growth period as depositors shifting away their funds into safer institutions or non-banks institutions as well as following the economic slowdown trends
- The banking system needs to deal with fierce competition of the shadow banking system : entities or activities structured outside the regular banking mechanism that perform bank-like functions such as credit intermediation or funding sources (with bank corporate clients with refinancing rates lower or similar to the banks themselves and of course without financial regulatory restrictions and risk control). Size of the shadow banking system is evaluated to $67 trillion in 2011 according to the Financial Stability Board (FSB), this estimation is based on a proxy measure for non-credit intermediation in Australia, Canada, Japan, Korea, UK, US and the Euro area.

## Principal Sources of Funding

After 2007, financial groups have further improved the diversification of funding sources as the crisis has proven that limited mix of funds may turn out to be risky if these sources run dry all of a sudden.

2 forms to obtain funding for banks :

## Asset-based Funding Sources

The asset contribution to funding requirement depends on the bank ability to convert easily its assets to cash without loss.

- Cash-flows : as the primary source of asset side funding, occur when investments mature or through amortization of loans (periodic principal and interest cash-flows) and mortgage-backed securities
- Pledging of assets: in order to secure borrowings or line commitments. This practice induces a close management of these assets hold as collateral
- Liquidation of assets or sale of subsidiaries or lines of business (other form of shortening of assets can be also to reduce new loans origination)
- Securitization of assets as the bank originates loans with the intent to transform into pools of loans and selling them to investors

## Liability and Equity Funding Sources

## Retail Funding

From customers and small businesses and seen as stable sources with poor sensitivity level to market interest rates and bank's financial conditions.

- Deposit account
- Transaction accounts
- Savings accounts
- Public deposit
- Current account

## Wholesale Funding

- Borrowing funds under secured and unsecured debt obligations (volatile and subordinated liabilities that are purchased by rate sensitive investors)
    - Short-term:

        - High-grade securities (otherwise the counterparty or broker/ dealer will not accept the collateral or charge high haicut on collateral) sold under repurchase agreement : repo transaction that helps create leverage and short-term liabilities collateralised with longer maturity assets
        - Debt instruments such as commercial paper (promissory note such as Asset-backed commercial paper program or ABCP)
    - Longer terms : collateralized loans and issuance of debt securities such as straight or covered bonds
- Other form of deposit
    - Certificate of deposit
    - Money market deposit
    - Brokered deposit (in the US banking industry)
    - Parent company deposit
    - Deposit from banks
- Support from legacy governments and central bank facilities.Such as Long Term Refinancing Operations (LTRO) in the Eurozone where the ECB provides financing to Eurozone banks (on 29 February 2012, the last LTRO has contained €529,5 billion 36-months maturity low-interest loans with 800 banks participants)

## Equity Funds or Raising Capital

- Common stock
- Preferred stock
- Retained earnings

## Putting an Operative Plan for the Normal Daily Operations and Ongoing Business Activities

This plan needs to embrace all available funding sources and requires an integrated approach with the strategic business planning process. The objective is to provide realistic projection of funding future under various set of assumptions. This strategy includes :

## Assessment of Possible Funding Sources

Main characteristics :

- Concentrations level between funding sources

- Sensitivity to interest-rate and credit risk volatility
- Ability and speed to renew or replace the funding source at favorable terms (evaluation of the possibility to lengthening its maturity for liability source)
- For borrowed funds, documentation of a plan defining repayment of the funds and terms including call features, prepayment penalties, debt covenants...
- Possible early redemption option of the source
- Diversification of sources, tenors, investors base and types, currencies and to collateralization requirements (with limits by counterparty, secured versus unsecured level of the market funding, instrument types, securitization vehicles, geographic market and investor types)
- Costs : a bank can privilegiate interest bearing deposit products for retail clients as it is still considered as a cheap form of stable funding but the fierce competition between banks to attract a big market share has increased the acquisition and operational costs generated to manage large volume treatment (personnel, advertising...)

**Liability sensitivity**

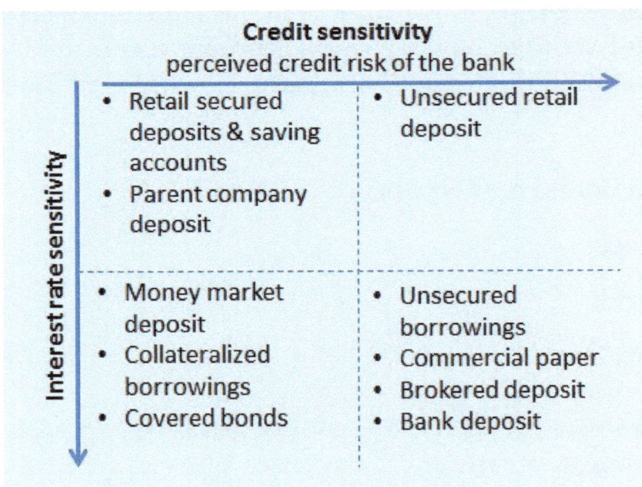


Funding requirement-liability sensitivity table

Dependencies to endogenous (bank specific events such as formulas, asset allocation, funding methods) / exogenous (investment returns, market volatility, inflation, bank ratings) factors that will influence the bank ability to access one particular source.

## Setting for Each Source an Action Plan and Assessment of the Bank's Exposure to Changes

Once the bank has established a list of potential sources based on their characteristics and risk/ reward analysis, it should monitor the link between its funding strategy and market conditions or systemic events.

For simplification, the diversify available sources are divided into 3 main time categories:

- Short-term
- Medium-term
- Long-term period

Key aspects to take into account :

1. Assessment of the likehood of funding deficiencies or cost increase across time periods. In case for example, position on the wholesale funding, providers often require liquid assets as collateral. If that collaterals become less liquid or difficult to evaluate, wholesale funds providers may arbitrate no more funding extension maturity
2. Explanation of the objective, purpose and strategy behind each funding source chosen : a bank may borrow on a long-term basis to fund real estate loans
3. Monitoring of the bank capacity to raise each funds quickly and without bad cost effects as well as the monitoring of the dependence factors affecting its capacity to raise them
4. Maintenance of a constant relation with funding market as market access is critical and affects the ability to both raise new funds and liquid assets. This access to market is expressed first by identification and building of strong relationships with current and potential key providers of funding (even if the bank is solliciting also brokers or third parties to raise funds)
5. As a prudent measure, the choice of any source has to be demonstrated with the effective ability to access the source for the bank. If the bank has never experienced to sold loans in the past or securitization program, it should not anticipate using such funding strategies as a primary source of liquidity

## Liquidity Reserve or Highly Liquid Assets Stock

This reserve can also referred to liquidity buffer and represents as the first line of defense in a liquidity crisis before intervention of any measures of the contingency funding plan. It consists of a stock of highly liquid assets without legal, regulatory constraints (the assets need to be readily available and not pledged to payments or clearing houses, we call them cashlike assets). They can include :

- High grade collateral received under repo

- Collateral pledged to the central bank for emergency situation
- Trading assets if they are freely disposable (not used as collateral)

Key actions to undertake :

1. To maintain a central data repository of these unemcombered liquid assets
2. To invest in liquid assets for purely precautionary motives during normal time of business and not during first signs of market turbulence
3. To apply, if possible (smaller banks may suffer from a lack of internal model intelligence), both an economic and regulatory liquidity assets holding position. The LCR (Liquidity Coverage Ratio), one of the new Basel III ratios in that context can represent an excellent 'warning indicator' for monitoring the dedicated level and evolution of the dedicated stock of liquid assets. Indeed, the LCR addresses the sufficiency of a stock of high quality liquid assets to meet short-term liquidity needs under a specified acute stress scenario. It identifies the amount of unencumbered, high quality liquid assets an institution holds that can be used to offset the net cash outflows it would encounter under an acute 30-days stress scenario specified by supervisors. In light of the stricter LCR eligible assets definition, the economic approach could include a larger bulk of other liquid assets (in particular in the trading book)
4. To adapt (scalability approach) the stock of the cushion of liquid assets according to stress scenarios (scenarios including estimation on loss or impairment of unsecured/ secured funding sources, contractual or non contractual cashflows as well as among others withdrawal stickiness measures). As an example, a bank may decide to use high liquid sovereign debt instruments in entering into repurchase transaction in response to one severe stress scenario
5. To evaluate the cost of maintening dedicated stock of liquid assets portfolio as the negative carry between the yield of this portfolio and its penalty rate (cost of funding or rate at which the bank may obtain funding on the financial markets or the interbank market). This negative carry of this high liquid portfolio assets will be then allocated to the respective business lines that are creating the need for such liquidity reserve

## Contingency Funding Plan

As the bank should not assume that business will always continue as it is the current business process, the institution needs to explore emergency sources of funds and formalise a contingency plan. The purpose is to find alternative backup sources of funding to those that occur within the normal course of operations.

Dealing with Contingency Funding Plan (CFP) is to find adequate actions as regard to low-probability and high-impact events as opposed to high-probability and low-impact into the day-to-day management of funding sources and their usage within the bank.

To do so, the bank needs to perform the hereafter tasks :

## Identification of Plausible Stress Events

Bank specific events : generally linked to bank's business activities and arising from credit, market, operational, reputation or strategic risk. These aspects can be expressed as the inability :

- To fund asset growth
- To renew or replace maturing liabilities
- To use off-balance sheet commitments given
- To hold back unexpected large deposit withdrawals

External events :

- Changes in economic conditions
  - Changes in price volatility of securities
  - Negative press coverage
  - Disruption in the markets from which the bank obtains funds

## Estimation of the Severity Levels, Occurrence and Duration of those Stress Events on the Bank Funding Structure

This assessment is realised in accordance with the bank current funding structure to establish a clear view on their impacts on the 'normal' funding plan and therefore evaluate the need for extra funding.

This quantitative estimation of additional funding ressources under stress events is declined for:

- Each relevant level of the bank (consolidated level to solo and business lines ones)
- Within the 3 main time categories horizon : short-term (focus on intraday, daily, weekly operations), medium to long-term

In addition, analysis are conducted to evaluate the threat of those stress events on the bank earnings, capital level, business activities as well as the balance sheet composition.

| Contingency Funding plan- Monitoring report | | |
|---|---|---|
| Stress event | Warning indicators | Monitoring tasks |
| External credit rating downgrade (or significant changes in short to long-term debt ratings) | Rating agency credit watch for potential downgrades<br>Widening credit spreads on senior subordinated debts<br>Fast decline in Credit Default Swap and bank stock price | Maket watch or rating agency reports<br>Debt and credit spreads<br>stock performance |
| Deterioration of the bank's asset quality | Deteriorating trend in loan performance, default and recovery level, non-performing portfolio trends | Loan provision level and trends<br>Volumes and trends in loan sales (quality level of the credit portfolios, attrition rate...) |
| High and consistent operating losses | Decline in earning performance | Margin and profitability reports and trends |
| Inability to access funds into normal conditions<br>Restriction by traditional providers to funding extension requests<br>Difficulty in accessing long-term debt markets | Rising funding costs in a stable market<br>Difficulties to set repo agreement into normal access (in term of haircut or collateral acceptance)<br>Counterpary reluctance to off-balance sheet products<br>Increase margin requirements<br>Concentration trends in high-cost funding | Wire transfer activity reportsr<br>Collateral management report<br>Benchmark analysis of the traditional bank's funding market<br>Funding capacity reports by funding typology<br>Funding source concentration report |
| Large withdrawal of clients deposit<br>Rapid redemption of Certficate of Deposits | Significant declines in clients deposits<br>Highest stickiness level of the deposit trend (volatile level)<br>Increased early redemption of CDs | Vault cash management reports<br>Cash-flow projection and run-off reports<br>CD early redemption report |
| Inability to sell assets | Increasing spreads on assets<br>Deterioration in asset market values | Asset impairment reports<br>Pricing trend analysis |

Examples of Contingent Funding Plan stress events

The bank need, in accordance, to develop a monitoring process to :

- Detect early sign of events that could degenerate into crisis situation through set of warning indicators or triggers
- Build an escalation scheme via reporting and action plan in order to provide precautionary measure before any material risk materialized

## Overview of Potential and Viable Contingent Funding Sources and Build Up of a Central Inventory

Such inventory includes :

- The dedicated liquidity reserve (stock of highly liquid assets that can follow the Basel III new liquidity ratios LCR/ NSFR strict liquid asset definition)
- Other unencombered liquid assets (i.e.,those contained in the trading book) and in relation to economic liquidity reserve view. They can represent :
    - Additional unsecured or secured funding (possible use of securities lending and borrowing)
    - Access to central bank reserves
    - Reduction plan of assets
    - Additional sale plan of unemcombered assets

## Determination of the Contingent Funding Sources Value According to Stressed Scenario Events

- Stressed haircut applied
- Variation around cash-flow projection

- Erosion level of the funding ressources
- Confidence level to gain access to the funding markets (tested market access)
- Monetization possibility of less liquid assets such as real-estate or mortgage loans with linked operational procedures and legal structure to put in place if any (as well as investor base, prices applied, transfer of servicing rights, recourse debt or not)

## Setting of an Administrative Structure and Crisis-management Team

The last key aspect of an effective Contingency Funding Plan relates to the management of potential crisis with a dedicated team in charge to provide :

- Action plan to take during a given level of stress
- Communication scheme with counterparties, large investors, Central Bank and regulators involved
- Reports and escalation process
- Link with other contingent activities such as the Business Continuity Planning of the bank

## Managing the ALM Profile Generated by the Funding Requirements

| Gap management report -By business line | | | | | | | | | |
|---|---|---|---|---|---|---|---|---|---|
| Time buckets | Overnight | Overnight to one week | One week to one month | One month to three months | Three months to six months | Six months to 12 months | Over 12 months | Non rate sensitive | Total |
| Assets | | | | | | | | | |
| Investments | | | | | | | | | |
| MBS | 0 | 0 | 120 | 180 | 145 | 130 | 5 | | 580 |
| Other securities | 0 | 0 | 1627 | | | | | | 1627 |
| Swap | 0 | 0 | 0 | 0 | 0 | 0 | 0 | | 0 |
| Commercial loans | | | | | | | | | |
| Fixed | 45 | 650 | 1000 | 3000 | 3450 | 3000 | 7675 | | 18820 |
| Variables | 500 | 230 | 670 | 1456 | 1690 | 3500 | 3904 | | 11950 |
| Consumer loans | | | | | | | | | 0 |
| Fixed | 0 | 230 | 570 | 720 | 850 | 760 | 456 | | 3586 |
| Variables | 0 | 345 | 560 | 722 | 899 | 700 | 433 | | 3659 |
| Real estate loans | | | | | | | | | 0 |
| Fixed | 0 | 0 | 1240 | 2400 | 3600 | 3900 | 14500 | | 25640 |
| Variables | 0 | 0 | 170 | 2400 | 6790 | 8000 | 15890 | | 33250 |
| Overdrafts & advances to custumers | 300 | 400 | 171 | 0 | 0 | 0 | 0 | | 871 |
| Reverse repurchase agreements | 2800 | 670 | 95 | 0 | 0 | 0 | 0 | | 3565 |
| Available for sale financial assets | 400 | 700 | 250 | 506 | | | | | 1856 |
| Non earning assets | | | | | | | | 6900 | 6900 |
| Total assets | 4045 | 3225 | 6473 | 11384 | 17424 | 19990 | 42863 | 6900 | 112304 |
| % | 3,6 | 2,9 | 5,8 | 10,1 | 15,5 | 17,8 | 38,2 | 6,1 | 100,0 |

ALM funding report requirement

The objective is to settle an approach of the asset-liabilitiy profile of the bank in accordance with its funding requirement. In fact, how effectively balancing the funding sources and uses with regard to liquidity, interest rate management, funding diversification and the type of business-model the bank is conducting (for example business based on a majority of short-term movements with high frequency changement of the asset profile) or the type of activities of the respective business lines (market making business is requiring more flexible liquidity profile than traditional bank activities)

| | | | | | | | | | |
|---|---|---|---|---|---|---|---|---|---|
| **Liabilities** | | | | | | | | | |
| Demand deposit | | | | | | | | 15600 | 15600 |
| Interest-bearing Deposits | 1200 | 3403 | 4405 | 4789 | 4985 | 5009 | 8900 | | 32691 |
| Wholesale funding | | | | | | | | | 0 |
| Long-short term borrowings | 2100 | 2344 | 2990 | 2523 | 1381 | | 4670 | | 16008 |
| Debt securitities in issue | 0 | 2000 | 2355 | 4370 | 2200 | 2080 | | | 13005 |
| Non funding liabilities | | | | | | | | 5000 | 5000 |
| Capital | | | | | | | | 30000 | 30000 |
| **Total liabilities** | **3300** | **7747** | **9750** | **11682** | **8566** | **7089** | **13570** | **50600** | **112304** |
| | 2,9 | 6,9 | 8,7 | 10,4 | 7,6 | 6,3 | 12,1 | 45,1 | 100,0 |
| Periodic Gap / Mismatch (Liabilities-Assets) | -745 | **4522** | **3277** | **298** | -8858 | -12901 | -29293 | **43700** | **109267** |
| Gap as % of total funding | 0,7 | 4,0 | 2,9 | -0,3 | 7,9 | 11,5 | 26,1 | 38,9 | |
| Gap as % of total gap | 0,7 | 4,1 | 3,0 | -0,3 | 8,1 | 11,8 | 26,8 | 40,0 | 100 |
| Gap limit as % of total funding | 20 | 20 | 20 | 20 | 20 | 20 | 20 | | |
| Limit breach | No | No | No | No | No | No | Yes | | |
| Cumulative gap | -745 | 3777 | 7054 | 7352 | -1506 | -14407 | -43700 | 0 | |
| Cumulative gap as % of total funding | -0,7% | 3,4% | 6,3% | 6,5% | -1,3% | -12,8% | -38,9% | 0,0% | |
| Marginal gap | -745 | 5267 | -1245 | -2979 | -9156 | -4043 | -16392 | | |
| Periodic assets / total assets | 3,6% | 2,9% | 5,8% | 10,1% | 15,5% | 17,8% | 38,2% | 6,1% | 100% |
| Periodic liabilities / total liabilities | 2,9% | 6,9% | 8,7% | 10,4% | 7,6% | 6,3% | 12,1% | 45,1% | 100% |

ALM funding report requirement - Liabilities and gap profile

## ALM Report

Funding report summarises the total funding needs and sources with the objective to dispose of a global view where the forward funding requirement lies at the time of the snapshot. The report breakdown is at business line level to a consolidatedone on the firm-wide level. As a widespread standard, a 20% gap tolerance level is applied in each time bucket meaning that gap within each time period defined can support no more than 20% of total funding.

- Marginal gap : difference between change in assets and change in liabilities for a given time period to the next (known also as incremental gap)
- Gap as % of total gap : to prevent an excessive forward gap developing in one time period

## Funding Cost Allocation or Fund Transfer Pricing Concept

The effect of terming out funding is to produce a cost of funds, the objective is to :

- Set an internal price estimation of the cost of financing needed for the coming periods
- Assign it to users of funds

This is the concept of Fund Transfer Pricing (FTP) a process within ALM context to ensure that business lines are funded with adequate tenors and that are charged and accountable in adequation to their current or future estimated situation.

3

# Fixed Assets: An Integrated Study

Fixed asset is the property that cannot be converted into cash. They can be of two types: freehold assets and leasehold assets. Fixed asset register and fixed-asset turnover are important topics in regard with the subject matter. This chapter has been carefully written to provide an easy understanding of the varied facets of fixed asset.

## Fixed Asset

Fixed assets, also known as tangible assets or property, plant, and equipment (PP&E), is a term used in accounting for assets and property that cannot easily be converted into cash. This can be compared with current assets such as cash or bank accounts, which are described as liquid assets. In most cases, only tangible assets are referred to as fixed. IAS 16 (International Accounting Standard) defines Fixed Assets as assets whose future economic benefit is probable to flow into the entity, whose cost can be measured reliably. Fixed assets belong to one of 2 types: "Freehold Assets" – assets which are purchased with legal right of ownership and used, and "Leasehold Assets" – assets used by owner without legal right for a particular period of time.

Moreover, a fixed/non-current asset can also be defined as an asset not directly sold to a firm's consumers/end-users. As an example, a baking firm's current assets would be its inventory (in this case, flour, yeast, etc.), the value of sales owed to the firm via credit (i.e. debtors or accounts receivable), cash held in the bank, etc. Its non-current assets would be the oven used to bake bread, motor vehicles used to transport deliveries, cash registers used to handle cash payments, etc. While these non-current assets have value, they are not directly sold to consumers and cannot be easily converted to cash.

These are items of value that the organization has bought and will use for an extended period of time; fixed assets normally include items such as land and buildings, motor vehicles, furniture, office equipment, computers, fixtures and fittings, and plant and machinery. These often receive favorable tax treatment (depreciation allowance) over short-term assets.

It is pertinent to note that the cost of a fixed asset is its purchase price, including import duties and other deductible trade discounts and rebates. In addition, cost attributable to bringing and installing the asset in its needed location and the initial estimate of dismantling and removing the item if they are eventually no longer needed on the location.

The primary objective of a business entity is to make profit and increase the wealth of its owners. In the attainment of this objective it is required that the management will exercise due care and diligence in applying the basic accounting concept of "Matching Concept". Matching concept is simply matching the expenses of a period against the revenues of the same period.

The use of assets in the generation of revenue is usually more than a year, i.e. long term. It is therefore obligatory that in order to accurately determine the net income or profit for a period depreciation is charged on the total value of asset that contributed to the revenue for the period in consideration and charge against the same revenue of the same period. This is essential in the prudent reporting of the net revenue for the entity in the period.

Net book value of an asset is basically the difference between the historical cost of that asset and its associated depreciation. From the foregoing, it is apparent that in order to report a true and fair position of the financial jurisprudence of an entity it is relatable to record and report the value of fixed assets at its net book value. Apart from the fact that it is enshrined in Standard Accounting Statement (SAS) 3 and IAS 16 that value of asset should be carried at the net book value, it is the best way of consciously presenting the value of assets to the owners of the business and potential investor.

## Depreciating a Fixed Asset

Depreciation is, simply put, the expense generated by the uses of an asset. It is the wear and tear of an asset or diminution in the historical value owing to usage. Further to this; it is the cost of the asset less any salvage value over its estimated useful life. A fixed asset can be depreciated using the straight line method which is the most common form of depreciation.

## Fixed Asset Register

A fixed asset register (FAR) is essentially nothing more than a list of fixed assets that belong to an accounting entity. Traditionally the fixed asset register was maintained in a written format by a bookkeeper using a book that was set aside specifically for that purpose. Nowadays it is more often held in electronic format in an accounting system.

The main purpose of a fixed asset register is to keep track of the book value of the assets and allow depreciation to be calculated and recorded for both management and taxation purposes. A secondary purpose is to allow for the easy identification of an asset by assigning each asset a unique ID which may be printed on labels in the form of a barcode.

## Fixed-asset Turnover

Fixed-asset turnover is the ratio of sales (on the profit and loss account) to the value of fixed assets (on the balance sheet). It indicates how well the business is using its fixed assets to generate sales.

$$Fixed\ Asset\ Turnover = \frac{Net\ sales}{Average\ net\ fixed\ assets}$$

Generally speaking, the higher the ratio, the better, because a high ratio indicates the business has less money tied up in fixed assets for each unit of currency of sales revenue. A declining ratio may indicate that the business is over-invested in plant, equipment, or other fixed assets.

In A.A.T. assessments this financial measure is calculated in two different ways.

1. Total Asset Turnover Ratio = Revenue / Total Assets

2. Net Asset Turnover Ratio = Revenue / (Total Assets - Current Liabilities)

# Revaluation of Fixed Assets

A revaluation of fixed assets is an action that may be required to accurately describe the true value of the capital goods a business owns. This should be distinguished from planned depreciation, where the recorded decline in value of an asset is tied to its age.

Fixed assets are held by an enterprise for the purpose of producing goods or rendering services, as opposed to being held for resale for the normal course of business. An example, machines, buildings, patents or licenses can be fixed assets of a business.

The purpose of a revaluation is to bring into the books the fair market value of fixed assets. This may be helpful in order to decide whether to invest in another business. If a company wants to sell one of its assets, it is revalued in preparation for sales negotiations.

## Reasons for Revaluation

It is common to see companies revaluing their fixed assets. It is important to make the distinctions between a 'private' revaluation to a 'public' revaluation which is carried out in the financial reports. The purposes are varied:

- To show the true rate of return on capital employed.
- To conserve adequate funds in the business for replacement of fixed assets at the end of their useful lives. Provision for depreciation based on historic cost will show inflated profits and lead to payment of excessive dividends.

- To show the fair market value of assets which have considerably appreciated since their purchase such as land and buildings.
- To negotiate fair price for the assets of the company before merger with or acquisition by another company.
- To enable proper internal reconstruction, and external reconstruction.
- To issue shares to existing shareholders (rights issue or follow-on offering).
- To get fair market value of assets, in case of sale and leaseback transaction.
- When the company intends to take a loan from banks/financial institutions by mortgaging its fixed assets. Proper revaluation of assets would enable the company to get a higher amount of loan.
- Sale of an individual asset or group of assets.
- In financial firms revaluation reserves are required for regulatory reasons. They are included when calculating a firm's funds to give a fairer view of resources. Only a portion of the firm's total funds (usually about 20%) can be loaned or in the hands of any one counterparty at any one time (large exposures restrictions).
- To decrease the leverage ratio (the ratio of debt to equity).

## Methods of Revaluation of Fixed Assets

The common methods used in revaluing assets are:

### Indexation

Under this method, indices are applied to the cost value of the assets to arrive at the current cost of the assets. The Indices by the country's departments of Statistical Bureau or Economic Surveys may be used for the revaluation of assets.

### Current Market Price (CMP)

- Land values can be estimated by using recent prices for similar plots of land sold in the area. However, certain adjustments will have to be made for the plus and minus points of the land possessed by the company. This may be done with the assistance of brokers and agencies dealing in land, or by a licensed appraiser.
- Buildings values can be estimated by a realtor (real estate dealer) or Chartered Surveyor (in the UK) in a similar manner to land.
- Plant & Machinery: The CMP can be obtained from suppliers of the assets concerned. This may not be possible if brands are not available in the market due to closure of companies manufacturing them. Similarly, a direct CMP may not

be available for a model that has been discontinued or changed by the manufacturer. Comparison of assets to most similar types available for sale, new or used, can provide an estimate of value. CMP of an existing asset = CMP of comparable new asset x Remaining useful life of asset / Original useful life of asset.

## Appraisal Method

Under this method, technical experts are called in to carry out a detailed examination of the assets with a view to determining their fair market value. Proper appraisal is necessary when the company is taking out an insurance policy for protection of its fixed assets. It ensures that the fixed assets are neither over-insured nor under-insured. The factors which are considered in determining the value of an asset, are as follows:

- Date of purchase.
- Extent of use i.e. single shift, double shift, triple shift.
- Type of asset. Whether the asset is a general purpose or special purpose asset?
- Repairs & Maintenance policy of the enterprise.
- Availability of spares in the future, mainly in the case of imported machines.
- Future demand for the product manufactured by an asset.
- If the asset is part of a bigger fixed asset, the life of the latter is crucial.

## Selective Revaluation

Selective revaluation can be defined as revaluation of specific assets within a class or all assets within a specific location.

A manufacturing company may have its manufacturing facilities spread over different locations. Suppose it decides to undertake a revaluation of its plant & machinery. Selective revaluation will mean revaluing specific assets (such as boiler, heater, central air-conditioning system) at all locations, or revaluing all items of Plant & Machinery at a particular location only. Such revaluation will lead to unrepresentative amounts being shown in the Fixed Assets Register (FAR). In case of revaluation of specific assets of a class, while some assets will be shown at a revalued amount others will be shown at historic cost. The same will happen in case of revaluation of all assets of plant & machinery at a particular location only.

It is not consistent to value and depreciate fixed assets using different bases. Therefore, selective revaluation is generally not considered best practice.

## Preliminary Considerations

Revaluation will typically require liaison between the company's Production Department, Accounts Department, Technical Department and external appraisers. To commission the project they should set out their conclusions to the following questions:

- Why is the revaluation necessary?
- What is the most suitable method, taking into account the type of fixed assets, statutory requirements, availability of required information? Should the values arrived at by one method be crosschecked with the values derived from another method?
- What assets are to be revalued?
- What is the period within which the revaluation has to be completed?
- What guidelines should be laid down for the revaluation?
- What modifications will be required in the FAR to show revalued figures in place of historic figures? Similarly, depreciation will be computed twice. One taking into account the historic cost, and the other as per revalued figures.

## Upward Revaluation

The FASB in the U.S. does not allow upward revaluation of fixed assets to reflect fair market values although it is compulsory to account for impairment costs in fixed assets (downward revaluation of fixed assets) as per FASB Statement No. 144, Accounting for the Impairment or Disposal of Long-Lived Assets.

In other countries, upward revaluation is mainly done for fixed assets such as land, and real estate whose value keeps rising from year to year. It seems the concept of upward revaluation of fixed assets such as real estate has not been widely welcomed by a majority of companies in USA on account of fear of paying higher property and capital gains taxes. Further, the provision against upward restatement ensures conservative valuation.

The United Kingdom, Australia, and India allow upward revaluation in the values of fixed assets to bring them in consonance with fair market values. However, the law requires disclosure of the basis of revaluation, amount of revaluation made to each class of assets (for a specified period after the financial year in which revaluation is made), and other information. Similarly, law prohibits payment of dividend out of any reserve created as a result of upward revaluation of fixed assets. The law in Australia has been amended recently to allow for the payment of dividends from the increase in value of non-current assets in certain instances where a company meets other liquidity tests.

## Important Points

- The increase in value of fixed assets because of revaluation of fixed assets is credited to 'Revaluation Reserve', and is not available for distribution as dividend. Revaluation Reserve is treated as a Capital Reserve.

- The increase in depreciation arising out of revaluation of fixed assets is debited to revaluation reserve and the normal depreciation to Profit and Loss account.
- Selection of the most suitable method of revaluation is extremely important. The most used method is the appraisal method. Methods such as indexation, and reference to current market prices are also used. However, when these methods are used they are crosschecked with the values arrived at by using the appraisal method.revaluation of loans and bonds is also required;
- When any asset is sold that has previously been revalued, the revaluation within the carrying value is debited to the Revaluation Reserve.
- When assets are revalued, every Balance Sheet shall show for a specified period of years, the amount of increase / decrease made in respect of each class of assets. Similarly, the increased / decreased value shall be shown in place of the original cost.
- In case of land and buildings, revaluation is desirable as their value generally increases over time, and is carried out every 3 to 5 years. In case of plant & machinery, revaluation is carried out only if there is a strong case for it. In case of depreciable assets such as vehicles, furniture & fittings or office equipment, revaluation is not carried out.
- Revaluation should not result in the net book value of an asset exceeding its recoverable value.

## Downward Revaluation

Revaluation does not mean only an upward revision in the book values of the asset. It can also mean a downward revision (also called impairment) in the book values of the assets. However, any downward revision in the book values of the assets is immediately written off to the Profit & Loss account. Under IFRS, an asset is considered to be impaired (and is thus written down) if its carrying amount is greater than its recoverable amount. The recoverable amount is the greater of the asset's value in use (present value of future values) or net realizable value.

## Successive Revaluations

On upward revaluation of a fixed asset which has been previously subject to downward revaluation, an amount of the upward revaluation equal to the amount previously expensed is credited back to the Profit & Loss Account.

Example:

Machinery 'A' is purchased on 01-04-1999 for $100,000. It is depreciated using the Straight Line Method at the rate of 10% p.a.

| Particulars | First Revaluation | Second Revaluation |
|---|---|---|
| Nature of Revaluation | ▼ | ▲ |
| Date of Revaluation | 01-04-2001 | 01-04-2004 |
| Gross Cost | 100,000 | 93,750 |
| Less: Depreciation | 20,000 | 46,875 |
| Net Book Value | 80,000 | 46,875 |
| Revalued - Appraisal Method | 75,000 | 55,000 |
| Increase / (Decrease) in Net Book Value | (5,000) | 8,125 |
| Debit to Profit & Loss a/c | 5,000 | 0 |
| Credit to Profit & Loss a/c | 0 | 5,000 |
| Credit to Revaluation Reserve | 0 | 3,125 |

## IAS 16

International Accounting Standard 16 *Property, Plant and Equipment* or IAS 16 is an international financial reporting standard adopted by the International Accounting Standards Board (IASB). It concerns accounting for property, plant and equipment (known more generally as fixed assets), including recognition, determination of their carrying amounts, and the depreciation charges and impairment losses to be recognised in relation to them.

IAS 16 was issued in December 1993 by the International Accounting Standards Committee, the predecessor to the IASB. It was reissued in December 2003 and has been amended multiple times, most recently in May 2012.

### Overview

IAS 16 applies to property, plant and equipment (PPE). The standard itself defines PPE as "tangible items that are held for use in the production or supply of goods or services, for rental to others, or for administrative purposes; and are expected to be used during more than one [accounting] period."

The standard does not apply to assets classified as held for sale in accordance with IFRS 5 *Non-current Assets Held for Sale and Discontinued Operations* and assets which require more specialised accounting, such as biological (IAS 41 *Agriculture*), exploration and evaluation assets (IFRS 6 *Exploration for and Evaluation of Mineral Resources*), mineral rights and reserves such as oil, natural gas and similar non-regenerative resources.

### Recognition and Measurement

IAS 16 prescribes that an item of property, plant and equipment should be recognised (capitalised) as an asset if it is probable that the future economic benefits associated with the asset will flow to the entity and the cost of the asset can be measured reliably. Future economic benefits occur when the risks and rewards of the asset's ownership have passed to the entity.

The standard also discusses the accounting treatment of parts of property, plant and equipment which may require replacement at regular intervals and the capitalisation of inspection costs.

Items of property, plant and equipment should be measured at cost, which includes its original purchase price, any costs necessary to bring the asset to the location and condition for its intended use (e.g. site preparation, delivery and handling, installation, related professional fees for architects and engineers), and the estimated cost of dismantling and removing the asset and restoring the site.

## Measurement after Recognition

IAS 16 permits two accounting models for measurement of the asset in periods subsequent to its recognition, namely the *cost model* and the *revaluation model.*

- Under the *cost model*, the carrying amount of the asset is measured at cost less accumulated depreciation and eventual impairment (similar to the inventory's Lower of cost or market prudent principle). Under the cost model, the impairment is always recognised (debited) as expense.
- Under the *revaluation model*, the asset is carried at its revalued amount, being its fair value at the date of revaluation less subsequent depreciation and impairment, provided that fair value can be determined reliably.
    - If a revaluation results in an increase in value, it should be credited to equity (through other comprehensive income), unless it represents the reversal of a revaluation decrease of the same asset previously recognised as an expense, in which case it should be recognised as income.
    - An asset should also be impaired in accordance with IAS 36 *Impairment of Assets* if its recoverable amount falls below its carrying amount. Recoverable amount is the higher of an asset's fair value less costs to sell and its value in use (estimate of future cash flows the entity expects to derive from the asset). An impairment cost under the revaluation model is treated as a revaluation decrease (decrease of other comprehensive income) to the extent of previous revaluation surpluses. Any loss that takes the asset below historical depreciated cost is recognised in the income statement.

Depreciation: The depreciable amount (cost less residual value) should be allocated on a systematic basis over the asset's useful life. That is, the mark-down in value of the asset should be recognised as an expense in the income statement every accounting period throughout the asset's useful life. The useful life of the asset is determined by taking into account expected usage, physical wear and tear, technical or commercial obsolescence arising from changes in production or market demand and legal limits on its use. In addition, the depreciation in each accounting period of the asset's useful life should reflect the pattern which the asset's economic benefits are expected to be consumed by the entity.

## Derecognition

Items of property, plant and equipment are derecognised on disposal or when no future economic benefit is expected from its use. An entity should recognise any gain or loss on disposal in its income statement. The gain or loss on disposal is the difference between the proceeds received in exchange for the asset disposed and the carrying amount at the time of disposal.

## Disclosure

IAS 16 requires an entity to disclose in its financial statements for each class of property, plant and equipment:

- the basis for measuring carrying amount
- the depreciation method(s) used
- the useful lives or depreciation rates
- the gross carrying amount and accumulated depreciation and impairment losses
- a reconciliation of the carrying amount at the beginning and the end of the period, showing:
    - additions
    - disposals
    - acquisitions through business combinations
    - revaluation increases or decreases
    - impairment losses
    - reversals of impairment losses
    - depreciation
    - net foreign exchange differences on translation
    - other movements

# 4

# A Brief Introduction to Liquid Assets

Liquid assets are assets that can be bought and sold without much effect to the price of the asset. The most liquid asset is cash. Liquidation is the process of exchanging a less liquid asset to a more liquid asset. The topics elaborated in this chapter will help in gaining a better perspective about liquid assets.

## Liquid Assets

Gold is a substance with high market liquidity, as it may be sold quickly without having to reduce the price.

In business, economics or investment, liquid assets is a market's ability to purchase or sell an asset without causing drastic change in the asset's price. Equivalently, an asset's market liquidity (or simply "an asset's liquidity") describes the asset's ability to sell quickly without having to reduce its price to a significant degree. Liquidity is about how big the trade-off is between the speed of the sale and the price it can be sold for. In a liquid market, the trade-off is mild: selling quickly will not reduce the price much. In a relatively illiquid market, selling it quickly will require cutting its price by some amount.

Money, or cash, is the most liquid asset, because it can be "sold" for goods and services instantly with no loss of value. There is no wait for a suitable buyer of the cash. There is no trade-off between speed and value. It can be used immediately to perform economic actions like buying, selling, or paying debt, meeting immediate wants and needs.

If an asset is moderately (or very) liquid, it has moderate (or high) liquidity. In an alternative definition, liquidity can mean the amount of cash and cash equivalents. If a business has moderate liquidity, it has a moderate amount of very liquid assets. If a business has sufficient liquidity, it has a sufficient amount of very liquid assets and the ability to meet its payment obligations.

An act of exchanging a less liquid asset for a more liquid asset is called liquidation. Often liquidation is trading the less liquid asset for cash, also known as selling it. An asset's liquidity can change. For the same asset, its liquidity can change through time or between different markets, such as in different countries. The change in the asset's liquidity is just based on the market liquidity for the asset at the particular time or in the particular country, etc. The liquidity of a product can be measured as how often it is bought and sold.

Liquidity is defined formally in many accounting regimes and has in recent years been more strictly defined. For instance, the US Federal Reserve intends to apply quantitative liquidity requirements based on Basel III liquidity rules as of fiscal 2012. Bank directors will also be required to know of, and approve, major liquidity risks personally. Other rules require diversifying counterparty risk and portfolio stress testing against extreme scenarios, which tend to identify unusual market liquidity conditions and avoid investments that are particularly vulnerable to sudden liquidity shifts.

## Overview

This old church building for sale in Cheshire, England, has relatively low liquidity. It could be sold in a matter of days at a low price, but it could take several years to find a buyer who is willing to pay a reasonable price.

A liquid asset has some or all of the following features: It can be sold rapidly, with minimal loss of value, any time within market hours. The essential characteristic of a liquid market is that there are always ready and willing buyers and sellers. It is similar to, but distinct from, market depth, which relates to the trade-off between quantity being sold and the price it can be sold for, rather than the liquidity trade-off between speed of sale and the price it can be sold for. A market may be considered both deep and liquid if there are ready and willing buyers and sellers in large quantities.

An illiquid asset is an asset which is not readily salable (without a drastic price reduction, and sometimes not at any price) due to uncertainty about its value or the lack of a market in which it is regularly traded. The mortgage-related assets which resulted in the subprime mortgage crisis are examples of illiquid assets, as their value was not readily determinable despite being secured by real property. Before the crisis, they had moderate liquidity because it was believed that their value was generally known.

Speculators and market makers are key contributors to the liquidity of a market, or asset. Speculators are individuals or institutions that seek to profit from anticipated increases or decreases in a particular market price. Market makers seek to profit by charging for immediacy of execution: either implicitly by earning a bid/ask spread or explicitly by charging execution commissions. By doing this, they provide the capital needed to facilitate the liquidity. The risk of illiquidity need not apply only to individual investments: whole portfolios are subject to market risk. Financial institutions and asset managers that oversee portfolios are subject to what is called "structural" and "contingent" liquidity risk. Structural liquidity risk, sometimes called funding liquidity risk, is the risk associated with funding asset portfolios in the normal course of business. Contingent liquidity risk is the risk associated with finding additional funds or replacing maturing liabilities under potential, future stressed market conditions. When a central bank tries to influence the liquidity (supply) of money, this process is known as open market operations.

## Effect on Asset Values

The market liquidity of assets affects their prices and expected returns. Theory and empirical evidence suggests that investors require higher return on assets with lower market liquidity to compensate them for the higher cost of trading these assets. That is, for an asset with given cash flow, the higher its market liquidity, the higher its price and the lower is its expected return. In addition, risk-averse investors require higher expected return if the asset's market-liquidity risk is greater. This risk involves the exposure of the asset return to shocks in overall market liquidity, the exposure of the asset own liquidity to shocks in market liquidity and the effect of market return on the asset's own liquidity. Here too, the higher the liquidity risk, the higher the expected return on the asset or the lower is its price.

One example of this is comparison of assets with and without a liquid secondary market. The liquidity discount is the reduced promised yield or expected return for such assets, like the difference between newly issued U.S. Treasury bonds compared to off the run treasuries with the same term to maturity. Initial buyers know that other investors are less willing to buy off-the-run treasuries, so the newly issued bonds have a higher price (and hence lower yield).

## Futures

In the futures markets, there is no assurance that a liquid market may exist for offsetting a commodity contract at all times. Some future contracts and specific delivery months tend to have increasingly more trading activity and have higher liquidity than others. The most useful indicators of liquidity for these contracts are the trading volume and open interest.

There is also dark liquidity, referring to transactions that occur off-exchange and are therefore not visible to investors until after the transaction is complete. It does not contribute to public price discovery.

## Banking

In banking, liquidity is the ability to meet obligations when they come due without incurring unacceptable losses. Managing liquidity is a daily process requiring bankers to monitor and project cash flows to ensure adequate liquidity is maintained. Maintaining a balance between short-term assets and short-term liabilities is critical. For an individual bank, clients' deposits are its primary liabilities (in the sense that the bank is meant to give back all client deposits on demand), whereas reserves and loans are its primary assets (in the sense that these loans are owed to the bank, not by the bank). The investment portfolio represents a smaller portion of assets, and serves as the primary source of liquidity. Investment securities can be liquidated to satisfy deposit withdrawals and increased loan demand. Banks have several additional options for generating liquidity, such as selling loans, borrowing from other banks, borrowing from a central bank, such as the US Federal Reserve bank, and raising additional capital. In a worst-case scenario, depositors may demand their funds when the bank is unable to generate adequate cash without incurring substantial financial losses. In severe cases, this may result in a bank run. Most banks are subject to legally mandated requirements intended to help avoid a liquidity crisis.

Banks can generally maintain as much liquidity as desired because bank deposits are insured by governments in most developed countries. A lack of liquidity can be remedied by raising deposit rates and effectively marketing deposit products. However, an important measure of a bank's value and success is the cost of liquidity. A bank can attract significant liquid funds. Lower costs generate stronger profits, more stability, and more confidence among depositors, investors, and regulators.

## Stock Market

In the market, liquidity has a slightly different meaning, although still tied to how easily assets, in this case shares of stock, can be converted to cash. The market for a stock is said to be liquid if the shares can be rapidly sold and the act of selling has little impact on the stock's price. Generally, this translates to where the shares are traded and the level of interest that investors have in the company. Another way to judge liquidity in a company's stock is to look at the bid/ask spread. For liquid stocks, such as Microsoft or General Electric, the spread is often just a few pennies – much less than 1% of the price. For illiquid stocks, the spread can be much larger, amounting to a few percent of the trading price. In today's stock market, high-frequency trading firms purport of themselves to contribute to nearly 50% of all liquidity.

Liquidity positively impacts the stock market. When stock prices rise, it is said to be due to a confluence of extraordinarily high levels of liquidity on household and business balance sheets, combined with a simultaneous normalization of liquidity preferences. On the margin, this drives a demand for equity investments.

## Proxies

One way to calculate the liquidity of the banking system of a country is to divide liquid assets to short term liabilities.

## Current Ratio

The current ratio is a liquidity ratio that measures whether or not a firm has enough resources to meet its short-term obligations. It compares a firm's current assets to its current liabilities, and is expressed as follows:

$$\text{Current ratio} = \frac{\text{Current Assets}}{\text{Current Liabilities}}$$

The current ratio is an indication of a firm's liquidity. Acceptable current ratios vary from industry to industry. In many cases a creditor would consider a high current ratio to be better than a low current ratio, because a high current ratio indicates that the company is more likely to pay the creditor back. Large current ratios are not always a good sign for investors. If the company's current ratio is too high it may indicate that the company is not efficiently using its current assets or its short-term financing facilities.

If current liabilities exceed current assets the current ratio will be less than 1. A current ratio of less than 1 indicates that the company may have problems meeting its short-term obligations. Some types of businesses can operate with a current ratio of less than one however. If inventory turns into cash much more rapidly than the accounts payable become due, then the firm's current ratio can comfortably remain less than one. Inventory is valued at the cost of acquiring it and the firm intends to sell the inventory for more than this cost. The sale will therefore generate substantially more cash than the value of inventory on the balance sheet. Low current ratios can also be justified for businesses that can collect cash from customers long before they need to pay their suppliers

## Limitations of Current Ratio

1. The ratio is only useful when two companies are compared within industry because inter industry business operations differ substantially.

2. To determine liquidity, the current ratio is not as helpful as the quick ratio, because it includes all those assets that may not be easily liquidated, like prepaid expenses and inventory.

## Quick Ratio

In finance, the acid-test or quick ratio or liquidity ratio measures the ability of a company to use its *near cash* or quick assets to extinguish or retire its current liabilities immediately. Quick assets include those current assets that presumably can be quickly converted to cash at close to their book values. It is the ratio between quick or liquid assets and current liabilities.

A normal liquid ratio is considered to be 1:1. A company with a quick ratio of less than 1 cannot currently fully pay back its current liabilities.

This ratio is considered to be much better and reliable as a tool for assessment of liquidity position of firms.

### Formula

$$\text{Liquid Ratio} = \frac{\text{Liquid Assets}}{\text{Current Liabilities}}$$

### Formula

$$\text{Quick (Acid Test) Ratio} = \frac{\text{Cash and Cash Equivalent} + \text{Marketable Securities} + \text{Accounts Receivable}}{\text{Current Liabilities}}$$

Note that inventory is excluded from the sum of assets in the quick ratio, but included in the current ratio. Ratios are tests of viability for business entities but do not give a complete picture of the business' health. If a business has large amounts in accounts receivable which are due for payment after a long period (say 120 days), and essential business expenses and accounts payable due for immediate payment, the quick ratio may look healthy when the business is actually about to run out of cash. In contrast, if the business has negotiated fast payment or cash from customers, and long terms from suppliers, it may have a very low quick ratio and yet be very healthy.

Generally, the acid test ratio should be 1:1 or higher, however this varies widely by industry. In general, the higher the ratio, the greater the company's liquidity (i.e., the better able to meet current obligations using liquid assets).

## Reserve Requirement

The reserve requirement (or cash reserve ratio) is a central bank regulation employed by most, but not all, of the world's central banks, that sets the minimum amount of reserves that must be held by a commercial bank. The minimum reserve is generally determined by the central bank to be no less than a specified percentage of the amount of deposit liabilities the commercial bank owes to its customers. The commercial bank's reserves normally consist of cash owned by the bank and stored physically in the bank vault (vault cash), plus the amount of the commercial bank's balance in that bank's account with the central bank.

The required reserve ratio is sometimes used as a tool in monetary policy, influencing the country's borrowing and interest rates by changing the amount of funds available for banks to make loans with. Western central banks rarely increase the reserve requirements because it would cause immediate liquidity problems for banks with low excess reserves; they generally prefer to use open market operations (buying and selling government-issued bonds) to implement their monetary policy. The People's Bank of China uses changes in reserve requirements as an inflation-fighting tool, and raised the reserve requirement ten times in 2007 and eleven times since the beginning of 2010.

An institution that holds reserves in excess of the required amount is said to hold *excess reserves*.

## Effects on Money Supply

## The Conventional View

The theory that a reserve requirement can be used as a tool of monetary policy is frequently found in economics textbooks. Under the theory, higher the reserve requirement is set, the less funds banks will have to loan out , leading to lower money creation and perhaps to higher purchasing power of the money previously in use. Under this view, the effect is multiplied, because money obtained as loan proceeds can be re-deposited, and a portion of those deposits may again be loaned out, and so on. Under this theory, the effect on the money supply is governed by the following formulas:

$M_1 = MB * m$ : definitional relationship between monetary base $MB$ (bank reserves plus currency held by the non-bank public) the narrowly defined money supply, $M_1$,

$m = \frac{(1+c)}{(c+R)} = \frac{1+\frac{C}{D}}{\frac{C}{D}+R}$ : derived formula for the money multiplier $m$, the factor by which lending and re-lending leads $M_1$ to be a multiple of the monetary base:

where notationally,

$c =$ the currency ratio: the ratio of the public's holdings of currency (undeposited cash) to the public's holdings of demand deposits; and

$R =$ the total reserve ratio (the ratio of legally required plus non-required reserve holdings of banks to demand deposit liabilities of banks).

However, in the United States (and other countries except Brazil, China, India, Russia), the reserve requirements are generally not frequently altered to implement monetary policy because of the short-term disruptive effect on financial markets.

## The Endogenous Money View

Some economists dispute the conventional theory of the reserve requirement. Criticisms of the conventional theory are usually associated with theories of endogenous money.

Jaromir Benes and Michael Kumhof of the IMF Research Department report that the "deposit multiplier" of the undergraduate economics textbook, where monetary aggregates are created at the initiative of the central bank, through an initial injection of high-powered money into the banking system that gets multiplied through bank lending, turns the actual operation of the monetary transmission mechanism on its head. Benes and Kumhof assert that in most cases where banks ask for replenishment of depleted reserves, the central bank obliges. Under this view, reserves therefore impose no constraints, as the deposit multiplier is simply, in the words of Kydland and Prescott (1990), a myth. Under this theory, private banks almost fully control the money creation process.

## Required Reserves

### United States

In the United States, a reserve requirement (or liquidity ratio) is a minimum value, set by the Board of Governors of the Federal Reserve System, of the ratio of required reserves to a category of deposit liabilities (called the "Net Transaction Accounts" or "NTAs") owed by depository institutions to their customers (e.g., owed by commercial banks including U.S. branches of a foreign bank, savings and loan association, savings bank, credit union). The deposit liability categories currently subject to reserve requirements are mainly checking accounts. There is no reserve requirement on savings accounts and time deposit accounts owned by individuals. The total amount of all NTAs held by customers with U.S. depository institutions, plus the U.S. paper currency and coin currency held by the nonbank public, is called M1.

A depository institution can satisfy its reserve requirements by holding either vault cash or reserve deposits. An institution that is a member of the Federal Reserve System must hold its reserve deposits at a Federal Reserve Bank. Nonmember institutions can elect to hold their reserve deposits at a member institution on a pass-through basis.

A depository institution's reserve requirements vary by the dollar amount of NTAs held by customers of that institution. Effective November 17, 2015, institutions with net transactions accounts:

- Of less than $15.2 million have no minimum reserve requirement;
- Between $15.2 million and $110.2 million must have a liquidity ratio of 3% of NTAs;
- Exceeding $110.2 million must have a liquidity ratio of 10% of NTAs.

The threshold monetary amounts are recalculated annually according to a statutory formula.

Effective 27 December 1990, a liquidity ratio of zero has applied to CDs and time deposits, owned by entities other than households, and the Eurocurrency liabilities of depository institutions. Deposits owned by foreign corporations or governments are currently not subject to reserve requirements.

When an institution fails to satisfy its reserve requirements, it can make up its deficiency with reserves borrowed from a Federal Reserve Bank or from an institution holding reserves in excess of reserve requirements. Such loans are typically due in 24 hours or less.

An institution's overnight reserves, averaged over some maintenance period, must equal or exceed its average required reserves, calculated over the same maintenance period. If this calculation is satisfied, there is no requirement that reserves be held at any point in time. Hence reserve requirements play only a limited role in money creation in the United States. Since quantitative easing began in 2008, they have been even less important, as an enormous glut of excess reserves now exists (over the whole system, though in theory, individual banks may still run into temporary shortfalls).

The International Banking Act of 1978 requires branches of foreign banks operating in the United States to follow the same required reserve ratio standards.

## Countries without Reserve Requirements

Canada, the UK, New Zealand, Australia, Sweden and Hong Kong have no reserve requirements.

This does not mean that banks can - even in theory - create money without limit. On the contrary, banks are constrained by capital requirements, which are arguably more important than reserve requirements even in countries that have reserve requirements.

It also does not mean that a commercial bank's overnight reserves can become *negative*, in these countries. The central bank will *always* step in to lend the necessary reserves if necessary so that this does not happen; this is sometimes described as "defending the payment system". Historically a central bank might once have run out of reserves to lend and so have had to suspend redemptions, but this can no longer happen to modern central banks because of the end of the gold standard worldwide, which means that all nations use a fiat currency.

A zero reserve requirement cannot be explained by a theory that holds that monetary policy works by varying the quantity of money using the reserve requirement.

Even in the United States, which retains formal (though now mostly irrelevant) reserve requirements, the notion of controlling the money supply by targeting the quantity of base money fell out of favor many years ago, and now the pragmatic explanation of monetary policy refers to targeting the *interest rate* to control the broad money supply.

## United Kingdom

In the UK the term clearing banks is sometimes used, meaning banks that have direct access to the clearing system. However, for the purposes of clarity, the term *commercial banks* will be used for the remainder of this section.

The Bank of England, which is the central bank for the entire United Kingdom, previously held to a voluntary reserve ratio system, with no minimum reserve requirement set. In theory this meant that commercial banks could retain zero reserves. The average cash reserve ratio across the entire United Kingdom banking system, though, was higher during that period, at about 0.15% as of 1999.

From 1971 to 1980, the commercial banks all agreed to a reserve ratio of 1.5%. In 1981 this requirement was abolished.

From 1981 to 2009, each commercial bank set out its own monthly voluntary reserve target in a contract with the Bank of England. Both shortfalls and excesses of reserves relative to the commercial bank's own target over an averaging period of one day would result in a charge, incentivising the commercial bank to stay near its target, a system known as *reserves averaging*.

Upon the parallel introduction of quantitative easing and interest on excess reserves in 2009, banks were no longer required to set out a target, and so were no longer penalised for holding excess reserves; indeed, they were proportionally compensated for holding all their reserves at the Bank Rate (the Bank of England now uses the same interest rate for its bank rate, its deposit rate and its interest rate target). In the absence of an agreed target, the concept of excess reserves does not really apply to the Bank of England any longer, so it is technically incorrect to call its new policy "interest on excess reserves".

### Historical Changes in Reserve Ratios

In some countries, the *cash reserve ratios* have decreased over time; in some countries they have increased:

| Country | 1968 | 1978 | 1988 | 1998 |
|---|---|---|---|---|
| United Kingdom | 20.5 | 15.9 | 5.0 | 3.1 |
| Turkey | 58.3 | 62.7 | 30.8 | 18.0 |
| Germany | 19.0 | 19.3 | 17.2 | 11.9 |
| United States | 12.3 | 10.1 | 8.5 | 10.3 |
| India | 3 | 6 | 10 | 10-11 |

(Ratios are expressed in percentage points.)

## Liquidity Risk

Liquidity risk is a financial risk that for a certain period of time a given financial asset, security or commodity cannot be traded quickly enough in the market without impacting the market price.

### Types of Liquidity Risk

Market liquidity – An asset cannot be sold due to lack of liquidity in the market – essentially a sub-set of market risk. This can be accounted for by:

- Widening bid/offer spread
- Making explicit liquidity reserves
- Lengthening holding period for VaR calculations

Funding liquidity – Risk that liabilities:

- Cannot be met when they fall due
- Can only be met at an uneconomic price
- Can be name-specific or systemic

### Causes of Liquidity Risk

Liquidity risk arises from situations in which a party interested in trading an asset cannot do it because nobody in the market wants to trade for that asset. Liquidity risk becomes particularly important to parties who are about to hold or currently hold an asset, since it affects their ability to trade.

Manifestation of liquidity risk is very different from a drop of price to zero. In case of a drop of an asset's price to zero, the market is saying that the asset is worthless. However, if one party cannot find another party interested in trading the asset, this can potentially be only a problem of the market participants with finding each other. This is why liquidity risk is usually found to be higher in emerging markets or low-volume markets.

Liquidity risk is financial risk due to uncertain liquidity. An institution might lose liquidity if its credit rating falls, it experiences sudden unexpected cash outflows, or some other event causes counterparties to avoid trading with or lending to the institution. A firm is also exposed to liquidity risk if markets on which it depends are subject to loss of liquidity.

Market and funding liquidity risks compound each other as it is difficult to sell when other investors face funding problems and it is difficult to get funding when the collateral is hard to sell. Liquidity risk also tends to compound other risks. If a trading organization has a position in an illiquid asset, its limited ability to liquidate that position at short notice will compound its market risk. Suppose a firm has offsetting cash flows with two different counterparties on a given day. If the counterparty that owes it a payment defaults, the firm will have to raise cash from other sources to make its payment. Should it be unable to do so, it too will default. Here, liquidity risk is compounding credit risk.

A position can be hedged against market risk but still entail liquidity risk. This is true in the above credit risk example—the two payments are offsetting, so they entail credit risk but not market risk. Another example is the 1993 *Metallgesellschaft* debacle. Futures contracts were used to hedge an Over-the-counter finance OTC obligation. It is debatable whether the hedge was effective from a market risk standpoint, but it was the liquidity crisis caused by staggering margin calls on the futures that forced Metallgesellschaft to unwind the positions.

Accordingly, liquidity risk has to be managed in addition to market, credit and other risks. Because of its tendency to compound other risks, it is difficult or impossible to isolate liquidity risk. In all but the most simple of circumstances, comprehensive metrics of liquidity risk do not exist. Certain techniques of asset liability management can be applied to assessing liquidity risk. A simple test for liquidity risk is to look at future net cash flows on a day-by-day basis. Any day that has a sizeable negative net cash flow is of concern. Such an analysis can be supplemented with stress testing. Look at net cash flows on a day-to-day basis assuming that an important counterparty defaults.

Analyses such as these cannot easily take into account contingent cash flows, such as cash flows from derivatives or mortgage-backed securities. If an organization's cash flows are largely contingent, liquidity risk may be assessed using some form of scenario analysis. A general approach using scenario analysis might entail the following high-level steps:

- Construct multiple scenarios for market movements and defaults over a given period of time
- Assess day-to-day cash flows under each scenario.

Because balance sheets differ so significantly from one organization to the next, there is little standardization in how such analyses are implemented.

Regulators are primarily concerned about systemic implications of liquidity risk.

## Pricing of Liquidity Risk

Risk-averse investors naturally require higher expected return as compensation for liquidity risk. The liquidity-adjusted CAPM pricing model therefore states that, the higher an asset's market-liquidity risk, the higher its required return.

A common method for estimating the upper bound for a security illiquidity discount is by using a Lookback option, where the premia is equal to the difference between the maximum value of a security during a restricted trading period and its value at the end of the period. When the method is extended for corporate debt it is shown that liquidity risk increases with a bond credit risk.

## Measures of Liquidity Risk

## Liquidity Gap

Culp defines the liquidity gap as the net liquid assets of a firm. The excess value of the firm's liquid assets over its volatile liabilities. A company with a negative liquidity gap should focus on their cash balances and possible unexpected changes in their values.

As a static measure of liquidity risk it gives no indication of how the gap would change with an increase in the firm's marginal funding cost.

## Liquidity Risk Elasticity

Culp denotes the change of net of assets over funded liabilities that occurs when the liquidity premium on the bank's marginal funding cost rises by a small amount as the liquidity risk elasticity. For banks this would be measured as a spread over libor, for nonfinancials the LRE would be measured as a spread over commercial paper rates.

Problems with the use of liquidity risk elasticity are that it assumes parallel changes in funding spread across all maturities and that it is only accurate for small changes in funding spreads.

## Measures of Asset Liquidity

### Bid-offer Spread

The bid-offer spread is used by market participants as an asset liquidity measure. To compare different products the ratio of the spread to the product's bid price can be used. The smaller the ratio the more liquid the asset is.

This spread is composed of operational, administrative, and processing costs as well as the compensation required for the possibility of trading with a more informed trader.

### Market Depth

Hachmeister refers to market depth as the amount of an asset that can be bought and sold at various bid-ask spreads. Slippage is related to the concept of market depth. Knight and Satchell mention a flow trader needs to consider the effect of executing a large order on the market and to adjust the bid-ask spread accordingly. They calculate the liquidity cost as the difference of the execution price and the initial execution price.

### Immediacy

Immediacy refers to the time needed to successfully trade a certain amount of an asset at a prescribed cost.

### Resilience

Hachmeister identifies the fourth dimension of liquidity as the speed with which prices return to former levels after a large transaction. Unlike the other measures resilience can only be determined over a period of time.

## Managing Liquidity Risk

### Liquidity-adjusted Value at Risk

Liquidity-adjusted VAR incorporates exogenous liquidity risk into Value at Risk. It can be defined at VAR + ELC (Exogenous Liquidity Cost). The ELC is the worst expected half-spread at a particular confidence level.

Another adjustment, introduced in the 1970s with a regulatory precursor to today's VAR measures, is to consider VAR over the period of time needed to liquidate the portfolio. VAR can be calculated over this time period. The BIS mentions "a number of institutions are exploring the use of liquidity adjusted-VAR, in which the holding periods in the risk assessment are adjusted by the length of time required to unwind positions."

## Liquidity at Risk

Alan Greenspan (1999) discusses management of foreign exchange reserves and suggested a measure called Liquidity at risk. A country's liquidity position under a range of possible outcomes for relevant financial variables (exchange rates, commodity prices, credit spreads, etc.) is considered. It might be possible to express a standard in terms of the probabilities of different outcomes. For example, an acceptable debt structure could have an average maturity—averaged over estimated distributions for relevant financial variables—in excess of a certain limit. In addition, countries could be expected to hold sufficient liquid reserves to ensure that they could avoid new borrowing for one year with a certain ex ante probability, such as 95 percent of the time.

## Scenario Analysis-based Contingency Plans

The FDIC discuss liquidity risk management and write "Contingency funding plans should incorporate events that could rapidly affect an institution's liquidity, including a sudden inability to securitize assets, tightening of collateral requirements or other restrictive terms associated with secured borrowings, or the loss of a large depositor or counterparty." Greenspan's liquidity at risk concept is an example of scenario based liquidity risk management.

## Diversification of Liquidity Providers

If several liquidity providers are on call then if any of those providers increases its costs of supplying liquidity, the impact of this is reduced. The American Academy of Actuaries wrote "While a company is in good financial shape, it may wish to establish durable, ever-green (i.e., always available) liquidity lines of credit. The credit issuer should have an appropriately high credit rating to increase the chances that the resources will be there when needed."

## Derivatives

Bhaduri, Meissner and Youn discuss five derivatives created specifically for hedging liquidity risk:

- Withdrawal option: A put of the illiquid underlying at the market price.
- Bermudan-style return put option: Right to put the option at a specified strike.
- Return swap: Swap the underlying's return for LIBOR paid periodicially.
- Return swaption: Option to enter into the return swap.
- Liquidity option: "Knock-in" barrier option, where the barrier is a liquidity metric.

## Case Studies

### Amaranth Advisors LLC – 2006

Amaranth Advisors lost roughly $6bn in the natural gas futures market back in September 2006. Amaranth had a concentrated, undiversified position in its natural gas strategy. The trader had used leverage to build a very large position. Amaranth's positions were staggeringly large, representing around 10% of the global market in natural gas futures. Chincarini notes that firms need to manage liquidity risk explicitly. The inability to sell a futures contract at or near the latest quoted price is related to one's concentration in the security. In Amaranth's case, the concentration was far too high and there were no natural counterparties when they needed to unwind the positions. Chincarini (2006) argues that part of the loss Amaranth incurred was due to asset illiquidity. Regression analysis on the 3 week return on natural gas future contracts from August 31, 2006 to September 21, 2006 against the excess open interest suggested that contracts whose open interest was much higher on August 31, 2006 than the historical normalized value, experienced larger negative returns.

### Northern Rock – 2007

Northern Rock suffered from funding liquidity risk in September 2007 following the subprime crisis. The firm suffered from liquidity issues despite being solvent at the time, because maturing loans and deposits could not be renewed in the short-term money markets. In response, the FSA now places greater supervisory focus on liquidity risk especially with regard to "high-impact retail firms".

### LTCM – 1998

Long-Term Capital Management (LTCM) was bailed out by a consortium of 14 banks in 1998 after being caught in a cash-flow crisis when economic shocks resulted in excessive mark-to-market losses and margin calls. The fund suffered from a combination of funding and asset liquidity. Asset liquidity arose from LTCM failure to account for liquidity becoming more valuable (as it did following the crisis). Since much of its balance sheet was exposed to liquidity risk premium its short positions would increase in price relative to its long positions. This was essentially a massive, unhedged exposure to a single risk factor. LTCM had been aware of funding liquidity risk. Indeed, they estimated that in times of severe stress, cuts on AAA-rated commercial mortgages would increase from 2% to 10%, and similarly for other securitiles. In response to this, LTCM had negotiated long-term financing with margins fixed for several weeks on many of their collateralized loans. Due to an escalating liquidity spiral, LTCM could ultimately not fund its positions in spite of its numerous measures to control funding risk.

# Cash and Cash Equivalents

**The Procter & Gamble Company (PG)** - NYSE

**80.45** ↓0.09(0.11%) 23 Jun 1:30AM

Add to Portfolio

**Balance Sheet**

Get Balance Sheet for: GO

View: **Annual Data** | Quarterly Data

All numbers in thousands

| Period Ending | 30-Jun-2014 | 30-Jun-2013 | 30-Jun-2012 |
|---|---|---|---|
| **Assets** | | | |
| Current Assets | | | |
| Cash And Cash Equivalents | 8,558,000 | 5,947,000 | 4,436,000 |
| Short Term Investments | 2,128,000 | - | - |
| Net Receivables | 7,478,000 | 7,456,000 | 7,069,000 |
| Inventory | 6,759,000 | 6,909,000 | 6,721,000 |
| Other Current Assets | 6,694,000 | 3,678,000 | 3,684,000 |
| **Total Current Assets** | **31,617,000** | **23,990,000** | **21,910,000** |
| Long Term Investments | - | - | - |
| Property Plant and Equipment | 22,304,000 | 21,666,000 | 20,377,000 |
| Goodwill | 53,704,000 | 55,188,000 | 53,773,000 |
| Intangible Assets | 30,843,000 | 31,572,000 | 30,988,000 |
| Accumulated Amortization | - | - | - |
| Other Assets | 5,798,000 | 6,847,000 | 5,196,000 |
| Deferred Long Term Asset Charges | - | - | - |
| **Total Assets** | **144,266,000** | **139,263,000** | **132,244,000** |

Cash and Cash Equivalents are recorded as current assets

Cash and cash equivalents (CCE) are the most liquid current assets found on a business's balance sheet. Cash equivalents are short-term commitments "with temporarily idle cash and easily convertible into a known cash amount". An investment normally counts to be a cash equivalent when it has a short maturity period of 90 days or even less(if maturity period is more than 90 days (e.g., 100 days), then it will not be considered as cash and cash equivalents) from date of acquisition and when it carries an insignificant risk of changes in value. Equity investments mostly are excluded from cash equivalents, unless they are essentially cash equivalents, for instance, if the preferred shares acquired within a short maturity period and with specified recovery date.

One of the company's crucial health indicators is its ability to generate cash and cash equivalents. Company with a pp relatively higher net assets than cash and cash equivalents is mostly an indication of non-liquidity. For investors and companies cash and cash equivalents are generally counted to be "low risk and low return" investments and sometimes analysts can estimate company's ability to pay its bills in a short period of time by comparing CCE and current liabilities. Nevertheless, this can happen only if there are receivables that can be converted into cash immediately.

However, companies with a big value of cash and cash equivalents are targets for takeovers (by other companies), since their excess cash helps buyers to finance their acquisition. High cash reserves can also indicate that the company is not effective at deploying its CCE resources, whereas for big companies it might be a sign of preparation for substantial purchases. The opportunity cost of saving up CCE is the return on equity that company could earn by investing in a new product or service or expansion of business.

## Components of Cash

- Currency
- Coins
- Bank overdrafts normally are considered as financing activities. Nevertheless, where bank borrowings which are repayable on a demand form an integral part of company's cash management, bank overdrafts are considered to be a part of cash and cash equivalents.
- Cash in saving accounts is generally for the saving purposes so that they are not used for daily expenses.
- Cash in checking accounts allow to write checks and use electronic debit to access funds in the account.
- Money order is a financial instrument issued by government or financial institutions which is used by payee to receive cash on demand. The advantage of money orders over checks is that it is more trusted since it is always prepaid. They are acceptable for payment of personal or small business's debts and can be purchased for a small fee at many locations such as post office and grocery.
- Petty cash small amount of cash that is used for payment of insignificant expenses and the amount of it may vary depending on the organisation. For some entities $50 is adequate amount of cash, whereas for others the minimum sum should be $200. Petty cash funds must be safeguarded and recorded in order to avoid thefts. Often there is a custodian appointed who is responsible for the documentation of petty cash transactions.

## Components of Cash Equivalents

1969 $100,000 Treasury Bill

- Treasury bills are also called as "T- bills" and are a security issued by U.S Department of Treasury issues, so that company essentially lends money to the

U.S government. T- bills are sold in denominations of $1000 up to maximum amount of $5 million and generally they do not pay any interest rates, but are sold at a discount, their yield being the difference between purchase price and redemption value.

- Commercial paper is a bearer document which is used by big companies. The minimum amount permitted is £100,000 and this form of borrowing is not suitable for certain "entities". Finance companies sell 2/3 of their total commercial paper to the public, but there are also some companies which borrow less and sell their commercial paper to "paper dealers" who then re-sell the papers to the investors. A "round lot" for paper dealers is approximately £250,000.
- Marketable securities make business look more liquid, since they are also included in the calculation of current ratio. These securities are mostly traded on public exchange due to their ready price availability. There are two forms of Marketable Securities: Marketable Equity Securities and Marketable Debt Securities.
- Money Market funds are similar to checking accounts, but they mostly pay higher interest rates generated on deposited funds. Net asset Value (NAV) of Money Market funds maintains stable compared to other mutual funds and its share price is constant: $1.00 per share. For businesses, non-profit organizations and many other institutions MMF are very effective "vehicle" for cash management.
- Short-term government bonds are mostly issued by governments to support government's spending. They are mostly issued in country's domestic currency and in the U.S government bonds include the Saving bond, Treasury bond, Treasury inflation-protected securities and many others. Before investing into government bond investors should take into account political risk, inflation and interest rate risk.

## Calculation of Cash and Cash Equivalents

Cash and cash equivalents are listed on balance sheet as "current assets" and its value changes when different transactions are occurred.These changes are called "cash flows" and they are recorded on accounting ledger. For instance, if a company spends $300 on purchasing goods, this is recorded as $300 increase to its supplies and decrease in the value of CCE. These are few formulas that are used by analysts to calculate transactions related to cash and cash equivalents:

*Change in CCE = End of Year Cash and Cash equivalents - Beginning of Year Cash and Cash Equivalents.*

*Value of Cash and Cash Equivalents at the end of period = Net Cash Flow + Value of CCE at the period of beginning*

## Liquidity Measurement Ratios

- Current ratio is generally used to estimate company's liquidity by "deriving the proportion of current assets available to cover current liabilities". The main idea behind this concept is to decide whether current assets which also include cash and cash equivalents are available pay off its short term liabilities (taxes, notes payable and etc.)The higher current ratio is, the better is for the organisation.

$$\text{Current ratio} = \frac{\text{Current assets}}{\text{Current liabilities}}$$

- Quick ratio is liquidity indicator that defines current ratio by measuring the most liquid current assets in the company that are available to cover liabilities. Unlike to the current ratio, inventories and other assets that are difficult to convert into the cash are excluded from the calculation of quick ratio.

$$\text{Quick Ratio} = \frac{\text{Current Assets} - \text{Inventories}}{\text{Current Liabilities}}$$

- Cash ratio is more restrictive than above mentioned ratios because no other current assets than cash can be used to pay off current debt. Most of the creditors give importance to cash ratio of the company, since it give them idea whether the entity is able to maintain stable cash balances in order to pay off their current debts as they come due.

$$\text{Cash Ratio} = \frac{\text{Cash and Cash Equivalent}}{\text{Current Liabilities}}$$

## Restricted Cash

Restricted cash is the amount of cash and cash equivalent items which are restricted for withdrawal and usage. The restrictions might include legally restricted deposits, which are held as compensating balances against short-term borrowings, contacts entered into with others or entity statements of intention with regard to specific deposits; nevertheless, time deposits and short-term certificates of deposit are excluded from legally restricted deposits. Restricted cash can be also set aside for other purposes such as expansion of the entity, dividend funds or "retirement of long-term debt". Depending on its immateriality or materiality, restricted cash may be recorded as "cash" in the financial statement or it might be classified based on the date of availability disbursements.

Moreover, if cash is expected to be used within one year after the balance sheet date it can be classified as "current asset", but in a longer period of time it is mentioned as non- current asset. For example, a large machine manufacturing company receives an advance payment (deposit) from its customer for a machine that should be produced and shipped to another country within 2 months. Based on the customer contract the manufacturer should put the deposit into separate bank account and not withdraw or use the money until the equipment is shipped and delivered. This is a restricted cash, since manufacturer has the deposit, but he can not use it for operations until the equipment is shipped.

**Balance Sheet Data**
(in millions)

| | December 31, | | | | |
|---|---|---|---|---|---|
| | 2014 | 2013 | 2012 | 2011 | 2010 |
| Cash, cash equivalents and investments | $ 168.7 | $ 312.3 | $ 278.0 | $ 479.4 | $ 340.1 |
| Restricted cash | 2.0 | — | — | 71.2 | 182.1 |
| Property, plant and equipment, net | 1,589.1 | 1,654.0 | 1,678.3 | 1,350.1 | 1,008.3 |
| Total assets | 2,159.9 | 2,357.4 | 2,351.3 | 2,319.3 | 1,915.1 |
| Senior notes, net of unamortized discount | 498.5 | 597.0 | 596.5 | 596.1 | 595.7 |
| Federal coal lease obligations | 64.0 | 122.9 | 186.1 | 288.3 | 118.3 |
| Asset retirement obligations, net of current portion | 216.2 | 246.1 | 239.0 | 192.7 | 182.2 |
| Total liabilities | 1,072.1 | 1,355.4 | 1,420.3 | 1,568.9 | 1,383.9 |
| Total equity | 1,087.8 | 1,002.0 | 931.0 | 750.4 | 531.2 |

How Restricted Cash is presented in Balance Sheet

## References


- Ahorny, Joseph; Saunders, Anthony; Swary, Itzhak (1985). "The Effects of the International Banking Act on Domestic Bank Profitability and Risk". Journal of Money, Credit, and Banking. JSTOR. 17: 493–506. JSTOR 1992444
- Worstall, Tim (31 March 2014). "Michael Lewis Is Entirely Wrong About High Frequency Trading Hitting The Little Guy". Forbes. Retrieved 11 August 2014
- Nobes, Christopher (2006). Penguin Dictionary of Accounting. London: Penguin Books. p. 227. ISBN 978-0-14-102525-4
- Brunnermeier, Markus K.; Pedersen, Lasse Heje (2009). "Market Liquidity and Funding Liquidity". Review of Financial Studies. 22 (6): 2201–38. doi:10.1093/rfs/hhn098
- Acharya, V; Pedersen, L (2005). "Asset pricing with liquidity risk". Journal of Financial Economics. 77 (2): 375–410. doi:10.1016/j.jfineco.2004.06.007
- "Final Report of the Multidisciplinary Working Group on Enhanced Disclosure". Bank for International Settlements. April 2001. Retrieved August 8, 2012
- Longstaff, Francis A. (1995). "How Much Can Marketability Affect Security Values?". The Journal of Finance. 50 (5): 1767–74. doi:10.1111/j.1540-6261.1995.tb05197

- "Mr Greenspan discusses recent trends in the management of foreign exchange reserves" (pdf). Bank for International Settlements. April 29, 1999. Retrieved August 8, 2012
- Abudy, Menachem Meni; Raviv, Alon (2016). "How much can illiquidity affect corporate debt yield spread?". Journal of Financial Stability. 25: 58–69. doi:10.1016/j.jfs.2016.06.011
- Tracy, John A. (2004). How to Read a Financial Report: Wringing Vital Signs Out of the Numbers. John Wiley and Sons. p. 173. ISBN 0-471-64693-8
- Chincarini, Ludwig B. (2008). "Natural Gas Futures and Spread Position Risk: Lessons from the Collapse of Amaranth Advisors L.L.C". SSRN Electronic Journal. doi:10.2139/ssrn.1086865
- "FSA moves to enhance supervision in wake of Northern Rock". Financial Services Authority. March 26, 2008. Retrieved August 9, 2012
- Chincarini, Ludwig B. (2007). "The Amaranth Debacle: Failure of Risk Measures or Failure of Risk Management?". SSRN Electronic Journal. doi:10.2139/ssrn.952607
- Duffie, Darrell; Garleanu, Nicolae; Pedersen, Lasse Heje (2005). "Over-the-Counter Markets". Econometrica. 73 (6): 1815–47. doi:10.1111/j.1468-0262.2005.00639

# 5

# Investment and Investment Management

Investment is done with the intention of some benefit in the future. Investment management, P2P asset management, investment strategy, assets under management, global assets under management and separately managed account have been explained. This chapter is an overview of the subject matter incorporating all the major aspects of investment and investment management.

## Investment

To invest is to allocate money (or sometimes another resource, such as time) in the expectation of some benefit in the future.

In finance, the benefit from investment is called a return. The return may consist of capital gain or investment income, including dividends, interest, rental income etc., or a combination of the two. The projected economic return is the appropriately discounted value of the future returns. The historic return comprises the actual capital gain (or loss) or income (or both) over a period of time.

Investment generally results in acquiring an asset, also called an investment. If the asset is available at a price worth investing, it is normally expected either to generate income, or to appreciate in value, so that it can be sold at a higher price (or both).

Investors generally expect higher returns from riskier investments. Financial assets range from low-risk, low-return investments, such as high-grade government bonds, to those with higher risk and higher expected commensurate reward, such as emerging markets stock investments.

Investors, particularly novices, are often advised to adopt an investment strategy and diversify their portfolio. Diversification has the statistical effect of reducing overall risk.

### Related Terms

Investment differs from arbitrage, in which profit is generated without investing capital or bearing risk.

An investor may bear a risk of loss of some or all of their capital invested, whereas in saving (such as in a bank deposit) the risk of loss in nominal value is normally remote. (Note that if the currency of a savings account differs from the account holder's home currency, then there is the risk that the exchange rate between the two currencies will move unfavorably, so that the value in the account holder's home currency of the savings account decreases.)

Speculation involves a level of risk which is greater than most investors would generally consider justified by the expected return. An alternative characterization of speculation is its short-term, opportunistic nature.

## Famous Investors

Investors famous for their success include Warren Buffett. In March 2013 *Forbes* magazine, Warren Buffett ranked number 2 in their Forbes 400 list. Buffett has advised in numerous articles and interviews that a good investment strategy is long term and choosing the right assets to invest in requires due diligence.

Edward O. Thorp was a highly successful hedge fund manager in the 1970s and 1980s who spoke of a similar approach.

The investment principles of both of these investors have points in common with the Kelly criterion for money management. Numerous interactive calculators which use the Kelly criterion can be found online.

## Intermediaries and Collective Investments

Investments are often made indirectly through intermediary financial institutions. These intermediaries include pension funds, banks, and insurance companies. They may pool money received from a number of individual end investors into funds such as investment trusts, unit trusts, SICAVs, etc. to make large scale investments. Each individual investor holds an indirect or direct claim on the assets purchased, subject to charges levied by the intermediary, which may be large and varied.

Approaches to investment sometimes referred to in marketing of collective investments include dollar cost averaging and market timing.

## History

The Code of Hammurabi (around 1700 BC) provided a legal framework for investment, establishing a means for the pledge of collateral by codifying debtor and creditor rights in regard to pledged land. Punishments for breaking financial obligations were not as severe as those for crimes involving injury or death.

In the early 1900s purchasers of stocks, bonds, and other securities were described in media, academia, and commerce as speculators. By the 1950s, the term investment had come to denote the more conservative end of the securities spectrum, while speculation was applied by financial brokers and their advertising agencies to higher risk securities much in vogue at that time. Since the last half of the 20th century, the terms speculation and speculator have specifically referred to higher risk ventures.

## Value Investment

A value investor buys assets that they believe to be undervalued (and sells overvalued ones). To identify undervalued securities, a value investor uses analysis of the financial reports of the issuer to evaluate the security. Value investors employ accounting ratios, such as earnings per share and sales growth, to identify securities trading at prices below their worth.

Warren Buffett and Benjamin Graham are notable examples of value investors. Graham and Dodd's seminal work Security Analysis was written in the wake of the Wall Street Crash of 1929.

The price to earnings ratio (P/E), or earnings multiple, is a particularly significant and recognized fundamental ratio, with a function of dividing the share price of stock, by its earnings per share. This will provide the value representing the sum investors are prepared to expend for each dollar of company earnings. This ratio is an important aspect, due to its capacity as measurement for the comparison of valuations of various companies. A stock with a lower P/E ratio will cost less per share, than one with a higher P/E, taking into account the same level of financial performance; therefore, it essentially means a low P/E is the preferred option.

An instance, in which the price to earnings ratio has a lesser significance, is when companies in different industries are compared. An example; although, it is reasonable for a telecommunications stock to show a P/E in the low teens; in the case of hi-tech stock, a P/E in the 40s range, is not unusual. When making comparisons the P/E ratio can give you a refined view of a particular stock valuation.

For investors paying for each dollar of a company's earnings, the P/E ratio is a significant indicator, but the price-to-book ratio (P/B) is also a reliable indication of how much investors are willing to spend on each dollar of company assets. In the process of the P/B ratio, the share price of a stock is divided by its net assets; any intangibles, such as goodwill, are not taken into account. It is a crucial factor of the price-to-book ratio, due to it indicating the actual payment for tangible assets and not the more difficult valuation, of intangibles. Accordingly, the P/B could be considered a comparatively, conservative metric.

## Free Cash Flow and Capital Structure

Free cash flow measures the cash a company generates which is available to its debt and equity investors, after allowing for reinvestment in working capital and capital expenditure. High and rising free cash flow therefore tend to make a company more attractive to investors.

The debt-to-equity ratio is an indicator of capital structure. A high proportion of debt, reflected in a high debt-to-equity ratio, tends to make a company's earnings, free cash flow, and ultimately the returns to its investors, more risky or volatile. Investors compare a company's debt-to-equity ratio with those of other companies in the same industry, and examine trends in debt-to-equity ratios and free cash flow.

## EBITDA

A popular valuation metric is Earnings Before Interest, Tax, Depreciation and Amortization (EBITDA), with application for example to valuing unlisted companies and mergers and acquisitions.

For an attractive investment, for example a company competing in a high growth industry, an investor might expect a significant acquisition premium above book value or current market value, which values the company at several times the most recent EBITDA. A private equity fund for example may buy a target company for a multiple of its historical or forecasted EBITDA, perhaps as much as 6 or 8 times.

In certain cases, an EBITDA may be sacrificed by a company, in order for the pursuance of future growth; a strategy frequently used by corporate giants, such as, Amazon, Google and Microsoft, among others. This is a business decision that can impact negatively on buyout offers, founded on EBITDA and can be the cause of many negotiations, failing. It may be recognized as a valuation breach, with many investors maintaining that sellers are too demanding, while buyers are regarded as failing to realize the long-term potential of, expenditure or acquisitions.

## Capital Gains Taxes

The amount to pay in taxes for long term investments, investments that span over a year long term, and short term investments such as those that are below a year are different. The long term investments range from Zero to twenty percent for capital gains and they are regulated by what tax bracket you are in for income taxes. For the zero to fifteen percent income tax bracket you could qualify for the zero percent long-term capital gains rate. The next bracket is the fifteen to twenty percent income tax bracket where you are set at fifteen percent capital gains tax for long term investments. The next bracket is between twenty and 39.6 percent and that leads to a twenty percent capital gains tax however with these numbers you should add 3.8 percent for the health care surtax. The short term capital gains tax is also related to your total taxable income and is taxed at the same rate as your income and ranges from ten to 39.6 percent.

## Types of Financial Investment

Types of financial investments include:

- Alternative investments

- Traditional investments
- (Interested investment)

## Value Investing

Value investing is an investment paradigm which generally involves buying securities that appear underpriced by some form of fundamental analysis, though it has taken many forms since its inception. It derives from the ideas on investment that Benjamin Graham and David Dodd began teaching at Columbia Business School in 1928 and subsequently developed in their 1934 text *Security Analysis*. As examples, such securities may be stock in public companies that trade at discounts to book value or tangible book value, have high dividend yields, have low price-to-earning multiples or have low price-to-book ratios.

High-profile proponents of value investing, including Berkshire Hathaway chairman Warren Buffett, have argued that the essence of value investing is buying stocks at less than their intrinsic value. The discount of the market price to the intrinsic value is what Benjamin Graham called the "margin of safety". The intrinsic value is the discounted value of all future distributions. However, the future distributions and the appropriate discount rate can only be assumptions. ( Graham never recommended using future numbers, only past ones). For the last 25 years, Warren Buffett has taken the value investing concept even further with a focus on "finding an outstanding company at a sensible price" rather than generic companies at a bargain price.

Graham never used the phrase, "value investing" — the term was coined later to help describe his ideas and has resulted in significant misinterpretation of his principles, the foremost being that Graham simply recommended cheap stocks.

## History

### Benjamin Graham

Benjamin Graham (pictured) established value investing along with fellow professor David Dodd.

Value investing was established by Benjamin Graham and David Dodd, both professors at Columbia Business School and teachers of many famous investors. In Graham's book *The Intelligent Investor*, he advocated the important concept of margin of safety — first introduced in *Security Analysis*, a 1934 book he co-authored with David Dodd — which calls for an approach to investing that is focused on purchasing equities at prices less than their intrinsic values. In terms of picking or screening stocks, he recommended purchasing firms who have steady profits, are trading at low prices to book value, have low price-to-earnings (P/E) ratios, and who have relatively low debt.

## Further Evolution

However, the concept of value (as well as "book value") has evolved significantly since the 1970s. Book value is most useful in industries where most assets are tangible. Intangible assets such as patents, brands, or goodwill are difficult to quantify, and may not survive the break-up of a company. When an industry is going through fast technological advancements, the value of its assets is not easily estimated. Sometimes, the production power of an asset can be significantly reduced due to competitive disruptive innovation and therefore its value can suffer permanent impairment. One good example of decreasing asset value is a personal computer. An example of where book value does not mean much is the service and retail sectors. One modern model of calculating value is the discounted cash flow model (DCF), where the value of an asset is the sum of its future cash flows, discounted back to the present.

## Value Investing Performance

### Performance of Value Strategies

Value investing has proven to be a successful investment strategy. There are several ways to evaluate its success. One way is to examine the performance of simple value strategies, such as buying low PE ratio stocks, low price-to-cash-flow ratio stocks, or low price-to-book ratio stocks. Numerous academics have published studies investigating the effects of buying value stocks. These studies have consistently found that value stocks outperform growth stocks and the market as a whole.

### Performance of Value Investors

Simply examining the performance of the best known value investors would not be instructive, because investors do not become well known unless they are successful. This introduces a selection bias. A better way to investigate the performance of a group of value investors was suggested by Warren Buffett, in his May 17, 1984 speech that was published as The Superinvestors of Graham-and-Doddsville. In this speech, Buffett examined the performance of those investors who worked at Graham-Newman Corporation and were thus most influenced by Benjamin Graham. Buffett's conclusion is identical to that of the academic research on simple value investing strategies—value investing is, on average, successful in the long run.

During about a 25-year period (1965–90), published research and articles in leading journals of the value ilk were few. Warren Buffett once commented, "You couldn't advance in a finance department in this country unless you thought that the world was flat."

## Well-known Value Investors

### Ben Graham's Students

Benjamin Graham is regarded by many to be the father of value investing. Along with David Dodd, he wrote *Security Analysis*, first published in 1934. The most lasting contribution of this book to the field of security analysis was to emphasize the quantifiable aspects of security analysis (such as the evaluations of earnings and book value) while minimizing the importance of more qualitative factors such as the quality of a company's management. Graham later wrote *The Intelligent Investor*, a book that brought value investing to individual investors. Aside from Buffett, many of Graham's other students, such as William J. Ruane, Irving Kahn, Walter Schloss, and Charles Brandes went on to become successful investors in their own right.

Irving Kahn was one of Graham's teaching assistants at Columbia University in the 1930s. He was a close friend and confidant of Graham's for decades and made research contributions to Graham's texts *Security Analysis*, *Storage and Stability*, *World Commodities and World Currencies* and *The Intelligent Investor*. Kahn was a partner at various finance firms until 1978 when he and his sons, Thomas Graham Kahn and Alan Kahn, started the value investing firm, Kahn Brothers & Company. Irving Kahn remained chairman of the firm until his death at age 109.

Walter Schloss was another Graham-and-Dodd disciple. Schloss never had a formal education. When he was 18, he started working as a runner on Wall Street. He then attended investment courses taught by Ben Graham at the New York Stock Exchange Institute, and eventually worked for Graham in the Graham-Newman Partnership. In 1955, he left Graham's company and set up his own investment firm, which he ran for nearly 50 years. Walter Schloss was one of the investors Warren Buffett profiled in his famous Superinvestors of Graham-and-Doddsville article.

Christopher H. Browne of Tweedy, Browne was well known for value investing. According to the *Wall Street Journal*, Tweedy, Browne was the favorite brokerage firm of Benjamin Graham during his lifetime; also, the Tweedy, Browne Value Fund and Global Value Fund have both beat market averages since their inception in 1993. In 2006, Christopher H. Browne wrote *The Little Book of Value Investing* in order to teach ordinary investors how to value invest.

Peter Cundill was a well-known Canadian value investor who followed the Graham teachings. His flagship Cundill Value Fund allowed Canadian investors access to fund management according to the strict principles of Graham and Dodd. Warren Buffett had indicated that Cundill had the credentials he's looking for in a chief investment officer.

## Warren Buffett & Charlie Munger

Graham's most famous student, however, is Warren Buffett, who ran successful investing partnerships before closing them in 1969 to focus on running Berkshire Hathaway. Charlie Munger joined Buffett at Berkshire Hathaway in the 1970s and has since worked as Vice Chairman of the company. Buffett has credited Munger with encouraging him to focus on long-term sustainable growth rather than on simply the valuation of current cash flows or assets.

## Other Columbia Business School Value Investors

Columbia Business School has played a significant role in shaping the principles of the *Value Investor*, with professors and students making their mark on history and on each other. Ben Graham's book, *The Intelligent Investor*, was Warren Buffett's bible and he referred to it as "the greatest book on investing ever written." A young Warren Buffett studied under Ben Graham, took his course and worked for his small investment firm, Graham Newman, from 1954 to 1956. Twenty years after Ben Graham, Roger Murray arrived and taught value investing to a young student named Mario Gabelli. About a decade or so later, Bruce Greenwald arrived and produced his own protégés, including Paul Sonkin—just as Ben Graham had Buffett as a protégé, and Roger Murray had Gabelli.

## Mutual Series and Franklin Templeton Disciples

Mutual Series has a well-known reputation of producing top value managers and analysts in this modern era. This tradition stems from two individuals: Max Heine, founder of the well regarded value investment firm Mutual Shares fund in 1949 and his protégé legendary value investor Michael F. Price. Mutual Series was sold to Franklin Templeton Investments in 1996. The disciples of Heine and Price quietly practice value investing at some of the most successful investment firms in the country. Franklin Templeton Investments takes its name from Sir John Templeton, another contrarian value oriented investor.

Seth Klarman, a Mutual Series alum, is the founder and president of The Baupost Group, a Boston-based private investment partnership, and author of *Margin of Safety, Risk Averse Investing Strategies for the Thoughtful Investor*, which since has become a value investing classic. Now out of print, *Margin of Safety* has sold on Amazon for $1,200 and eBay for $2,000.

## Other Value Investors

Laurence Tisch, who led Loews Corporation with his brother, Robert Tisch, for more than half a century, also embraced value investing. Shortly after his death in 2003 at age 80, Fortune wrote, "Larry Tisch was the ultimate value investor. He was a brilliant contrarian: He saw value where other investors didn't -- and he was usually right." By 2012, Loews Corporation, which continues to follow the principles of value investing, had revenues of $14.6 billion and assets of more than $75 billion.

Michael Larson is the Chief Investment Officer of Cascade Investment, which is the investment vehicle for the Bill & Melinda Gates Foundation and the Gates personal fortune. Cascade is a diversified investment shop established in 1994 by Gates and Larson. Larson graduated from Claremont McKenna College in 1980 and the Booth School of Business at the University of Chicago in 1981. Larson is a well known value investor but his specific investment and diversification strategies are not known. Larson has consistently outperformed the market since the establishment of Cascade and has rivaled or outperformed Berkshire Hathaway's returns as well as other funds based on the value investing strategy.

Martin J. Whitman is another well-regarded value investor. His approach is called safe-and-cheap, which was hitherto referred to as financial-integrity approach. Martin Whitman focuses on acquiring common shares of companies with extremely strong financial position at a price reflecting meaningful discount to the estimated NAV of the company concerned. Whitman believes it is ill-advised for investors to pay much attention to the trend of macro-factors (like employment, movement of interest rate, GDP, etc.) because they are not as important and attempts to predict their movement are almost always futile. Whitman's letters to shareholders of his Third Avenue Value Fund (TAVF) are considered valuable resources "for investors to pirate good ideas" by Joel Greenblatt in his book on special-situation investment *You Can Be a Stock Market Genius*.

Joel Greenblatt achieved annual returns at the hedge fund Gotham Capital of over 50% per year for 10 years from 1985 to 1995 before closing the fund and returning his investors' money. He is known for investing in special situations such as spin-offs, mergers, and divestitures.

Charles de Vaulx and Jean-Marie Eveillard are well known global value managers. For a time, these two were paired up at the First Eagle Funds, compiling an enviable track record of risk-adjusted outperformance. For example, Morningstar designated them the 2001 "International Stock Manager of the Year" and de Vaulx earned second place from Morningstar for 2006. Eveillard is known for his Bloomberg appearances where he insists that securities investors never use margin or leverage. The point made is that margin should be considered the anathema of value investing, since a negative price move could prematurely force a sale. In contrast, a value investor must be able and willing to be patient for the rest of the market to recognize and correct whatever pricing issue created the momentary value. Eveillard correctly labels the use of margin or leverage as speculation, the opposite of value investing.

Other notable value investors include: Mason Hawkins, Whitney Tilson, Mohnish Pabrai, Li Lu, Guy Spier and Tom Gayner who manages the investment portfolio of Markel Insurance.

## Criticism

Value stocks do not always beat growth stocks, as demonstrated in the late 1990s. Moreover, when value stocks perform well, it may not mean that the market is inefficient, though it may imply that value stocks are simply riskier and thus require greater returns.

An issue with buying shares in a bear market is that despite appearing undervalued at one time, prices can still drop along with the market. Conversely, an issue with not buying shares in a bull market is that despite appearing overvalued at one time, prices can still rise along with the market.

Also, one of the biggest criticisms of price centric Value Investing is that an emphasis on low prices (and recently depressed prices) regularly misleads retail investors; because fundamentally low (and recently depressed) prices often represent a fundamentally sound difference (or change) in a company's relative financial health. To that end, Warren Buffett has regularly emphasized that "it's far better to buy a wonderful company at a fair price, than to buy a fair company at a wonderful price."

In 2002, Stanford accounting professor Joseph Piotroski developed the "F-Score", which discriminates higher potential members within a class of value candidates. The F-Score aims to discover additional value from signals in a firm's series of annual financial statements, after initial screening of static measures like book-to-market value. The F-Score formula inputs financial statements and awards points for meeting predetermined criteria. Piotroski retrospectively analyzed a class of high book-to-market stocks in the period 1976-1996, and demonstrated that high F-Score selections increased returns by 7.5% annually versus the class as a whole. The American Association of Individual Investors examined 56 screening methods in a retrospective analysis of the financial crisis of 2008, and found that only F-Score produced positive results.

Another issue is the method of calculating the "intrinsic value". Some analysts believe that two investors can analyze the same information and reach different conclusions regarding the intrinsic value of the company, and that there is no systematic or standard way to value a stock. In other words, a value investing strategy can only be considered successful if it delivers excess returns after allowing for the risk involved, where risk may be defined in many different ways, including market risk, multi-factor models or idiosyncratic risk.

## Alternative Investment

A British 1 shilling embossed stamp, typical of the type included in an investment portfolio of stamps.

An alternative investment is an investment in asset classes other than stocks, bonds, and cash. The term is a relatively loose one and includes tangible assets such as precious metals, art, wine, antiques, coins, or stamps and some financial assets such as real estate, commodities, private equity, distressed securities, hedge funds, carbon credits, venture capital, film production, financial derivatives, and cryptocurrencies. Investments in real estate and forestry are also often termed alternative despite the ancient use of such real assets to enhance and preserve wealth. In the last century, fancy color diamonds have emerged as an alternative investment class as well. Alternative investments are to be contrasted with traditional investments.

## Research

There is a wide variety of literature on alternative investments; however, this term has been used broadly and can also refer to financial alternatives such as derivatives or other alternatives such as energy. It is difficult to find research on the investment characteristics of tangible alternatives such as art or wine due primarily to a lack of good quality data. The Goizueta Business School at Emory University has established the Emory Center for Alternative Investments to provide research and a forum for discussion regarding private equity, hedge fund, and venture capital investments. William Baumol used the repeat sale method in a 1986 paper in *The American Economic Review*, comparing the prices of 500 paintings sold over 410 years, concluding that the average annual return on art was 0.55% (after taking inflation into account). A master's thesis by Dennis Kundu and Alexander Raza studied the return on investment on high-quality oil paintings sold in Sweden between 1985 and 2016, and found the average return to be merely 0.6% annually.

As with any investment, it's important to do your homework, but in the case of many alternative investments, some specialist knowledge on the specific asset is often needed. Therefore, it's important that would-be investors have a reputable broker or investment company on their side with demonstrable success in their asset class arena, which are happy to work with you to identify your ideal investment solutions.

## Access to Alternative Investments

In recent years, the growth of alternative finance has opened up new avenues to investing in alternatives. These include the following:

### Equity Crowdfunding

Equity crowdfunding platforms allow "the crowd" to review early-stage investment opportunities presented by entrepreneurs and take an equity stake in the business. Typically an online platform acts as a broker between investors and founders. These platforms differ greatly in the types of opportunities they will offer up to investors, how much due diligence is performed, degree of investor protections available, minimum investment size and so on. Equity crowdfunding platforms have seen a significant amount of success in the UK and, with the passing of JOBS Act Title III in early 2016, are now picking up steam in the US.

### Investor-led Crowdfunding

The investor-led model was introduced by UK-based crowdfunding platform SyndicateRoom and makes it necessary for any startup seeking funding to first be vetted by an experienced investor that is also investing a significant amount (25% or more) of the target round.

### SEIS and EIS Funds

Only available in the UK, SEIS funds and EIS funds present a tax-efficient way of investing in early-stage ventures. These work much like venture capital funds, with the added bonus of receiving government tax incentives for investing and loss relief protection should the companies invested in fail. Such funds help to diversify investor exposure by investing into multiple early ventures. Fees are normally charged by the management team for participating in the fund, and these can end up totalling anywhere between 15% and 40% of the fund value over the course of its life.

### Private Equity

Private equity consists of large-scale private investments into unlisted companies in return for equity. Private funds are typically formed by combining funds from institutional investors such as high-net-worth individuals, insurance companies, pension funds etc. Funds are used alongside borrowed money and the money of the private equity firm itself to invest in businesses they believe to have high growth potential. In Europe, venture capital, buy-ins and buy-outs are considered private equity.

## Investors

The *Merrill Lynch/Cap Gemini Ernst & Young World Wealth Report 2003*, based on 2002 data, showed high-net-worth individuals, as defined in the report, to have 10% of their financial assets in alternative investments. For the purposes of the report, alternative investments included "structured products, luxury valuables and collectibles, hedge funds, managed futures, and precious metals". By 2007, this had reduced to 9%. No recommendations were made in either report about the amount of money investors *should* place in alternative investments.

A Good Delivery bar, the standard for trade in the major international gold markets.

## Characteristics

Alternative investments are sometimes used as a way of reducing overall investment risk through diversification.

Some of the characteristics of alternative investments may include:

- Low correlation with traditional financial investments such as stocks and bonds
- It may be difficult to determine the current market value of the asset
- Alternative investments may be relatively illiquid
- Costs of purchase and sale may be relatively high
- There may be limited historical risk and return data
- A high degree of investment analysis may be required before buying

## Liquid Alts

Liquid alternatives ("alts") are alternative investments that provide daily liquidity. Liquid alternative investments should produce returns uncorrelated to GDP growth, must have protection against systemic market risk and should be too small to create new systemic risks for the market. Hedge funds may be included in this category; however, traditional hedge funds may have liquidity limitations, and the term is usually used for registered mutual funds which use hedge fund strategies such as long-short equity investments.

## United States

Liquid alternatives became popular in the late 2000s, growing from $124 billion in assets under management 2010 to $310 billion in 2014. However, in 2015 only $85 million was added, with 31 closed funds and a high-profile underperformance by the largest long-short equity fund at the time, Marketfield Fund.

In 2014 there were an estimated 298 liquid alternative funds with strategies such as long-short equity funds; event driven, relative value, tactical trading (including managed futures), and multi-strategy. This number does not include option income funds, tactical shorting and leveraged indexed funds.

There has been expressed skepticism over the complexity of liquid alts and the lack of able portfolio managers.

## Traditional Investments

An old stock certificate from Poland with most of the coupons still attached.

The notion of traditional investments refers to putting money into well-known assets (such as bonds, cash, real estate, and equity shares) with the expectation of capital appreciation, dividends, and interest earnings. Traditional investments are to be contrasted with alternative investments.

## Bonds

Here the investor purchases debt issued by companies or governments which promises to pay an annual return until the debt is repaid. The value of the investment changes as the level of general interest rates fluctuates, causing the bond to become more or less valuable.

## Cash

In cash investing, money is typically invested in short-term, low-risk investment vehicles like certificates of deposit, money market funds, and high yield bank accounts.

## Real Estate

In real estate, money is used to purchase property for the purpose of holding, reselling or leasing for income and there is an element of capital risk.

## Residential Real Estate

Investment in residential real estate is the most common form of real estate investment measured by number of participants because it includes property purchased as a primary residence. In many cases the buyer does not have the full purchase price for a property and must borrow additional money from a bank, finance company or private lender.

## Commercial Real Estate

Commercial real estate consists of apartments, office buildings, retail space, hotels, warehouses, and other commercial properties. Investors may purchase commercial property outright, with the help of a loan, or collectively through a real estate fund.

## Real Estate Investment Trusts

Investment in real estate investment trusts (REITs) is like investing in a pool of real estate that the company manages.

## Stocks and Shares

This involves purchasing a share in the equity of a company in the hope that the share price will increase. Purchasing a share in the company is the same as owning part of the company. Stock investing can come in the form of buying individual stocks, mutual funds, index funds and exchange traded funds (ETFs).

## Investment Management

Investment management is the professional asset management of various securities (shares, bonds and other securities) and other assets (e.g., real estate) in order to meet specified investment goals for the benefit of the investors. Investors may be institutions (insurance companies, pension funds, corporations, charities, educational establishments etc.) or private investors (both directly via investment contracts and more commonly via collective investment schemes e.g. mutual funds or exchange-traded funds).

The term asset management is often used to refer to the investment management of collective investments, while the more generic fund management may refer to all forms of institutional investment as well as investment management for private investors. Investment managers who specialize in *advisory* or *discretionary* management on behalf of (normally wealthy) private investors may often refer to their services as money management or portfolio management often within the context of so-called "private banking".

The provision of investment management services includes elements of financial statement analysis, asset selection, stock selection, plan implementation and ongoing monitoring of investments. Coming under the remit of financial services many of the world's largest companies are at least in part investment managers and employ millions of staff.

The term fund manager (or investment advisor in the United States) refers to both a firm that provides investment management services and an individual who directs fund management decisions.

According to a Boston Consulting Group study, the assets managed professionally for fees reached an all-time high of US$62.4 trillion in 2012, after remaining flat-lined since 2007. Furthermore, these industry assets under management were expected to reach US$70.2 trillion at the end of 2013 as per a Cerulli Associates estimate.

The global investment management industry is highly concentrated in nature, in a universe of about 70,000 funds roughly 99.7% of the US fund flows in 2012 went into just 185 funds. Additionally, a majority of fund managers report that more than 50% of their inflows go to only three funds.

### Industry Scope

The business of investment has several facets, the employment of professional fund managers, research (of individual assets and asset classes), dealing, settlement, marketing, internal auditing, and the preparation of reports for clients. The largest financial fund managers are firms that exhibit all the complexity their size demands. Apart from the people who bring in the money (marketers) and the people who direct investment (the fund managers), there are compliance staff (to ensure accord with legislative and regulatory constraints), internal auditors of various kinds (to examine internal systems and controls), financial controllers (to account for the institutions' own money and costs), computer experts, and "back office" employees (to track and record transactions and fund valuations for up to thousands of clients per institution).

## Key Problems of Running such Businesses

Key problems include:

- revenue is directly linked to market valuations, so a major fall in asset prices can cause a precipitous decline in revenues relative to costs;
- above-average fund performance is difficult to sustain, and clients may not be patient during times of poor performance;
- successful fund managers are expensive and may be headhunted by competitors;
- above-average fund performance appears to be dependent on the unique skills of the fund manager; however, clients are loath to stake their investments on the ability of a few individuals- they would rather see firm-wide success, attributable to a single philosophy and internal discipline;
- analysts who generate above-average returns often become sufficiently wealthy that they avoid corporate employment in favor of managing their personal portfolios.

## Representing the Owners of Shares

Institutions often control huge shareholdings. In most cases they are acting as fiduciary agents rather than principals (direct owners). The owners of shares theoretically have great power to alter the companies via the voting rights the shares carry and the consequent ability to pressure managements, and if necessary out-vote them at annual and other meetings.

In practice, the ultimate owners of shares often do not exercise the power they collectively hold (because the owners are many, each with small holdings); financial institutions (as agents) sometimes do. There is a general belief that shareholders – in this case, the institutions acting as agents—could and should exercise more active influence over the companies in which they hold shares (e.g., to hold managers to account, to ensure Board's effective functioning). Such action would add a pressure group to those (the regulators and the Board) overseeing management.

However, there is the problem of how the institution should exercise this power. One way is for the institution to decide, the other is for the institution to poll its beneficiaries. Assuming that the institution polls, should it then: (i) Vote the entire holding as directed by the majority of votes cast? (ii) Split the vote (where this is allowed) according to the proportions of the vote? (iii) Or respect the abstainers and only vote the respondents' holdings?

The price signals generated by large active managers holding or not holding the stock may contribute to management change. For example, this is the case when a large active manager sells his position in a company, leading to (possibly) a decline in the stock price, but more importantly a loss of confidence by the markets in the management of the company, thus precipitating changes in the management team.

Some institutions have been more vocal and active in pursuing such matters; for instance, some firms believe that there are investment advantages to accumulating substantial minority shareholdings (i.e. 10% or more) and putting pressure on management to implement significant changes in the business. In some cases, institutions with minority holdings work together to force management change. Perhaps more frequent is the sustained pressure that large institutions bring to bear on management teams through persuasive discourse and PR. On the other hand, some of the largest investment managers—such as BlackRock and Vanguard—advocate simply owning every company, reducing the incentive to influence management teams. A reason for this last strategy is that the investment manager prefers a closer, more open and honest relationship with a company's management team than would exist if they exercised control; allowing them to make a better investment decision.

The national context in which shareholder representation considerations are set is variable and important. The USA is a litigious society and shareholders use the law as a lever to pressure management teams. In Japan it is traditional for shareholders to be low in the 'pecking order,' which often allows management and labor to ignore the rights of the ultimate owners. Whereas US firms generally cater to shareholders, Japanese businesses generally exhibit a *stakeholder* mentality, in which they seek consensus amongst all interested parties (against a background of strong unions and labour legislation).

## Size of the Global Fund Management Industry

Conventional assets under management of the global fund management industry increased by 10% in 2010, to $79.3 trillion. Pension assets accounted for $29.9 trillion of the total, with $24.7 trillion invested in mutual funds and $24.6 trillion in insurance funds. Together with alternative assets (sovereign wealth funds, hedge funds, private equity funds and exchange traded funds) and funds of wealthy individuals, assets of the global fund management industry totalled around $117 trillion. Growth in 2010 followed a 14% increase in the previous year and was due both to the recovery in equity markets during the year and an inflow of new funds.

The US remained by far the biggest source of funds, accounting for around a half of conventional assets under management or some $36 trillion. The UK was the second largest centre in the world and by far the largest in Europe with around 8% of the global total.

## Philosophy, Process and People

The 3-P's (Philosophy, Process and People) are often used to describe the reasons why the manager is able to produce above average results.

- Philosophy refers to the overarching beliefs of the investment organization. For example: (i) Does the manager buy growth or value shares, or a combination of the two (and why)? (ii) Do they believe in market timing (and on what evidence)? (iii) Do they rely on external research or do they employ a team of researchers? It is helpful if any and all of such fundamental beliefs are supported by proof-statements.
- Process refers to the way in which the overall philosophy is implemented. For example: (i) Which universe of assets is explored before particular assets are chosen as suitable investments? (ii) How does the manager decide what to buy and when? (iii) How does the manager decide what to sell and when? (iv) Who takes the decisions and are they taken by committee? (v) What controls are in place to ensure that a rogue fund (one very different from others and from what is intended) cannot arise?
- People refers to the staff, especially the fund managers. The questions are, Who are they? How are they selected? How old are they? Who reports to whom? How deep is the team (and do all the members understand the philosophy and process they are supposed to be using)? And most important of all, How long has the team been working together? This last question is vital because whatever performance record was presented at the outset of the relationship with the client may or may not relate to (have been produced by) a team that is still in place. If the team has changed greatly (high staff turnover or changes to the team), then arguably the performance record is completely unrelated to the existing team (of fund managers).

## Investment Managers and Portfolio Structures

At the heart of the investment management industry are the managers who invest and divest client investments.

A certified company investment advisor should conduct an assessment of each client's individual needs and risk profile. The advisor then recommends appropriate investments.

## Asset Allocation

The different asset class definitions are widely debated, but four common divisions are stocks, bonds, real estate and commodities. The exercise of allocating funds among these assets (and among individual securities within each asset class) is what investment management firms are paid for. Asset classes exhibit different market dynamics, and different interaction effects; thus, the allocation of money among asset classes will have a significant effect on the performance of the fund. Some research suggests that allocation among asset classes has more predictive power than the choice of individual holdings in determining portfolio return. Arguably, the skill of a successful investment manager resides in constructing the asset allocation, and separate individual holdings, so as to outperform certain benchmarks (e.g., the peer group of competing funds, bond and stock indices).

## Long-term Returns

It is important to look at the evidence on the long-term returns to different assets, and to holding period returns (the returns that accrue on average over different lengths of investment). For example, over very long holding periods (e.g. 10+ years) in most countries, equities have generated higher returns than bonds, and bonds have generated higher returns than cash. According to financial theory, this is because equities are riskier (more volatile) than bonds which are themselves more risky than cash.

## Diversification

Against the background of the asset allocation, fund managers consider the degree of diversification that makes sense for a given client (given its risk preferences) and construct a list of planned holdings accordingly. The list will indicate what percentage of the fund should be invested in each particular stock or bond. The theory of portfolio diversification was originated by Markowitz (and many others). Effective diversification requires management of the correlation between the asset returns and the liability returns, issues internal to the portfolio (individual holdings volatility), and cross-correlations between the returns.

## Investment styles

There are a range of different styles of fund management that the institution can implement. For example, growth, value, growth at a reasonable price (GARP), market neutral, small capitalisation, indexed, etc. Each of these approaches has its distinctive features, adherents and, in any particular financial environment, distinctive risk characteristics. For example, there is evidence that growth styles (buying rapidly growing earnings) are especially effective when the companies able to generate such growth are scarce; conversely, when such growth is plentiful, then there is evidence that value styles tend to outperform the indices particularly successfully.

Large asset managers are increasingly profiling their equity portfolio managers to trade their orders more effectively. While this strategy is less effective with small-cap trades, it has been effective for portfolios with large-cap companies.

## Performance Measurement

Fund performance is often thought to be the acid test of fund management, and in the institutional context, accurate measurement is a necessity. For that purpose, institutions measure the performance of each fund (and usually for internal purposes components of each fund) under their management, and performance is also measured by external firms that specialize in performance measurement. The leading performance measurement firms (e.g. Frank Russell in the US or BI-SAM in Europe) compile aggregate industry data, e.g., showing how funds in general performed against given indices and peer groups over various time periods.

In a typical case (let us say an equity fund), then the calculation would be made (as far as the client is concerned) every quarter and would show a percentage change compared with the prior quarter (e.g., +4.6% total return in US dollars). This figure would be compared with other similar funds managed within the institution (for purposes of monitoring internal controls), with performance data for peer group funds, and with relevant indices (where available) or tailor-made performance benchmarks where appropriate. The specialist performance measurement firms calculate quartile and decile data and close attention would be paid to the (percentile) ranking of any fund.

Generally speaking, it is probably appropriate for an investment firm to persuade its clients to assess performance over longer periods (e.g., 3 to 5 years) to smooth out very short-term fluctuations in performance and the influence of the business cycle. This can be difficult however and, industry wide, there is a serious preoccupation with short-term numbers and the effect on the relationship with clients (and resultant business risks for the institutions).

An enduring problem is whether to measure before-tax or after-tax performance. After-tax measurement represents the benefit to the investor, but investors' tax positions may vary. Before-tax measurement can be misleading, especially in regimens that tax realised capital gains (and not unrealised). It is thus possible that successful active managers (measured before tax) may produce miserable after-tax results. One possible solution is to report the after-tax position of some standard taxpayer.

## Risk-adjusted Performance Measurement

Performance measurement should not be reduced to the evaluation of fund returns alone, but must also integrate other fund elements that would be of interest to investors, such as the measure of risk taken. Several other aspects are also part of performance measurement: evaluating if managers have succeeded in reaching their objective, i.e. if their return was sufficiently high to reward the risks taken; how they compare to their peers; and finally whether the portfolio management results were due to luck or the manager's skill. The need to answer all these questions has led to the development of more sophisticated performance measures, many of which originate in modern portfolio theory. Modern portfolio theory established the quantitative link that exists between portfolio risk and return. The Capital Asset Pricing Model (CAPM) developed by Sharpe (1964) highlighted the notion of rewarding risk and produced the first performance indicators, be they risk-adjusted ratios (Sharpe ratio, information ratio) or differential returns compared to benchmarks (alphas). The Sharpe ratio is the simplest and best known performance measure. It measures the return of a portfolio in excess of the risk-free rate, compared to the total risk of the portfolio. This measure is said to be absolute, as it does not refer to any benchmark, avoiding drawbacks related to a poor choice of benchmark. Meanwhile, it does not allow the separation of the performance of the market in which the portfolio is invested from that of the manager. The information ratio is a more general form of the Sharpe ratio in which the risk-free asset is replaced by a benchmark portfolio. This measure is relative, as it evaluates portfolio performance in reference to a benchmark, making the result strongly dependent on this benchmark choice.

Portfolio alpha is obtained by measuring the difference between the return of the portfolio and that of a benchmark portfolio. This measure appears to be the only reliable performance measure to evaluate active management. In fact, we have to distinguish between normal returns, provided by the fair reward for portfolio exposure to different risks, and obtained through passive management, from abnormal performance (or outperformance) due to the manager's skill (or luck), whether through market timing, stock picking, or good fortune. The first component is related to allocation and style investment choices, which may not be under the sole control of the manager, and depends on the economic context, while the second component is an evaluation of the success of the manager's decisions. Only the latter, measured by alpha, allows the evaluation of the manager's true performance (but then, only if you assume that any outperformance is due to skill and not luck).

Portfolio return may be evaluated using factor models. The first model, proposed by Jensen (1968), relies on the CAPM and explains portfolio returns with the market index as the only factor. It quickly becomes clear, however, that one factor is not enough to explain the returns very well and that other factors have to be considered. Multi-factor models were developed as an alternative to the CAPM, allowing a better description of portfolio risks and a more accurate evaluation of a portfolio's performance. For example, Fama and French (1993) have highlighted two important factors that characterize a company's risk in addition to market risk. These factors are the book-to-market ratio and the company's size as measured by its market capitalization. Fama and French therefore proposed three-factor model to describe portfolio normal returns (Fama–French three-factor model). Carhart (1997) proposed to add momentum as a fourth factor to allow the short-term persistence of returns to be taken into account. Also of interest for performance measurement is Sharpe's (1992) style analysis model, in which factors are style indices. This model allows a custom benchmark for each portfolio to be developed, using the linear combination of style indices that best replicate portfolio style allocation, and leads to an accurate evaluation of portfolio alpha.

### Education or Certification

Increasingly, international business schools are incorporating the subject into their course outlines and some have formulated the title of 'Investment Management' or 'Asset Management' conferred as specialist bachelor's degrees (e.g. Cass Business School, London). Due to global cross-recognition agreements with the 2 major accrediting agencies AACSB and ACBSP which accredit over 560 of the best business school programs, the Certification of MFP Master Financial Planner Professional from the American Academy of Financial Management is available to AACSB and ACBSP business school graduates with finance or financial services-related concentrations. For people with aspirations to become an investment manager, further education may be needed beyond a bachelors in business, finance, or economics. Designations, such as the Chartered Investment Manager (CIM) in Canada, are required for practitioners in the investment management industry. A graduate degree or an investment qualification such as the Chartered Financial Analyst designation (CFA) may help in having a career in investment management.

There is no evidence that any particular qualification enhances the most desirable characteristic of an investment manager, that is the ability to select investments that result in an above average (risk weighted) long-term performance. The industry has a tradition of seeking out, employing and generously rewarding such people without reference to any formal qualifications.

## Assets Under Management

Assets under management (AUM), sometimes called funds under management (FUM), measures the total market value of all the financial assets which a financial institution such as a mutual fund, venture capital firm, or brokerage house manages on behalf of its clients and themselves.

### Overview

Assets under management (AUM) is very popular within the financial industry as a measure of size and success of an investment management firm, compared with its history of assets under management in previous periods, and compared with the firm's competitors. Methods of calculating AUM vary between firms. Investment management companies generally charge their clients fees as a proportion of assets under management, so assets under management, combined with the firm's average fee rate, are the key factors indicating an investment management company's top line revenue. The fee structure depends on the contract between each client and the firm or fund.

Assets under management rise and fall. They may increase when investment performance is positive, or when new customers and new assets are brought into the firm. Rising AUM normally increases the fees which the firm generates.

Conversely, AUM are reduced by negative investment performance, as well as redemptions or withdrawals, including fund closures, client defections and other generally adverse events. Lower AUM tend to result in lower fees generated.

### AUM Includes

Assets under management includes:

- Capital raised from investors;
- Capital belonging to the principals of the fund management firm.

For example, if fund managers contribute $2B of their own capital to the fund and raise additional $10B from investors, their AUM is $12B.

## Investment Strategy

An investment strategy is a set of rules, behaviors or procedures, designed to guide an investor's selection of an investment portfolio. Individuals have different profit objectives, and their individual skills make different tactics and strategies appropriate. Some choices involve a tradeoff between risk and return. Most investors fall somewhere in between, accepting some risk for the expectation of higher returns.

### Strategies

No strategy: Investors who don't have a strategy have been called Sheep. Arbitrary choices modeled on throwing darts at a page (referencing earlier decades when stock prices were listed daily in the newspapers) have been called Blind Folded Monkeys Throwing Darts. This famous test had debatable outcomes.

Active vs Passive: Passive strategies like buy and hold and passive indexing are often used to minimize transaction costs. Investors don't believe it is possible to time the market. Active strategies such as momentum trading are an attempt to outperform benchmark indexes. Investors believe they have the better than average skills.

Momentum Trading: One strategy is to select investments based on their recent past performance. There is evidence both for and against this strategy.

Buy and Hold: This strategy involves buying company shares or funds and hold them for a long period. It is a long term investment strategy, based on the concept that in the long run equity markets give a good rate of return despite periods of volatility or decline. This viewpoint also holds that market timing, that one can enter the market on the lows and sell on the highs, does not work or does not work for small investors, so it is better to simply buy and hold.

Long Short Strategy: A long short strategy consists of selecting a universe of equities and ranking them according to a combined alpha factor. Given the rankings we long the top percentile and short the bottom percentile of securities once every re-balancing period.

Indexing: Indexing is where an investor buys a small proportion of all the shares in a market index such as the S&P 500, or more likely, an index mutual fund or an exchange-traded fund (ETF). This can be either a passive strategy if held for long periods, or an active strategy if the index is used to enter and exit the market quickly.

Pairs Trading: Pairs trade is a trading strategy that consists of identifying similar pairs of stocks and taking a linear combination of their price so that the result is a stationary time-series. We can then compute z-scores for the stationary signal and trade on the spread assuming mean reversion: short the top asset and long the bottom asset.

Value vs Growth: Value investing strategy looks at the intrinsic value of a company and value investors seek stocks of companies that they believed are undervalued. Growth investment strategy looks at the growth potential of a company and when a company that has expected earning growth that is higher than companies in the same industry or the market as a whole, it will attract the growth investors who are seeking to maximize their capital gain.

Dividend growth investing: This strategy involves investing in company shares according to the future dividends forecast to be paid. Companies that pay consistent and predictable dividends tend to have less volatile share prices. Well-established dividend-paying companies will aim to increase their dividend payment each year, and those who make an increase for 25 consecutive years are referred to as a dividend aristocrat. Investors who reinvest the dividends are able to benefit from compounding of their investment over the longer term, whether directly invested or through a Dividend Reinvestment Plan (DRIP).

Dollar cost averaging: The dollar cost averaging strategy is aimed at reducing the risk of incurring substantial losses resulted when the entire principal sum is invested just before the market falls.

Contrarian investment: A contrarian investment strategy consists of selecting good companies in time of down market and buying a lot of shares of that company in order to make a long-term profit. In time of economic decline, there are many opportunities to buy good shares at reasonable prices. But, what makes a company good for shareholders? A good company is one that focuses on the long term value, the quality of what it offers or the share price. This company must have a durable competitive advantage, which means that it has a market position or branding which either prevents easy access by competitors or controls a scarce raw material source. Some examples of companies that response to these criteria are in the field of insurance, soft drinks, shoes, chocolates, home building, furniture and many more. We can see that there is nothing "fancy" or special about these fields of investment: they are commonly used by each and every one of us. Many variables must be taken into consideration when making the final decision for the choice of the company. Some of them are:

- The company must be in a growing industry.
- The company cannot be vulnerable to competition.
- The company must have its earnings on an upward trend.
- The company must have a consistent returns on invested capital.
- The company must be flexible to adjust prices for inflation.

Smaller companies: Historically medium sized companies have outperformed large cap companies on the Stock market. Smaller companies again have had even higher returns. The very best returns by market cap size historically are from micro-cap companies. Investors using this strategy buy companies based on their small market cap size on the stock exchange. One of the greatest investors Warren Buffet made money in small companies early in his career combining it with value investing. He bought small companies with low P/E ratios and high assets to market cap.

## Asset Allocation

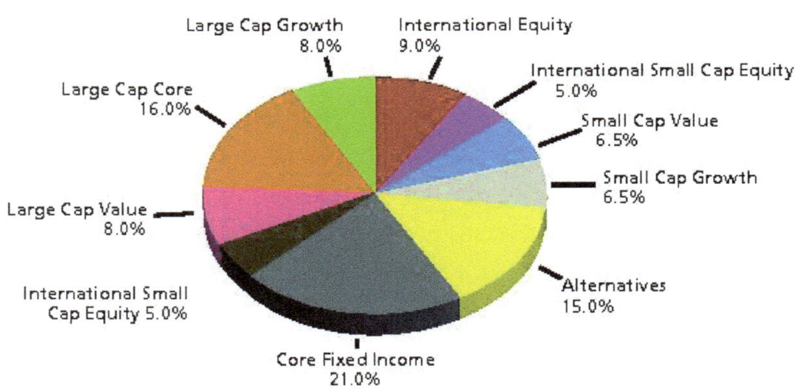


Investment portfolio with a diverse asset allocation

Asset allocation is the rigorous implementation of an investment strategy that attempts to balance risk versus reward by adjusting the percentage of each asset in an investment portfolio according to the investor's risk tolerance, goals and investment time frame.

## Description

Many financial experts argue that asset allocation is an important factor in determining returns for an investment portfolio. Asset allocation is based on the principle that different assets perform differently in different market and economic conditions.

A fundamental justification for asset allocation is the notion that different asset classes offer returns that are not perfectly correlated, hence diversification reduces the overall risk in terms of the variability of returns for a given level of expected return. Asset diversification has been described as "the only free lunch you will find in the investment game". Academic research has painstakingly explained the importance of asset allocation and the problems of active management.

Although risk is reduced as long as correlations are not perfect, it is typically forecast (wholly or in part) based on statistical relationships (like correlation and variance) that existed over some past period. Expectations for return are often derived in the same way.

When such backward-looking approaches are used to forecast future returns or risks using the traditional mean-variance optimization approach to asset allocation of modern portfolio theory (MPT), the strategy is, in fact, predicting future risks and returns based on history. As there is no guarantee that past relationships will continue in the future, this is one of the "weak links" in traditional asset allocation strategies as derived from MPT. Other, more subtle weaknesses include the "butterfly effect", by which seemingly minor errors in forecasting lead to recommended allocations that are grossly skewed from investment mandates and/or impractical—often even violating an investment manager's "common sense" understanding of a tenable portfolio-allocation strategy.

## Asset Classes

An asset class is a group of economic resources sharing similar characteristics, such as riskiness and return. There are many types of assets that may or may not be included in an asset allocation strategy.

## Traditional Assets

The "traditional" asset classes are *stocks*, *bonds*, and *cash*:

- Stocks: value, dividend, growth, or sector-specific (or a "blend" of any two or more of the preceding); large-cap versus mid-cap, small-cap or micro-cap; domestic, foreign (developed), emerging or frontier markets

- Bonds (fixed income securities more generally): investment-grade or junk (high-yield); government or corporate; short-term, intermediate, long-term; domestic, foreign, emerging markets
- Cash and cash equivalents (e.g., deposit account, money market fund)

Allocation among these three provides a starting point. Usually included are hybrid instruments such as convertible bonds and preferred stocks, counting as a mixture of bonds and stocks.

## Alternative Assets

Other alternative assets that may be considered include:

- Commodities: precious metals, nonferrous metals, agriculture, energy, others.
- Commercial or residential real estate (also REITs)
- Collectibles such as art, coins, or stamps
- Insurance products (annuity, life settlements, catastrophe bonds, personal life insurance products, etc.)
- Derivatives such as long-short or market neutral strategies, options, collateralized debt, and futures
- Foreign currency
- Venture capital
- Private equity
- Distressed securities

## Allocation Strategy

There are several types of asset allocation strategies based on investment goals, risk tolerance, time frames and diversification. The most common forms of asset allocation are: strategic, dynamic, tactical, and core-satellite.

## Strategic Asset Allocation

The primary goal of a strategic asset allocation is to create an asset mix that seeks to provide the optimal balance between expected risk and return for a long-term investment horizon. Generally speaking, strategic asset allocation strategies are agnostic to economic environments, i.e., they do not change their allocation postures relative to changing market or economic conditions.

## Dynamic Asset Allocation

Dynamic asset allocation is similar to strategic asset allocation in that portfolios are built by allocating to an asset mix that seeks to provide the optimal balance between expected risk and return for a long-term investment horizon. Like strategic allocation strategies, dynamic strategies largely retain exposure to their original asset classes; however, unlike strategic strategies, dynamic asset allocation portfolios will adjust their postures over time relative to changes in the economic environment.

## Tactical Asset Allocation

Tactical asset allocation is a strategy in which an investor takes a more active approach that tries to position a portfolio into those assets, sectors, or individual stocks that show the most potential for perceived gains. While an original asset mix is formulated much like strategic and dynamic portfolio, tactical strategies are often traded more actively and are free to move entirely in and out of their core asset classes.

## Core-satellite Asset Allocation

Core-Satellite allocation strategies generally contain a 'core' strategic element making up the most significant portion of the portfolio, while applying a dynamic or tactical 'satellite' strategy that makes up a smaller part of the portfolio. In this way, core-satellite allocation strategies are a hybrid of the strategic and dynamic/tactical allocation strategies mentioned above.

## Asset Allocation Fund

A fund that holds more than one asset class is called an asset allocation fund. This includes many types such as "balanced fund" and so on.

## Academic Studies

In 1986, Gary P. Brinson, L. Randolph Hood, and SEI's Gilbert L. Beebower (BHB) published a study about asset allocation of 91 large pension funds measured from 1974 to 1983. They replaced the pension funds' stock, bond, and cash selections with corresponding market indexes. The indexed quarterly return were found to be higher than pension plan's actual quarterly return. The two quarterly return series' linear correlation was measured at 96.7%, with shared variance of 93.6%. A 1991 follow-up study by Brinson, Singer, and Beebower measured a variance of 91.5%. The conclusion of the study was that replacing active choices with simple asset classes worked just as well as, if not even better than, professional pension managers. Also, a small number of asset classes was sufficient for financial planning. Financial advisors often pointed to this study to support the idea that asset allocation is more important than all other concerns, which the BHB study lumped together as "market timing". One problem with the

Brinson study was that the cost factor in the two return series was not clearly discussed. However, in response to a letter to the editor, Hood noted that the returns series were gross of management fees.

In 1997, William Jahnke initiated debate on this topic, attacking the BHB study in a paper titled *The Asset Allocation Hoax*. The Jahnke discussion appeared in the *Journal of Financial Planning* as an opinion piece, not a peer reviewed article. Jahnke's main criticism, still undisputed, was that BHB's use of quarterly data dampens the impact of compounding slight portfolio disparities over time, relative to the benchmark. One could compound 2% and 2.15% quarterly over 20 years and see the sizable difference in cumulative return. However, the difference is still 15 basis points (hundredths of a percent) per quarter; the difference is one of perception, not fact.

In 2000, Ibbotson and Kaplan used five asset classes in their study *Does Asset Allocation Policy Explain 40, 90, or 100 Percent of Performance?* The asset classes included were large-cap US stock, small-cap US stock, non-US stock, US bonds, and cash. Ibbotson and Kaplan examined the 10-year return of 94 US balanced mutual funds versus the corresponding indexed returns. This time, after properly adjusting for the cost of running index funds, the actual returns again failed to beat index returns. The linear correlation between monthly index return series and the actual monthly actual return series was measured at 90.2%, with shared variance of 81.4%. Ibbotson concluded 1) that asset allocation explained 40% of the variation of returns across funds, and 2) that it explained virtually 100% of the level of fund returns. Gary Brinson has expressed his general agreement with the Ibbotson-Kaplan conclusions.

In both studies, it is misleading to make statements such as "asset allocation explains 93.6% of investment return". Even "asset allocation explains 93.6% of quarterly performance variance" leaves much to be desired, because the shared variance could be from pension funds' operating structure. Hood, however, rejects this interpretation on the grounds that pension plans in particular cannot cross-share risks and that they are explicitly singular entities, rendering shared variance irrelevant. The statistics were most helpful when used to demonstrate the similarity of the index return series and the actual return series.

A 2000 paper by Meir Statman found that using the same parameters that explained BHB's 93.6% variance result, a hypothetical financial advisor with perfect foresight in *tactical* asset allocation performed 8.1% better per year, yet the strategic asset allocation still explained 89.4% of the variance. Thus, explaining variance does not explain performance. Statman says that strategic asset allocation is movement *along* the efficient frontier, whereas tactical asset allocation involves movement *of* the efficient frontier. A more common sense explanation of the Brinson, Hood, and Beebower study is that asset allocation explains more than 90% of the volatility of returns of an overall portfolio, but will not explain the ending results of your portfolio over long periods of time. Hood notes in his review of the material over 20 years, however, that explaining performance over time is possible with the BHB approach but was not the focus of the original paper.

Bekkers, Doeswijk and Lam (2009) investigate the diversification benefits for a portfolio by distinguishing ten different investment categories simultaneously in a mean-variance analysis as well as a market portfolio approach. The results suggest that real estate, commodities, and high yield add most value to the traditional asset mix of stocks, bonds, and cash. A study with such a broad coverage of asset classes has not been conducted before, not in the context of determining capital market expectations and performing a mean-variance analysis, neither in assessing the global market portfolio.

Doeswijk, Lam and Swinkels (2012) (2014) argue that the portfolio of the average investor contains important information for strategic asset allocation purposes. This portfolio shows the relative value of all assets according to the market crowd, which one could interpret as a benchmark or the optimal portfolio for the average investor. The authors determine the market values of equities, private equity, real estate, high yield bonds, emerging debt, non-government bonds, government bonds, inflation linked bonds, commodities, and hedge funds. For this range of assets, they estimate the invested global market portfolio for the period 1990-2012. For the main asset categories equities, real estate, non-government bonds and government bonds they extend the period to 1959-2012.

Doeswijk, Lam and Swinkels (2017) show that the market portfolio realizes a compounded real return of 4.38% with a standard deviation of 11.6% from 1960 until 2015. In the inflationary period from 1960 to 1979, the compounded real return of the GMP is 2.27%, while this is 5.57% in the disinflationary period from 1980 to 2015. The reward for the average investor is a compounded return of 3.24%-points above the saver's.

## Performance Indicators

McGuigan described an examination of funds that were in the top quartile of performance during 1983 to 1993. During the second measurement period of 1993 to 2003, only 28.57% of the funds remained in the top quartile. 33.33% of the funds dropped to the second quartile. The rest of the funds dropped to the third or fourth quartile.

In fact, low cost was a more reliable indicator of performance. Bogle noted that an examination of five-year performance data of large-cap blend funds revealed that the lowest cost quartile funds had the best performance, and the highest cost quartile funds had the worst performance.

## Return Versus Risk Trade-off

In asset allocation planning, the decision on the amount of stocks versus bonds in one's portfolio is a very important decision. Simply buying stocks without regard of a possible bear market can result in panic selling later. One's true risk tolerance can be hard to gauge until having experienced a real bear market with money invested in the market. Finding the proper balance is key.

| Cumulative return after inflation from 2000-to-2002 bear market | |
|---|---|
| 80% stock / 20% bond | −34.35% |
| 70% stock / 30% bond | −25.81% |
| 60% stock / 40% bond | −19.99% |
| 50% stock / 50% bond | −13.87% |
| 40% stock / 60% bond | −7.46% |
| 30% stock / 70% bond | −0.74% |
| 20% stock / 80% bond | +6.29% |

| Projected 10-year Cumulative return after inflation (stock return 8% yearly, bond return 4.5% yearly, inflation 3% yearly | |
|---|---|
| 80% stock / 20% bond | 52% |
| 70% stock / 30% bond | 47% |
| 60% stock / 40% bond | 42% |
| 50% stock / 50% bond | 38% |
| 40% stock / 60% bond | 33% |
| 30% stock / 70% bond | 29% |
| 20% stock / 80% bond | 24% |

The tables show why asset allocation is important. It determines an investor's future return, as well as the bear market burden that he or she will have to carry successfully to realize the returns.

## Problems with Asset Allocation

There are various reasons why asset allocation fails to work.

- Investors do not use asset allocation.
- Investors agree to asset allocation, but after some good returns they decide that they really wanted more risk.
- Investors agree to asset allocation, but after some bad returns they decide that they really wanted less risk.
- Investors' risk tolerance is not knowable ahead of time.
- Security selection within asset classes will not necessarily produce a risk profile equal to the asset class.
- The long-run behavior of asset classes does not guarantee their shorter-term behavior.

## Cyclical Tactical Asset Allocation

Stock price and bond yield movements are connected to changes in the economic environment. The cyclical approach to Tactical asset allocation involves monitoring the economic environment for patterns that have historically led to trends in stock market movements. Guidelines to these patterns can be followed to ascertain changes in market direction to a varying level of accuracy. This is very helpful to an investment decision because an exact reversal point is practically impossible to determine. Investors can use this information to improve their performance by modifying their strategic asset allocations.

In this way, an investor with an asset mix of stocks and bonds could use the cyclical approach to tactical asset allocation to rebalance their the amount of money invested in each in a favorable manner based on the economic cycle. For example, the investor could increase the allocation in bonds and decrease the allocation in equities when it is expected that the economy is heading into a recession. Historically, bonds have outperformed stocks in recessionary periods.

## Dynamic Asset Allocation

Dynamic asset allocation is a strategy used by investment products such as hedge funds, mutual funds, credit derivatives, index funds, principal protected notes (also known as guaranteed linked notes) and other structured investment products to achieve exposure to various investment opportunities and provide 100% principal protection.

Dynamic asset allocation includes CPPI, which consists of a guarantee, notionally related to a zero-coupon bond and an underlying investment. Assets are dynamically shifted (or allocated) between these two components depending largely on the performance of the underlying investments.

In some cases, certain products can use a borrowing facility to enhance exposure if the underlying investments experience strong returns. If the underlying investments decline in value, CPPI automatically deleverages, reducing exposure in falling markets.

The term 'Dynamic Asset Allocation' (DAA) can also refer to an investment strategy that seeks to produce high total returns irrespective of the performance of market indices using the tools of Tactical asset allocation/Global tactical asset allocation (TAA/GTAA) around a strategic benchmark. Indeed, many investment firms and commentators use the terms TAA, DAA, and GTAA interchangeably.

In the arena of institutional asset management DAA mandates tend to have absolute return targets that are not related to market index returns (e.g. USD LIBOR + 500bps), while TAA mandates will tend to have performance targets that reference market indices (e.g. 50% S&P 500/ 50% Barclays Capital Aggregate Bond Index + 200bps).

## Global Tactical Asset Allocation

Global Tactical Asset Allocation, or GTAA, is a top-down investment strategy that attempts to exploit short-term mis-pricings among a global set of assets. The strategy focuses on general movements in the market rather than on performance of individual securities.

## Hedge Funds and Asset Allocation

GTAA is believed to be derived from, and share some characteristics of, global macro hedge funds and tactical asset allocation (TAA). Global macro hedge funds, like GTAA, seek to profit from taking positions in major world equity, bond or currency markets. However, the two differ in the fact that global macro has been characterized by large, undiversified bets, while modern GTAA strategies are generally well-diversified and operate with risk controls. TAA decisions undertaken by managers of multi-asset funds, like GTAA decisions, are intended to enhance investment outcomes by overweighting and underweighting asset classes based on their expected performance over relatively short time periods (usually 3 to 6 months). While TAA, within multi-asset funds, is restricted to the asset classes contained in the fund's strategic asset allocation, GTAA strategies enjoys the privilege of accessing a broader opportunity set.

## Strategies

The modern global tactical asset allocation program is composed of two separate strategies: strategic rebalancing and overlay. The strategic rebalancing element of GTAA program is designed to remove any unintentional asset allocation risk which can be caused by various factors, including: drift risk, which occurs when the value of underlying portfolio holdings moves away from the strategic benchmark due to differences in asset class returns, due to changes in asset valuation, cash holdings, currency deviations from stock selection, unintentional country deviations within underlying stock/ bond portfolios, manager of benchmark transitions, and contributions to and redemptions from the portfolio. The overlay element of GTAA program is designed to capture excess return through intentional, opportunistic, long and short positions in asset classes and countries. The GTAA strategy can be viewed as making two major types of decisions: The first type is asset class timing, including stocks vs. bonds vs. cash, small-cap vs. large-cap stocks, value vs. growth stocks, emerging vs. developed stocks and bonds, etc. This kind of decision making is often referred to as TAA. The second type of decision is known as country or sector decisions within asset classes, including country selection in developed and emerging equity, as well as fixed income and currency markets. These are the global relative-value decisions which give meaning to the "G" in GTAA and distinguish the strategy from traditional market timing.

## Portfolios

It is widely known that many institutional investment portfolios remain dominated by equity and interest rate risk, and that these allocations tend to remain motionless regardless of market conditions. Therefore, there is reason to establish a portfolio of alternative alpha sources, and GTAA represents just that, for myriad reasons: the performance differentials between asset classes are frequently substantial, the derivative instruments used in GTAA are, for the most part, highly liquid and transaction costs are low. The volume of assets managed with a focus on relative performance of asset classes is low compared to that focused on finding opportunities within asset classes, and a number of managers with very impressive teams, processes and track records can be identified. Furthermore, the analysis and decision making involved in GTAA is focused on cross-market comparisons which proves to differ from the comparison of securities within given markets. Accordingly, GTAA should be a good diversifier, particularly within an alpha portfolio.

GTAA strategies provide investors with a series of exposures that may not otherwise be prevalent in their portfolios. Managing these exposures provides an opportunity for the generation of returns that share low correlations with other sources of active return, and they can also be expected to lead to more reliable added value.

## Tactical Asset Allocation

Tactical asset allocation (TAA) is a dynamic investment strategy that actively adjusts a portfolio's asset allocation. The goal of a TAA strategy is to improve the risk-adjusted returns of passive management investing.

## Strategy Descriptions

TAA strategies can be either discretionary or systematic.

## Discretionary

In discretionary tactical asset allocation strategies, an investor modifies his asset allocation according to the valuation of the markets in which they are invested. Thus, someone who invested heavily in stocks might reduce their position when they perceive that other securities, such as bonds, are poised to outperform stocks. Unlike stock picking, in which the investor predicts which individual stocks will perform well, tactical asset allocation involves only judgments of the future return of complete markets or sectors. As such, some practitioners perceive it as a natural supplement to mutual fund investing, including passive management investing.

## Systematic

Systematic tactical asset allocation strategies use a quantitative investment model to systematically exploit inefficiencies or temporary imbalances in equilibrium values among different asset classes. They are often based on known financial market anomalies (inefficiencies) that are supported by academic and practitioner research. For example, many systematic TAA strategies use quantitative Trend Following or Relative Strength techniques to produce excess returns. These both aim to capitalize on momentum, a well-known market anomaly.

## Considerations

The efficient-market hypothesis would imply that tactical asset allocation cannot increase risk-adjusted returns, since markets are already efficiently priced. If a tactical approach were found that could increase returns without an increase in risk, investors would flock to that inefficiency, and the advantage would go away. Many investors do not accept this hypothesis, however, and believe that inefficiencies in the market persist and can be exploited.

Many factors determine the success of a TAA strategy. The investor needs to have the necessary knowledge, practical investment skills, dedication, and discipline to design and/or execute a successful tactical strategy. The specific market anomalies on which the strategy is based may change or disappear in the future. Other factors such as risk tolerance, market timing, portfolio size, investment expenses, etc. may also affect the portfolio performance.

## Criticism

Investors who utilize the tactical asset allocation strategy generally want to hedge risk in a volatile market. However, Larry Swedroe of CBS MoneyWatch described the strategy as an attempt to time the market, and provides an excuse for managers to increase revenue from trading fees due to the frequent activity the strategy requires. In a study conducted by Morningstar, Inc., they examined the "net annualized return, standard deviation, Sharpe ratio, and maximum drawdown from July 31, 2010, to December 31, 2011," of 163 tactical funds. They concluded that only a small percentage of firms outperformed the Vanguard Balanced Index, the exceptions being PIMCO and GMO (Grantham, Mayo, Van Otterloo) Global Asset Allocation. Updated to June 2013, they found that 20 percent of funds beat the Vanguard Balanced Index Fund, and just four had a better Sharpe ratio.

## Socially Responsible Investing

Socially responsible investing (SRI), or social investment, also known as sustainable, socially conscious, "green" or ethical investing, is any investment strategy which seeks to consider both financial return and social good to bring about a social change.

Recently, it has also become known as "sustainable investing" or "responsible investing". There is also a subset of SRI known as "impact investing", devoted to the conscious creation of social impact through investment.

Alternative Energy: One of many forms of sustainable investing

In general, socially responsible investors encourage corporate practices that promote environmental stewardship, consumer protection, human rights, and diversity. Some avoid businesses involved in alcohol, tobacco, fast food, gambling, pornography, weapons, contraception/abortifacients/abortion, fossil fuel production or the military. The areas of concern recognized by the SRI practitioners are sometimes summarized under the heading of ESG issues: environment, social justice, and corporate governance.

"Socially responsible investing" is one of several related concepts and approaches that influence and, in some cases govern, how asset managers invest portfolios. The term "socially responsible investing" sometimes narrowly refers to practices that seek to avoid harm by screening companies included in an investment portfolio. However, the term is also used more broadly to include more proactive practices such as impact investing, shareholder advocacy and community investing. According to investor Amy Domini, shareholder advocacy and community investing are pillars of socially responsible investing, while doing only negative screening is inadequate.

## History

The origins of socially responsible investing may date back to the Religious Society of Friends (Quakers). In 1758, the Quaker Philadelphia Yearly Meeting prohibited members from participating in the slave trade – buying or selling humans.

One of the most articulate early adopters of SRI was John Wesley (1703–1791), one of the founders of Methodism. Wesley's sermon "The Use of Money" outlined his basic tenets of social investing – i.e. not to harm your neighbor through your business practices and to avoid industries like tanning and chemical production, which can harm the health of workers. Some of the best-known applications of socially responsible investing were religiously motivated. Investors would avoid "sinful" companies, such as those associated with products such as guns, liquor, and tobacco.

The modern era of socially responsible investing evolved during the political climate of the 1960s. During this time, socially concerned investors increasingly sought to address equality for women, civil rights, and labor issues. Economic development projects started or managed by Dr. Martin Luther King, like the Montgomery Bus Boycott and the Operation Breadbasket Project in Chicago, established the beginning model for socially responsible investing efforts. King combined ongoing dialog with boycotts and direct action targeting specific corporations. Concerns about the Vietnam War were incorporated by some social investors. Many people living during the era remember a picture in June 1972 of a naked nine-year-old girl, Phan Thị Kim Phúc, running towards a photographer screaming, her back burning from the napalm dropped on her village. That photograph channeled outrage against Dow Chemical, the manufacturer of napalm, and prompted protests across the country against Dow Chemical and other companies profiting from the Vietnam War.

During the 1950s and 1960s, trade unions deployed multi-employer pension fund monies for targeted investments. For example, the United Mine Workers fund invested in medical facilities, and the International Ladies' Garment Workers' Union (ILGWU) and International Brotherhood of Electrical Workers (IBEW) financed union-built housing projects. Labor unions also sought to leverage pension stocks for shareholder activism on proxy fights and shareholder resolutions. In 1978, SRI efforts by pension funds was spurred by *The North will Rise Again: Pensions, Politics, and Power in the 1980s* and the subsequent organizing efforts of authors Jeremy Rifkin and Randy Barber. By 1980, presidential candidates Jimmy Carter, Ronald Reagan and Jerry Brown advocated some type of social orientation for pension investments.

SRI had an important role in ending the apartheid government in South Africa. International opposition to apartheid strengthened after the 1960 Sharpeville massacre. In 1971, Reverend Leon Sullivan (at the time a board member for General Motors) drafted a code of conduct for practicing business in South Africa which became known as the Sullivan Principles. However, reports documenting the application of the Sullivan Principles said that US companies were not trying to lessen discrimination in South Africa. Due to these reports and mounting political pressure, cities, states, colleges, faith-based groups and pension funds throughout the US began divesting from companies operating in South Africa. In 1976, the United Nations imposed a mandatory arms embargo against South Africa. From the 1970s to the early 1990s, large institutions avoided investment in South Africa under apartheid. The subsequent negative flow of investment eventually forced a group of businesses, representing 75% of South African employers, to draft a charter calling for an end to apartheid. While the SRI efforts alone did not bring an end to apartheid, it did focus persuasive international pressure on the South African business community.

The mid and late 1990s saw the rise of SRI's focus on a diverse range of other issues, including tobacco stocks, mutual fund proxy disclosure, and other diverse focuses.

Since the late 1990s, SRI has become increasingly defined as a means to promote environmentally sustainable development. Many investors consider effects of global climate change a significant business and investment risk. CERES was founded in 1989 by Joan Bavaria and Dennis Hayes, coordinator of the first Earth Day, as a network for investors, environmental organizations, and other public interest groups interested in working with companies to address environmental concerns.

Since 1989, representatives from the SRI industry have gathered at the annual SRI in the Rockies Conference to exchange ideas and gain momentum for new initiatives. This conference is produced by First Affirmative Financial Network, an investment advisory firm that specializes in sustainable and responsible investing. The conference has attracted over 550 persons annually since 2006.

The first sell-side brokerage in the world to offer SRI research was the Brazilian bank Unibanco. The service was launched in January 2001 by Unibanco SRI analyst Christopher Wells from the São Paulo headquarters of the bank. It was targeted at SRI funds in Europe and the US, although it was sent to non-SRI funds both in and out of Brazil. The research was about environmental and social issues (but not governance issues) regarding companies listed in Brazil. It was sent for free to Unibanco's clients. The service lasted until mid-2002.

Two good things came out this research:

1. The idea was picked up by Mike Tyrrell, who worked at Jupiter, an SRI fund manager in London, and who developed it into something much bigger and better at HSBC and then Citigroup.

2. ABN AMRO's operation in Brazil used this research to create the first SRI fund in an emerging market, launched in November 2001. As of late 2008, this fund, called Fundo Ethical, was the Brazilian operation's biggest and best performing stock fund of any kind. (ABN AMRO's operation in Brazil was bought by Santander in 2007.)

Drawing on the industry's experience using divestment as a tool against apartheid, the Sudan Divestment Task Force was established in 2006 in response to the genocide occurring in the Darfur region of the Sudan. Support from the US government followed with the Sudan Accountability and Divestment Act of 2007.

More recently, some social investors have sought to address the rights of indigenous peoples around the world who are affected by the business practices of various companies. The 2007, SRI in the Rockies Conference held a special pre-conference specifically to address the concerns of indigenous peoples. Healthy working conditions, fair wages, product safety, and equal opportunity employment also remain headline concerns for many social investors. In the mid-2010s, some funds developed gender lens investing strategies to promote workplace equity and general welfare of women and girls.

## Current Strategies

Socially responsible investing is a growing market in both the US and Europe. In particular, it has become an important principle guiding the investment strategies of various funds and accounts.

## Government-controlled Funds

Government-controlled funds such as pension funds are often very large players in the investment field, and are being pressured by the citizenry and by activist groups to adopt investment policies which encourage ethical corporate behavior, respect the rights of workers, consider environmental concerns, and avoid violations of human rights. One outstanding endorsement of such policies is The Government Pension Fund of Norway, which is mandated to avoid "investments which constitute an unacceptable risk that the Fund may contribute to unethical acts or omissions, such as violations of fundamental humanitarian principles, serious violations of human rights, gross corruption or severe environmental damages."

Many pension funds are currently under pressure to disinvest from the arms company BAE Systems, partially due to a campaign run by the Campaign Against Arms Trade (CAAT). Liverpool City Council has passed a successful resolution to disinvest from the company, but a similar attempt by the Scottish Green Party in Edinburgh City Council was blocked by the Liberal Democrats.

## Mutual Funds and ETFs

Socially responsible mutual funds counted by the 2014 Trends Report increased in number to 415 in 2014, up from 333 in 2012, 250 in 2010, 173 in 2005 & 2007, 189 in 2003, and 167 in 2001. The overall number of mutual funds incorporating environmental, social and corporate governance (ESG) has increased four-fold increase since 2012. Additionally, 20 exchange-traded funds (ETFs) that incorporate ESG criteria were identified with $3.5 billion in assets at the end of 2011, an increase from the 8 ETFs with $2.25 billion in net assets identified in its 2007 report—the first Trends report to track ETFs . Unlike the Employee Retirement Income Security Act of 1974 (ERISA), which severely limits the extent to which socially responsible goals can be considered in managing corporate and Taft-Hartley pension assets (due to ERISA's overriding goal of protecting employees' pensions), registered investment companies can take these factors into account so long as the disclosure and other requirements of the Investment Company Act of 1940 are met. US SIF maintains charts describing the socially responsible mutual funds offered by its member firms.

## Separately Managed Accounts

According to the 2014 Report on US Sustainable, Responsible and Impact Investing

Trends, among separate account managers, 214 distinctive separate account vehicles or strategies, with $433 billion in assets, incorporated ESG factors into investment analysis. Where a separate account is subject to ERISA, there are legal limitations on the extent to which investment decisions can be based on factors other than maximizing plan participants' economic returns.

## Shareholder Advocacy

Shareholder resolutions are filed by a wide variety of institutional investors, including public pension funds, faith-based investors, socially responsible mutual funds, and labor unions. In 2004, faith-based organizations filed 129 resolutions, while socially responsible funds filed 56 resolutions.

Regulations governing shareholder resolutions vary from country to country. In the United States, they are determined primarily by the Securities and Exchange Commission, which regulates mutual funds and applies the 1940 Act and by the Department of Labor, which regulates certain plans and applies ERISA.

These regulatory regimes require pension plans and mutual funds to disclose how they voted on behalf of their investors. U.S. shareholders have organized various groups to facilitate jointly filing resolutions. These include the Council of Institutional Investors, the Interfaith Center on Corporate Responsibility, and the US SIF.

From 2012 to 2014, more than 200 US institutions and investment management firms filed or co-filed proposals. These institutions and money managers collectively controlled $1.72 trillion in assets at the end of 2013. The top categories of environmental and social issues from 2012 to 2014 were political contributions and climate change and environmental issues.

## Community Investing

Community investing, a subset of socially responsible investing, allows for investment directly into community-based organizations. Community investing institutions use investor capital to finance or guarantee loans to individuals and organizations that have historically been denied access to capital by traditional financial institutions. These loans are used for housing, small business creation, and education or personal development in the US, or are made available to local financial institutions abroad to finance international community development. The community investing institution typically provides training and other types of support and expertise to ensure the success of the loan and its returns for investors.

Community investing grew almost 5% from 2012 to 2014. Assets held and invested locally by community development financial institutions (CDFIs) based in the US totaled $64.3 billion at the start of 2014, up from $61.4 billion in 2012.

## Investing Strategies

## Investing in Capital Markets

Social investors use several strategies to maximize financial return and attempt to maximize social good. These strategies seek to create change by shifting the cost of capital down for sustainable firm and up for the non-sustainable ones. The proponents argue that access to capital is what drives the future direction of development.

## Negative Screening

Negative screening excludes certain securities from investment consideration based on social or environmental criteria. For example, many socially responsible investors screen out tobacco company investments.

The longest-running SRI index, the Domini 400—now the MSCI KLD 400—was started in May 1990. It has continued to perform competitively —with average annualized total returns of 9.51% through December 2009 compared with 8.66% for the S&P 500.

Despite this impressive growth, it has long been commonly perceived that SRI brings smaller returns than unrestricted investing. So-called "sin stocks", including purveyors of tobacco, alcohol, gambling and defense contractors, were banned from portfolios on moral or ethical grounds. And shutting out entire industries hurts performance, the critics said. However, in a comprehensive study, financial economists Lobe, Roithmeier, and Walkshäusl taking the position of the *advocatus diaboli*, answer the question whether to invest in a socially responsible way – or not? They create a set of global and domestic sin indexes consisting of 755 publicly traded socially irresponsible stocks around the world belonging to the Sextet of Sin: adult entertainment, alcohol, gambling, nuclear power, tobacco, and weapons. They compare their stock market performance directly with a set of virtue comparables consisting of the most important international socially responsible investment indexes. They find no compelling evidence that ethical and unethical screens lead to a significant difference in their financial performance, which is in contrast with the results of prior studies on sinful investing.

## Divestment

Divesting is the act of removing stocks from a portfolio based on mainly ethical, non-financial objections to certain business activities of a corporation. Recently, CalSTRS (California State Teachers' Retirement System) announced the removal of more than $237 million in tobacco holdings from its investment portfolio after 6 months of financial analysis and deliberations.

## Shareholder Activism

Shareholder activism efforts attempt to positively influence corporate behavior. These efforts include initiating conversations with corporate management on issues of concern, and submitting and voting proxy resolutions. These activities are undertaken with the belief that social investors, working cooperatively, can steer management on a course that will improve financial performance over time and enhance the well being of the stockholders, customers, employees, vendors, and communities. Recent movements have also been reported of "investor relations activism", in which investor relations firms assist groups of shareholder activists in an organized push for change within a corporation; this is done typically by leveraging their enhanced knowledge of the corporation, its management (often via direct relationships), and the securities laws as a whole. Hedge funds are also major activist investors; while some pursue socially responsible investing goals, many simply are seeking to maximize fund returns. Pension plans subject to ERISA are somewhat more constrained in their ability to engage in shareholder activism or the use of plan assets to promote public policy positions; any expenditure of plan assets must be aimed at enhancing participants' retirement income.

## Shareholder Engagement

A less vocal subtype of shareholder activism, shareholder engagement requires extensive monitoring of the non-financial performance of all portfolio companies. In shareholder engagement dialogues, investees receive constructive feedback on how to improve ESG issues within their sphere of influence.

## Positive Investing

Positive investing is the new generation of socially responsible investing. It involves making investments in activities and companies believed to have a positive social impact. Positive investing suggested a broad revamping of the industry's methodology for driving change through investments. This investment approach allows investors to positively express their values on corporate behavior issues such as social justice and the environment through stock selection – without sacrificing portfolio diversification or long-term performance. Positive screening pushes the idea of sustainability, not just in the narrow environmental or humanitarian sense, but also in the sense of a company's long-term potential to compete and succeed. In 2015, Morgan Stanley conducted a review of 10,000 funds and concluded "strong sustainability" investments outperformed weak sustainability investments, tackling the idea of a trade-off between positive impact and financial return. while the Global Impact Investing Network's 2015 report on benchmarks and returns in impact investing in private equity and venture capital found market-rate or market-beating returns were common in impact investments.

## Impact Investing

Impact Investing is the alternative investment (ie private equity) approach to Positive investing. In 2014, the UK's presidency of the G8 created a Social Impact Investment Task Force which produced a series of reports that defined impact investing as "those that intentionally target specific social objectives along with a financial return and measure the achievement of both." Impact investing, capitalizes businesses that potentially provide social or environmental impact at a scale that purely philanthropic interventions usually cannot reach. This capital may be in a range of forms including private equity, debt, working capital lines of credit, and loan guarantees. Examples in recent decades include many investments in microfinance, community development finance, and clean technology. Impacting investing has its roots in the venture capital community, and an investor will often take active role mentoring or leading the growth of the company or start-up.

## Community Investment

By investing *directly* in an institution, rather than purchasing stock, an investor is able to create a greater social impact: Money spent purchasing stock accrues to the stock's previous owner and may not generate social good, while money invested in a community institution is put to work. For example, money invested in a Community Development Financial Institution may be used by that institution to alleviate poverty or inequality, spread access to capital to under-served communities, support economic development or green business, or create other social good. In 1984, Trillium Asset Management's founder, Joan Bavaria, invited Chuck Matthei of the Institute for Community Economics (ICE), an organization that helps communities create and sustain land trusts, to a meeting of US SIF. It is likely that this was the first time a nonprofit organization with a loan fund would meet directly with SRI managers. Trillium clients began investing in ICE later that year.

## Global Context

Socially responsible investing is a global phenomenon. With the international scope of business itself, social investors frequently invest in companies with international operations. As international investment products and opportunities have expanded, so have international SRI products. The ranks of social investors are growing throughout developed and developing countries. In 2006, the United Nations Environment Programme launched its Principles for Responsible Investment which provide a framework for investors to incorporate environmental, social, and governance (ESG) factors into the investment process. PRI has more than 1,500 signatories managing more than US$60 trillion of assets.

## Ethical Investment in the UK

In 1985, Friends Provident launched the first ethically screened investment fund with criteria which excluded tobacco, arms, alcohol and oppressive regimes. Since 1985, over 90 investment funds have launched offering a wide range of investment criteria; both negatively screened and with positive investment criteria i.e. investing into companies involved in promoting sustainability.

Since 1985, most of the major investment organizations have launched ethical and socially responsible funds, although this has led to a great deal of discussion and debate over the use of the term "ethical" investment. This is because each of the fund management organizations tend to apply a slightly different approach to running their funds.

In recent years there has been growth in the market for high social impact investments; this is a style of investing where the businesses receiving investment have social or environmental goals as a primary purpose.

UK institutions are also getting more involved in social investing through impact investing funds, with those such as Deutsche Bank and NESTA, alongside other institutions such as Big Issue Invest, which is part of The Big Issue group.

As of June 2014, EIRIS estimated that there was over £13.5 billion invested in Britain's green and ethical retail funds. This estimate is based on around 85 UK domiciled green or ethical retail funds and it seeks to not include UK money invested in ethical funds domiciled outside of the UK.

## In Higher Education

In 2007, the Dwight Hall organization at Yale University launched the first undergraduate-run socially responsible investment fund in the United States, known as the Dwight Hall Socially Responsible Investment Fund.

## Strategic Sustainable Investing

Strategic sustainable investing (SSI) is an investment strategy that recognizes and rewards leading companies that are moving society towards sustainability. SSI relies on a consensus-based scientific definition of sustainability, and the assumption that '*Backcasting from Principles of Sustainability*', whereby a vision of a sustainable future is set as the reference point for developing strategic actions, is the preferred approach to strategically move a company towards sustainability. It was developed by researchers at the Blekinge Institute of Technology in Sweden.

## The Strategic Sustainable Investment System

SSI outlines that the financial investment will offer a competitive risk-adjusted return, while providing investment capital to companies that are actively attempting to become more sustainable. It implies lower exposure to sustainability-related risks and it considers financial metrics together with environmental, social, and governance (ESG) aspects, as well as strategy analyses to educate investment decision-making.

Characteristics of SSI:

- Lower sustainability risk exposure

- A definition of sustainability based on scientific consensus
- Primarily driven by movement towards sustainability
- Considers financial, ESG, and strategy analysis

SSI operates by prioritizing investment capital allocation to companies that are taking the lead in shifting away from unsustainable behaviour towards new ways of doing business. This capital allocation will provide an incentive for companies to move forward in a sustainable direction. This movement is reported in corporate social responsibility (CSR) and other extra-financial reports, but is also recorded in traditional areas of a firm's financial balance sheets.

By incorporating sustainability investment and returns into traditional financial reporting, a clearer picture of the bottom-line impact of a company's actions towards sustainability is made available. In this positive reinforcing loop, greater investor returns and increased movement towards sustainability are generated with every cycle.

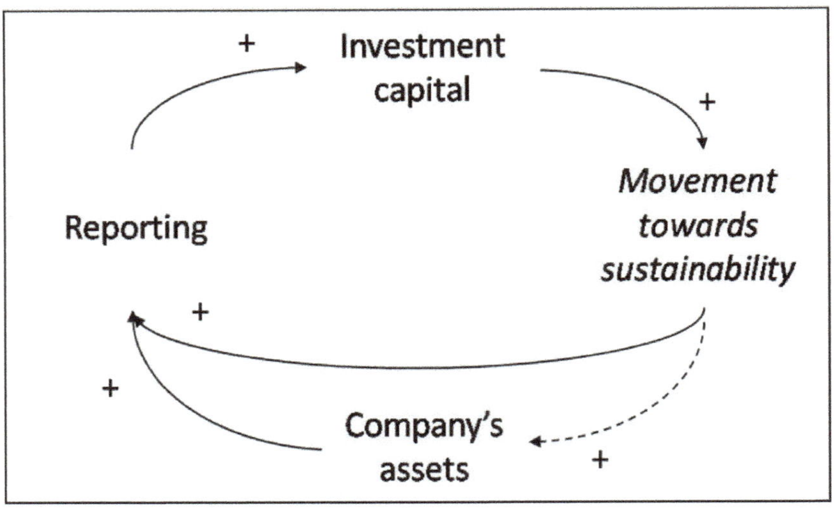


Causal loop diagram illustrating the strategic sustainable investment

Institutional investors, such as mutual and pension funds, take a longer-term position on investments and are thus ideally suited to incorporate SSI strategies.

## Theory Background

The theoretical foundation of SSI is strongly linked to *strategic sustainable development*, made popular by The Natural Step and its founder Dr. Karl-Henrik Robèrt.

This strategy resembles socially responsible investing (SRI), a growing practice amongst ethical investors. Nevertheless, SSI recognizes the gaps of SRI pointed by several academics and practitioners and presents some alternatives.

*Main differences between traditional investment strategies, SRI and SSI:*

| | Traditional | SRI | SSI |
|---|---|---|---|
| **Sustainability definition** | sustainability is not considered | Lack of clear definition | A definition based on scientific consensus |
| **Primary driver** | Maximize Return on Investment | Ethical values | Movement towards sustainability |
| **Analysis performed** | Financial analysis | ESG analysis<br>Financial analysis | ESG analysis<br>Financial analysis<br>Strategy analysis |
| **Sustainability risk exposure** | Higher exposure | Variable exposure | Lower exposure |

## SSI Analysis Tool

In order to evolve current SRI and traditional investment practices into Strategic Sustainable Investment, two gaps must be considered:

a. The recognition of companies with true leading strategies for a sustainable future
b. A robust and well defined link must be made between movement towards sustainability and higher investment returns

The SSI analysis tool addresses the first gap by measuring a company's strategy for addressing sustainability. It allows investors to recognize which companies are leading the transition in a new direction, and which are most likely to be strong performers in tomorrow's market.

This tool is divided in two main parts: the emerging sustainability issue (esi) chart and the strategy analysis component:

## ESI Chart

| | Assessment Categories | | |
|---|---|---|---|
| **Sustainability Issues** | **Urgency** | **Severity** | **Systematic Contribution** |
| *{Issue}* | | | Local |
| *{Issue}* | | | Local Global |
| *{Issue}* | | | Global |
| *{Issue}* | | | Global |

ESI Chart Sample

The Sectoral Emerging Sustainability Issue (ESI) chart is used to identify which aspects of a determined market sector will become a socio-environmental problem. In the common sense, an issue is called 'emergent' when it gets media exposure. Instead, the Tool relies on scientific Principles of sustainability to identify what is emergent.

It exposes which Sustainability Issues present high risks for companies within that sector in the short-term; as well as which Issues will be emerging in the medium and long-terms. Due to differences within a sector, the Sectoral ESI Chart should be made as specific as needed, being flexible to account for various geographical locations and sub-sector subtleties.

The process of composing an ESI chart follows:

Once a sector is selected for an ESI analysis, a list of relevant sustainability issues is assembled. This baseline analysis will result in a list of issues outlining the subject sector's strengths and concerns that impact society and the environment. Next, prioritization colours are assigned to each sustainability issue: red for very high priority; orange for high priority; yellow for medium priority, and green for low priority according to its assessment in each of three categories: urgency, severity, and systematic contribution.

*Urgency* assesses the time frame pressing each Issue. The *severity* assesses the seriousness of the Issue, in terms of its potential consequences for the environment, society, and companies within that sector. The *systematic contribution* is used to gauge the sector's contribution to the overall Issue.

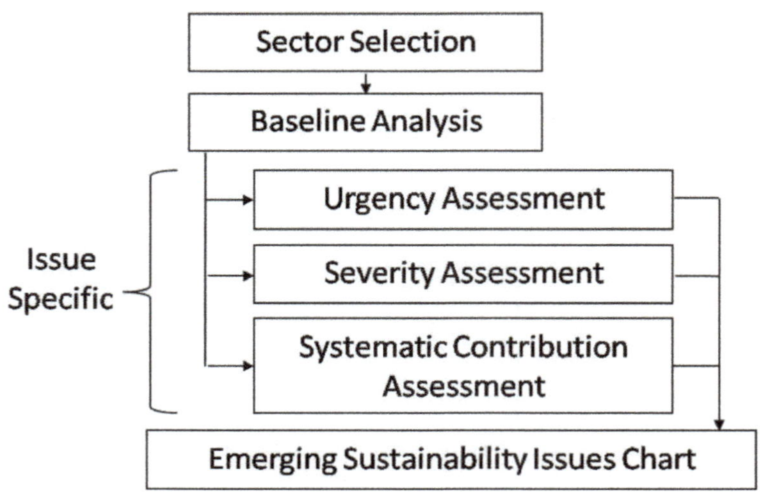


## Strategy Analysis Component

## Strategic Plan

The Strategic Plan element assesses the subject company's planned goals in relation to the emerging sustainability issue (ESI). The qualitative description includes, but is not limited to, information regarding: public commitments planned operational and business initiatives, political action/ lobbying, and third party partnerships (with NGOs, consultative firms etc.). There is also a comment on the subject company's core business in relation to the ESI; as this will assist in determining the subject company's exposure to the emerging risk.

## Strategic Actions

The strategic actions element looks at assessing the subject company's recent actions taken in relation to the emerging sustainability issue (ESI), thus determining whether the subject company is 'walking the talk' in comparison to the vision and goals outlined. The subject company's actions are seen through the lens of strategic sustainable development, and thus three questions are emphasized as a mental guideline:

a. Does this action provide a competitive return on investment (ROI)?

b. Is this action taking the subject company in the right direction?

c. Is this action a versatile platform?

## Strategy Analysis Graph

The strategy analysis graph shows the subject company's planned path for dealing with the ESI, tangible progress made, and if existent, government regulations. The trajectory of the subject company's planned path reveals the extent of their future risk exposure. This graph is placed in the center of the strategy analysis page.

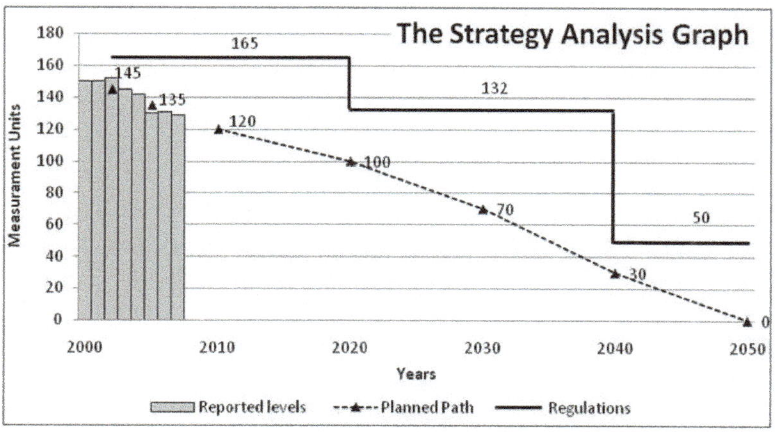


Sample of strategy analysis graph

## Assurance Assessment

The assurance assessment provides an overall impression of the validity of the information gathered. This assessment may be applied if the data is verified by an external third party, or if discrepancy is evident between different sources of information used on the report.

# P2P Asset Management

Peer-to-peer asset management is the practice of sharing investment strategies between unrelated individuals, or "peers", without going through a traditional financial intermediary such as a bank or other collective investment management vehicle.

## Overview

The rationale for P2P asset management is financial disintermediation. When multiple intermediaries participate in an investment management transaction, there is the potential for a conflict of interest between providers and buyers of the service, in a well documented sequence described in economic theory as the principal–agent problem. Intermediaries seek profit maximization. In the context of investment management, they offer the most attractive risk/return propositions to larger, more sophisticated customers. This maximizes their commission revenue for a given distribution effort. Further, given the option between two comparable investment opportunities, an intermediary enticed by investment management kickbacks will recommend the option most lucrative to him, perhaps at the expense of the best interests of non-sophisticated investors.

This regime is under regulatory and competitive pressure because it privileges large, sophisticated investors at the cost of the choice available to the relatively worse-off, and because incentives are against the most vulnerable element of the chain. The FCA (UK), have implemented the "treating customers fairly" policy, with wide ranging reforms such as the Retail Distribution Review, gradually banning "kickbacks" whereby providers of investment management services reward "independent" advisers who place their products.

Rather than the symptom - kickbacks and inadequate advice - new competitors tackle the issue - multiple intermediaries - by disrupting the intermediation chain. Propositions like Wealthfront (US) and Nutmeg (UK) leverage the reach of the Internet to pair a central provider of investment management services with end-customers online.

P2P Asset management takes dis-intermediation full circle. Rather than a central provider directing investors choices, an information exchange takes place between all investors, whereby the best performing strategies by all are made available to all. The first completely P2P provider is Darwinex (UK). Darwinex describe themselves as an exchange pairing providers with buyers of investment strategies, without intermediaries. Buyers pay providers with a share in their investment profits, with Darwinex acting as a central counter-party that independently lists the strategies for a public quoted price based off the underlying assets, rates strategy quality and manages investor risk.

P2P asset management offers the potential benefit vs. centralized providers that all participants crowdsource strategies that are independently rated in a competitive set-up.

## Characteristics

While peer-to-peer asset management shares some of the characteristics of traditional investment management services, owing to its innovative nature it is sometimes referred to as an alternative financial service.

The key characteristics of peer-to-peer asset management are:

- it is conducted for profit;
- it is open to all, without minimum investment volumes
- no necessary common bond or prior relationship between strategy providers and investors;
- intermediation by a peer-to-peer asset manager or strategy exchange;
- transactions take place on-line;
- Investors pick their chosen strategies without 3rd party advice;

Early peer-to-peer asset management was also characterized by disintermediation and reliance on social networks but features like "Social Trading" have started to fade. Since "Social Trading" disclosed live trades, investors learnt to replicate the strategies without compensation to the best providers, who then refused to publish them.

Popular providers of P2P asset management services such as Darwinex provide the following services:

- Brokerage and execution services for strategy providers to route their strategies to the market
- Rating services benchmarking strategies for desirable attributes like experience, risk management, discipline, timing, performance and scalability
- Risk management services shielding investors from unexpected deviations from target risk by the strategy providers
- Custody services - in segregated accounts with low risk counterparties
- Verifying investor identity, employment and income under customer protection legislation such as MiFID in Europe
- Processing payments from investors and carrying out the delivery versus payment payment to the providers agreeing to their strategy being replicated
- Regulatory cover (asset management is a regulated activity that only authorized persons may legally carry out) and legal compliance and reporting
- Attracting new providers and investors (marketing)

## History

P2P asset management is a recent industry. Growth by venture backed companies like Currensee or Covestor failed to satisfy their backers, and without additional funding, some were bought (Currensee).

Some customers argued that failure to independently manage the risk of the strategies or to protect the intellectual property of the providers breached the confidence chain required between strategy providers and investors.

## Legal Regulation

P2P asset managers broadly require two sets of regulatory permission. The first is to carry out brokerage services on behalf of traders and investors. The second is to manage investment strategies on behalf of retail or professional investors.

In the UK, these two permissions are the local implementation of MiFID regulation, referred to as "Dealing in investments as agent" for brokerage services, and "Dealing in investments as principal" and "Managing Investments" for the asset management side of the proposition. Further, permission is required for "Arranging safeguarding and administration of assets", which grants investors protection under the FCA Client Money Rules.

An important nuance is that P2P asset managers could suffer a conflict of interest, if in addition to acting in an agent capacity, providing investment management and brokerage services, they entered deals for their own account, acting as principals. This would stack their principal interests against the customers it served as agent. Traditional providers of financial services potentially suffering this conflict claim to overcome it by enforcing a Chinese wall.

P2P managers like Darwinex, tackle the issue at source by acting exclusively in an agent capacity. Customers may verify this restriction by ensuring that P2P managers hold the "matched principal restriction", whereby the regulator bans their engaging in any activity as a principal. A further test to identify conflicts of interest is to verify that execution services are provided at arms' length through 3rd parties (ideally recognized exchanges), at public prices.

## Advantages and Criticism

The main advantage of P2P asset management is the lack of intermediaries, which results in two structural advantages.

The first is that all incentives are aligned. The strategy provider can be certain that the strategy is not disclosed by the exchange because this would drop its prize to zero and hurt the exchange. The investor can be certain that the exchange will do its best to rate the strategies accurately, since it is the only way to ensure long term volumes.

The second advantage is that any profits achieved by the strategies are only shared between the strategy provider, the buyer, and the exchange. There is a single intermediary, without which the profit exchange is not possible, but no more.

Some have criticised P2P asset managers for the lack of "professional" asset management expertise by the strategy providers.

# Global Assets Under Management

Global assets under management consists of assets held by asset management firms, pension funds, sovereign wealth funds, hedge funds, and private equity funds.

## Assets by Classification

- AM - Asset Management Firm
- FOREX - Foreign Exchange Reserves
- HF - Hedge Fund
- MF - (Exchange Traded) Mutual Fund
- PEN - Pension Fund
- PE - Private Equity Firm
- SWF - Sovereign Wealth Fund
- UHNWI - (Billionaire) Ultra High-Net-Worth Individual

| Rank | Fund type | billions USD | Figures as of |
|---|---|---|---|
| — | Private wealth | $ 32,800 [1] | 2008 |
| 1 | Pension funds | $ 31,500 | 2011 |
| 2 | Insurance companies | $ 24,400 | 2011 |
| 3 | Mutual funds | $ 23,800 | 2011 |
| 4 | Real estate | $ 10,000 | 2006 |
| 5 | Foreign exchange reserves | $ 7,341 | February 2008 |
| 6 | Sovereign wealth funds | $ 3,980 | 2011 |
| 7 | Hedge funds | $ 2,845 | 2014 |
| 8 | Private equity funds | $ 1,600 | 2009 |
| 9 | REITs | $ 764 | 2007 |

## Assets by Company

| Investor Name | Type | Total assets (US$ billion) |
|---|---|---|
| Blackrock | AM | 4,700 |
| People's Bank of China | FOREX | 3,700 |
| The Vanguard Group | AM | 3,000 |
| Allianz Global Investors | AM | 2,213 |
| State Street Global Advisors | AM | 2,300 |
| Government Pension Investment Fund (Japan) | PEN | 1,370 |
| Bank of Japan | FOREX | 1,264 |
| Government Pension Fund - Global (Norway) | SWF | 893 |
| Government Pension Fund of Norway (Norway) | PEN | 856 |
| Civil Service Retirement and Disability Fund (United States) | PEN | 832 |
| Abu Dhabi Investment Authority (Abu Dhabi) | SWF | 773 |
| SAMA Foreign Holdings (Saudi Arabia) | SWF | 757 |
| Saudi Arabian Monetary Authority | FOREX | 745 |
| UBS Asset Management | AM | 680 |
| China Investment Corporation (China) | SWF | 653 |
| SAFE Investment Company (China) | SWF | 567 |
| Swiss National Bank | FOREX | 531 |
| Central Bank of the Russian Federation | FOREX | 429 |
| Stichting Pensioenfonds ABP (Netherlands) | PEN | 427 |
| National Pension Service (South Korea) | PEN | 400 |
| Canada Pension Plan Investment Board | AM | 278 |
| Barclays Inverse US Treasury Composite ETN (Blackrock) | MF | 211 |
| SPDR S&P 500 (State Street Global Advisors) | MF | 200 |
| Bridgewater Associates | HF | 78 |
| Bill Gates (Microsoft) | UHNWI | 76 |
| Carlos Slim (Grupo Carso/Telemex) | UHNWI | 72 |
| Core S&P 500 ETF (Blackrock) | MF | 70 |
| Man Group | HF | 65 |
| Amancio Ortega (Inditex Group) | UHNWI | 64 |
| Warren Buffett (Berkshire Hathaway) | UHNWI | 58 |
| iShare MSCI EAFE ETF (Blackrock) | MF | 54 |
| Total Stock Market ETF (the Vanguard Group) | MF | 50 |
| Larry Ellison (Oracle Corporation) | UHNWI | 48 |
| JP Morgan Asset Management | HF | 47 |
| Brevan Howard Asset Management | HF | 37 |
| TPG Capital | PE | 36 |

| Investor Name | Type | Total assets (US$ billion) |
|---|---|---|
| the Carlyle Group | PE | 33 |
| the Blackstone Group | PE | 30 |
| Och-Ziff Capital Management Group | HF | 29 |
| Kohlberg Kravis Roberts (KKR) | PE | 28 |
| Warburg Pincus | PE | 26 |

# Separately Managed Account

A separately managed account (SMA) is a term within the investment management industry encompassing several different types of investment accounts. For example, an SMA often is used to refer to an individual managed investment account often offered by a brokerage firm through one of their brokers or financial consultants and managed by independent investment management firms (often called money managers for short) and have varying fee structures. These particular types of SMAs may be called "wrap fee" or "dual contract" accounts, depending on their structure. There is no official designation for the SMA, but there are common characteristics that are represented in many types of SMA programs. These characteristics include an open structure or flexible investment security choices; multiple money managers; and a customized investment portfolio formulated for a client's specific investment objectives or desired restrictions.

## Description and History

The term "SMA" is used mostly in the U.S. brokerage industry for these types of arrangements whereby an account is managed by portfolio management resources within the firm, or more commonly, by an outside money management (investment advisory) firm along with an administrator. In this context, an SMA can be thought of as an investment vehicle similar to a mutual fund, in which the customer pays a fee to a money manager for its services managing the customer's investment. The important difference is that a mutual fund investor owns shares of a company that in turn owns other investments, whereas an SMA investor owns the invested assets directly in his own name. SMAs must abide by a number of requirements, set forth in Rule 3a-4 under the Investment Company Act of 1940, to ensure they are not deemed to be unregistered investment companies.

A similar type of account or arrangement is termed a "separately managed account", "separate account", or "private account" when opened directly with investment management firms, which are not brokerage firms. The term "separate account" in this context should not be confused with separate account of an insurance company.

SMAs were developed in the 1970s to accommodate accounts and clients who needed to meet specific objectives that did not fit within the constrictions of a mutual fund investment. It is the freedom of choice of professional managers, portfolio customization, objective investment advice for a set fee, diversification (or concentration should the client choose), tax efficiency and general flexibility that have made SMAs popular among informed investors.

Some people question if SMAs actually provide significant advantages in terms of risk/return over more typical portfolios. There is no clear answer, and without comprehensive data, any evidence is largely anecdotal.

The ownership structure of an SMA provides an investor some tax advantages over a similarly-invested mutual fund. After purchasing mutual fund shares, an investor will have a tax liability for any net capital gains in the mutual fund portfolio, even if the investments the fund sold for a gain were purchased before the investor owned the shares of the fund. This is known as an "unearned capital gain," and has a negative effect on the investor's return from his mutual fund investment. However, because assets in an SMA are owned by the investor directly, unearned capital gains are not possible. Further, an investor in an SMA typically has the ability to direct the investment manager to sell individual securities with the objective of raising capital gains or losses for tax planning purposes. This practice is known as "tax harvesting", and its objective is to attempt to equalize capital gains and losses across all of the investor's accounts for a given year in order to reduce capital gains taxes owed.

SMAs are popular with wealthier investors and their financial advisers as they are seen as exclusive, and offer investment options not available to those of more modest means. According to the *State of the Financial Advisory Industry: 2008* report, SMAs are popular picks among advisers at national broker/dealers and wealth managers. Advisers at national broker/dealers and wealth managers (defined as any financial adviser with a client asset minimum of $2 million or above) made much more aggressive allocations to SMAs than the average. The national broker/dealers allocated 29 percent to separately managed accounts, with 17 percent to mutual funds; wealth managers allocated 18 percent to separately managed accounts and 28 percent to mutual funds.

The financial scandals and market declines that occurred in 2008 have served as a catalyst for hedge fund investors to migrate towards SMAs. As such, the SMA is evolving to accommodate expected investor demand into such structures. Due to growing demands for SMAs in recent years, a number of technology vendors and solutions from innovators such as Scott_Kurland are facilitating the ability for SMA managers to scale their trading workflow to accommodate said growth. The unified managed account is an example of an improvement on the SMA structure as it links multiple managers and strategies to a single investor-controlled account. The configuration of the unified managed account allows whatever blend of managers selected by the investor to be more capital and operationally efficient than had the same blend been structured within an SMA or within a fund structure.

## Performance

| Average 2008 performance: separately managed accounts outperformed mutual funds | | | |
|---|---|---|---|
| **Type** | **SMA** | **Mutual funds** | **+ / -** |
| Large cap | -34.79 | -37.9 | 3.11 |
| Large cap growth | -38.44 | -40.9 | 2.46 |
| Large cap value | -34.94 | -37.38 | 2.44 |
| Middle cap | -37.13 | -39.68 | 2.55 |
| Small cap | -34.77 | -36.88 | 2.11 |
| Foreign large | -42.3 | -44.06 | 1.76 |
| Intermediate bond | 0.73 | -5.07 | 5.8 |

The *Wall Street Journal* reported that separately managed accounts performed much better than mutual funds in 2008, a year when the global stock market lost US$21 trillion in value.

Morningstar, Inc. found that SMAs outperformed mutual funds in 25 of 36 stock and bond market categories for not only 2008, but also 2006 and 2007. The *Wall Street Journal* cited top SMA performers including Robinson Value Management Ltd's Market Opportunity Composite Strategy, and PTI Securities & Futures LP's Protected Index Program. The *Wall Street Journal* added that SMAs work best for investors with at least $1 million or $2 million to spread among various SMA strategies. The story said that, "One reason SMAs may be outperforming mutual funds is that individual SMA strategies tend to have smaller amounts of assets than popular mutual funds, allowing them to trade more nimbly."

*Pensions & Investments*, a national US investment trade magazine, identified several of the top performing SMAs for 2008.

## References


- Firm Size, Book-to-Market Ratio, and Security Returns: A Holdout Sample of Financial Firms, by Lyon & Barber, 1997, Journal of Finance
- "Guide to Short-term vs Long-term Capital Gains Taxes (Brokerage Accounts, etc.)". Intuit Turbo Tax. Turbo Tax. Retrieved 19 November 2015
- Li, Xiaofei; Brooks, Chris; Miffre, Joelle (2009). "The value premium and time-varying volatility". Journal of Business Finance and Accounting. 36 (9-10): 1252–1272. ISSN 1468-5957. doi:10.1111/j.1468-5957.2009.02163
- Graham, Benjamin; Dodd, David (2002-10-31). Security Analysis: The Classic 1940 Edition (2 edition ed.). New York; London: McGraw-Hill Education. ISBN 9780071412285

- Krouse, Sarah (2015-12-31). "The Year the Hedge-Fund Model Stalled on Main Street". Wall Street Journal. ISSN 0099-9660. Retrieved 2016-06-16
- "Introduction To Dividends: Investing In Dividend Stocks | Investopedia". Investopedia. 2012-11-29. Retrieved 2016-11-29
- Gary P. Brinson, L. Randolph Hood, and Gilbert L. Beebower, Determinants of Portfolio Performance, The Financial Analysts Journal, July/August 1986
- Bekkers Niels, Doeswijk Ronald Q. and Lam Trevin, Strategic Asset Allocation: Determining the Optimal Portfolio with Ten Asset Classes , Journal of Wealth Management, Vol 12, No 3, pp 61-77, 2009
- "The premier industry conference for socially responsible investing in the United States of America". SRI in the Rockies. Retrieved 2013-07-25
- Holmberg, J and Robèrt, K-H "Backcasting from non-overlapping sustainability principles – a framework for strategic planning", International .Journal of Sustainable Development and World Ecology, 7:1–18. 2000
- Graham, Benjamin, Dodd, David (1934). Security Analysis New York: McGraw Hill Book Co., 4. ISBN 0-07-144820-9

# 6

# Depreciation: A Comprehensive Study

Depreciation is the decrease in the value of any asset. Some of the methods of depreciation are straight-line depreciation, annuity depreciation, doubling declining balance method, group depreciation method and composite depreciation method. The chapter on depreciation offers an insightful focus, keeping in mind the complex subject matter.

## Depreciation

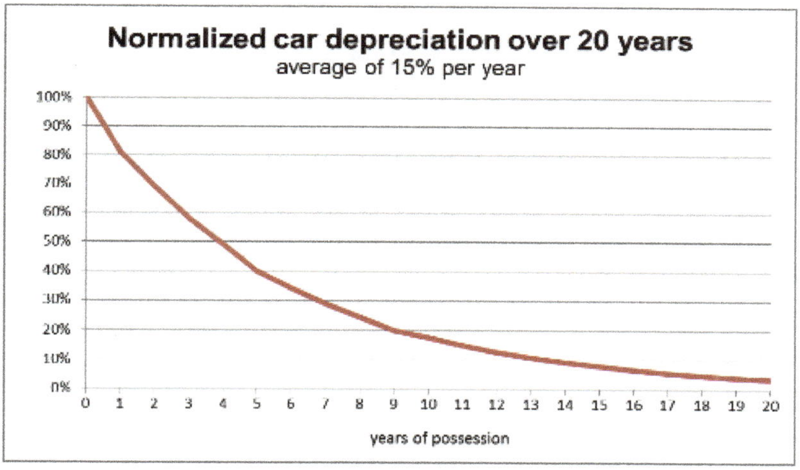


A typical vehicle depreciation over 20 years

- The decrease in value of assets (fair value depreciation)
- The allocation of the cost of assets to periods in which the assets are used (depreciation with the matching principle)

Depreciation is a method of reallocating the cost of a tangible asset over its useful life span of it being in motion. Businesses depreciate long-term assets for both tax and accounting purposes. The former affects the balance sheet of a business or entity, and the latter affects the net income that they report. Generally the cost is allocated, as depreciation expense, among the periods in which the asset is expected to be used. This expense is recognized by businesses for financial reporting and tax purposes. Methods of computing depreciation, and the periods over which assets are depreciated, may vary between asset types within the same business and may vary for tax purposes. These may be specified by law or accounting standards, which may vary by country. There are several standard methods of computing depreciation expense, including fixed percentage, straight line, and declining balance methods. Depreciation expense generally begins when the asset is placed in service. For example, a depreciation expense of 100 per year for five years may be recognized for an asset costing 500.

## Accounting Concept

In determining the profits (net income) from an activity, the receipts from the activity must be reduced by appropriate costs. One such cost is the cost of assets used but not immediately consumed in the activity. Such cost so allocated in a given period is equal to the reduction in the value placed on the asset, which is initially equal to the amount paid for the asset and subsequently may or may not be related to the amount expected to be received upon its disposal. Depreciation is any method of allocating such net cost to those periods in which the organization is expected to benefit from use of the asset. The asset is referred to as a depreciable asset. Depreciation is technically a method of allocation, not valuation, even though it determines the value placed on the asset in the balance sheet.

Any business or income producing activity using tangible assets may incur costs related to those assets. If an asset is expected to produce a benefit in future periods, some of these costs must be deferred rather than treated as a current expense. The business then records depreciation expense in its financial reporting as the current period's allocation of such costs. This is usually done in a rational and systematic manner. Generally this involves four criteria:

- cost of the asset,
- expected salvage value, also known as residual value of the assets,
- estimated useful life of the asset, and
- a method of apportioning the cost over such life.

## Depreciable Basis

Cost generally is the amount paid for the asset, including all costs related to acquisition. In some countries or for some purposes, salvage value may be ignored. The rules of some countries specify lives and methods to be used for particular types of assets. However, in most countries the life is based on business experience, and the method may be chosen from one of several acceptable methods.

## Net Basis

When a depreciable asset is sold, the business recognizes gain or loss based on net basis of the asset. This net basis is cost less depreciation.

## Impairment

Accounting rules also require that an impairment charge or expense be recognized if the value of assets declines unexpectedly. Such charges are usually nonrecurring, and may relate to any type of asset. Many companies consider write-offs of some of their long-lived assets because some property, plant, and equipment have suffered partial obsolescence. Accountants reduce the asset's carrying amount by its fair value. For example, if a company continues to incur losses because prices of a particular product or service are higher than the operating costs, companies consider write-offs of the particular asset. These write-offs are referred to as impairments. There are events and changes in circumstances might lead to impairment. Some examples are:

- Large amount of decrease in fair value of an asset.
- A change of manner in which the asset is used.
- Accumulation of costs that are not originally expected to acquire or construct an asset.
- A projection of incurring losses associated with the particular asset.

Events or changes in circumstances indicate that the company may not be able recover the carrying amount of the asset. In which case, companies use the recoverability test to determine whether impairment has occurred. The steps to determine are: 1. Estimate the future cash flow of asset. (from the use of the asset to disposition) 2. If the sum of the expected cash flow is less than the carrying amount of the asset, the asset is considered impaired.

## Depletion and Amortization

Depletion and amortization are similar concepts for minerals (including oil) and intangible assets, respectively.

## Effect on Cash

Depreciation expense does not require current outlay of cash. However, since depreciation is an expense to the P&L account, provided the enterprise is operating in a manner that covers its expenses (e.g. operating at a profit) depreciation is a source of cash in a statement of cash flows, which generally offsets the cash cost of acquiring new assets required to continue operations when existing assets reach the end of their useful lives.

## Accumulated Depreciation

While depreciation expense is recorded on the income statement of a business, its impact is generally recorded in a separate account and disclosed on the balance sheet as accumulated depreciation, under fixed assets, according to most accounting principles. Accumulated depreciation is known as a contra account, because it separately shows a negative amount that is directly associated with another account.

Without an accumulated depreciation account on the balance sheet, depreciation expense is usually charged against the relevant asset directly. The values of the fixed assets stated on the balance sheet will decline, even if the business has not invested in or disposed of any assets. The amounts will roughly approximate fair value. Otherwise, depreciation expense is charged against accumulated depreciation. Showing accumulated depreciation separately on the balance sheet has the effect of preserving the historical cost of assets on the balance sheet. If there have been no investments or dispositions in fixed assets for the year, then the values of the assets will be the same on the balance sheet for the current and prior year (P/Y).

## Methods of Depreciation

There are several methods for calculating depreciation, generally based on either the passage of time or the level of activity (or use) of the asset.

## Straight-line Depreciation

Straight-line depreciation is the simplest and most often used method. In this method, the company estimates the residual value (also known as salvage value or scrap value) of the asset at the end of the period during which it will be used to generate revenues (useful life). (The salvage value may be zero, or even negative due to costs required to retire it; however, for depreciation purposes salvage value is not generally calculated at below zero.) The company will then charge the same amount to depreciation each year over that period, until the value shown for the asset has reduced from the original cost to the salvage value.

Straight-line method:

$$\text{Annual Depreciation Expense} = \frac{\text{Cost of Fixed Asset} - \text{Residual Value}}{\text{Useful Life of Asset}(\textit{years})}$$

For example, a vehicle that depreciates over 5 years is purchased at a cost of $17,000, and will have a salvage value of $2000. Then this vehicle will depreciate at $3,000 per year, i.e. (17-2)/5 = 3. This table illustrates the straight-line method of depreciation. Book value at the beginning of the first year of depreciation is the original cost of the asset. At any time book value equals original cost minus accumulated depreciation.

book value = original cost − accumulated depreciation Book value at the end of year becomes book value at the beginning of next year. The asset is depreciated until the book value equals scrap value.

| Depreciation expense | Accumulated depreciation at year-end | Book value at year-end |
|---|---|---|
| | | (original cost) $17,000 |
| $3,000 | $3,000 | $14,000 |
| 3,000 | 6,000 | 11,000 |
| 3,000 | 9,000 | 8,000 |
| 3,000 | 12,000 | 5,000 |
| 3,000 | 15,000 | (scrap value) 2,000 |

If the vehicle were to be sold and the sales price exceeded the depreciated value (net book value) then the excess would be considered a gain and subject to depreciation recapture. In addition, this gain above the depreciated value would be recognized as ordinary income by the tax office. If the sales price is ever less than the book value, the resulting capital loss is tax deductible. If the sale price were ever more than the original book value, then the gain above the original book value is recognized as a capital gain.

If a company chooses to depreciate an asset at a different rate from that used by the tax office then this generates a timing difference in the income statement due to the difference (at a point in time) between the taxation department's and company's view of the profit.

In the UK used car pricing expert CAP regularly examine their data to find vehicles that devalue at a slower rate than others. They discuss the distinction and differences between percentage depreciate figures and real world cash depreciation to help motorists to reduce their long term costs. When buying a new vehicle it is important to consider if you are likely to change the car in the next three years (when most cars lose between 50% and 60% of their value) and the expected future value (also known as residual value). For example: "If you buy a car for £8,000 which 5 years later is only worth £2,000 you are actually going to have less value than if you had purchased a vehicle for £10,000 that 5 years later is worth £5,000.

## Doubling Declining Balance Method

Suppose a business has an asset with $1,000 original cost, $100 salvage value, and 5 years of useful life. First, the straight-line depreciation rate would be 1/5, i.e. 20% per year. Under the double-declining-balance method, double that rate, i.e. 40% depreciation rate would be used. The table below illustrates this:

| Depreciation rate | Depreciation expense | Accumulated depreciation | Book value at end of year |
|---|---|---|---|
| | | | original cost $1,000.00 |
| 40% | 400.00 | 400.00 | 600.00 |
| 40% | 240.00 | 640.00 | 360.00 |

| | | | |
|---|---|---|---|
| 40% | 144.00 | 784.00 | 216.00 |
| 40% | 86.40 | 870.40 | 129.60 |
| 129.60 - 100.00 | 29.60 | 900.00 | scrap value 100.00 |

When using the double-declining-balance method, the salvage value is not considered in determining the annual depreciation, but the book value of the asset being depreciated is never brought below its salvage value, regardless of the method used. Depreciation ceases when either the salvage value or the end of the asset's useful life is reached.

Since double-declining-balance depreciation does not always depreciate an asset fully by its end of life, some methods also compute a straight-line depreciation each year, and apply the greater of the two. This has the effect of converting from declining-balance depreciation to straight-line depreciation at a midpoint in the asset's life.

With the declining balance method, one can find the depreciation rate that would allow exactly for full depreciation by the end of the period, using the formula:

$$\text{depreciation rate} = 1 - \sqrt[N]{\frac{\text{residual value}}{\text{cost of fixed asset}}},$$

where N is the estimated life of the asset (for example, in years).

## Annuity Depreciation

Annuity depreciation methods are not based on time, but on a level of Annuity. This could be miles driven for a vehicle, or a cycle count for a machine. When the asset is acquired, its life is estimated in terms of this level of activity. Assume the vehicle above is estimated to go 50,000 miles in its lifetime. The per-mile depreciation rate is calculated as: ($17,000 cost - $2,000 salvage) / 50,000 miles = $0.30 per mile. Each year, the depreciation expense is then calculated by multiplying the number of miles driven by the per-mile depreciation rate.

## Sum-of-years-digits Method

Sum-of-years-digits is a depreciation method that results in a more accelerated write-off than the straight line method, and typically also more accelerated than the declining balance method. Under this method the annual depreciation is determined by multiplying the depreciable cost by a schedule of fractions.

Sum of the years' digits method of depreciation is one of the accelerated depreciation techniques which are based on the assumption that assets are generally more productive when they are new and their productivity decreases as they become old. The formula to calculate depreciation under SYD method is:

SYD Depreciation = Depreciable Base x (Remaining Useful Life/Sum of the Years' Digits)
Depreciable Base = Cost – Salvage Value

Example: If an asset has original cost of $1000, a useful life of 5 years and a salvage value of $100, compute its depreciation schedule.

First, determine years' digits. Since the asset has useful life of 5 years, the years' digits are: 5, 4, 3, 2, and 1.

Next, calculate the sum of the digits: 5+4+3+2+1=15

The sum of the digits can also be determined by using the formula $(n^2+n)/2$ where n is equal to the useful life of the asset in years. The example would be shown as $(5^2+5)/2=15$

Depreciation rates are as follows:

5/15 for the 1st year, 4/15 for the 2nd year, 3/15 for the 3rd year, 2/15 for the 4th year, and 1/15 for the 5th year.

| Depreciable base | Depreciation rate | Depreciation expense | Accumulated depreciation | Book value at end of year |
|---|---|---|---|---|
| | | | | **$1,000 (original cost)** |
| 900 | 5/15 | 300 =(900 x 5/15) | 300 | 700 |
| 900 | 4/15 | 240 =(900 x 4/15) | 540 | 460 |
| 900 | 3/15 | 180 =(900 x 3/15) | 720 | 280 |
| 900 | 2/15 | 120 =(900 x 2/15) | 840 | 160 |
| 900 | 1/15 | 60 =(900 x 1/15) | 900 | 100 (scrap value) |

## Units-of-production Depreciation Method

Under the units-of-production method, useful life of the asset is expressed in terms of the total number of units expected to be produced:

$$\text{Annual Depreciation Expense} = \frac{\text{Cost of Fixed Asset} - \text{Residual value}}{\text{Estimated Total Production}} \times \text{Actual Production}$$

Suppose, an asset has original cost $70,000, salvage value $10,000, and is expected to produce 6,000 units.

Depreciation per unit = ($70,000–10,000) / 6,000 = $10

10 × actual production will give the depreciation cost of the current year.

The table below illustrates the units-of-production depreciation schedule of the asset.

| Units of production | Depreciation cost per unit | Depreciation expense | Accumulated depreciation | Book value at end of year |
|---|---|---|---|---|
| | | | | $70,000 (original cost) |
| 1,000 | 10 | 10,000 | 10,000 | 60,000 |
| 1,100 | 10 | 11,000 | 21,000 | 49,000 |
| 1,200 | 10 | 12,000 | 33,000 | 37,000 |
| 1,300 | 10 | 13,000 | 46,000 | 24,000 |
| 1,400 | 10 | 14,000 | 60,000 | 10,000 (scrap value) |

Depreciation stops when book value is equal to the scrap value of the asset. In the end, the sum of accumulated depreciation and scrap value equals the original cost.

## Units of Time Depreciation

Units of time depreciation is similar to units of production, and is used for depreciation equipment used in mining or natural resource exploration, or cases where the amount the asset is used is not linear year to year.

A simple example can be given for construction companies, where some equipment is used only for some specific purpose. Depending on the number of projects, the equipment will be used and depreciation charged accordingly.

## Group Depreciation Method

The group depreciation method is used for depreciating multiple-asset accounts using a similar depreciation method. The assets must be similar in nature and have approximately the same useful lives.

## Composite Depreciation Method

The composite method is applied to a collection of assets that are not similar, and have different service lives. For example, computers and printers are not similar, but both are part of the office equipment. Depreciation on all assets is determined by using the straight-line-depreciation method.

| Asset | Historical cost | Salvage value | Depreciable cost | Life | Depreciation per year |
|---|---|---|---|---|---|
| Computers | $5,500 | $500 | $5,000 | 5 | $1,000 |
| Printers | $1,000 | $100 | $900 | 3 | $300 |
| Total | $6,500 | $600 | $5,900 | 4.5 | $1,300 |

Composite life equals the total depreciable cost divided by the total depreciation per year. $5,900 / $1,300 = 4.5 years.

Composite depreciation rate equals depreciation per year divided by total historical cost. $1,300 / $6,500 = 0.20 = 20%

Depreciation expense equals the composite depreciation rate times the balance in the asset account (historical cost). (0.20 * $6,500) $1,300. Debit depreciation expense and credit accumulated depreciation.

When an asset is sold, debit cash for the amount received and credit the asset account for its original cost. Debit the difference between the two to accumulated depreciation. Under the composite method no gain or loss is recognized on the sale of an asset. Theoretically, this makes sense because the gains and losses from assets sold before and after the composite life will average themselves out.

To calculate composite depreciation rate, divide depreciation per year by total historical cost. To calculate depreciation expense, multiply the result by the same total historical cost. The result, not surprisingly, will equal to the total depreciation per year again.

Common sense requires depreciation expense to be equal to total depreciation per year, without first dividing and then multiplying total depreciation per year by the same number.

## Tax Depreciation

Most income tax systems allow a tax deduction for recovery of the cost of assets used in a business or for the production of income. Such deductions are allowed for individuals and companies. Where the assets are consumed currently, the cost may be deducted currently as an expense or treated as part of cost of goods sold. The cost of assets not currently consumed generally must be deferred and recovered over time, such as through depreciation. Some systems permit full deduction of the cost, at least in part, in the year the assets are acquired. Other systems allow depreciation expense over some life using some depreciation method or percentage. Rules vary highly by country, and may vary within a country based on type of asset or type of taxpayer. Many systems that specify depreciation lives and methods for financial reporting require the same lives and methods be used for tax purposes. Most tax systems provide different rules for real property (buildings, etc.) and personal property (equipment, etc.).

## Capital Allowances

A common system is to allow a fixed percentage of the cost of depreciable assets to be deducted each year. This is often referred to as a capital allowance, as it is called in the United Kingdom. Deductions are permitted to individuals and businesses based on assets placed in service during or before the assessment year. Canada's Capital Cost Allowance are fixed percentages of assets within a class or type of asset. Fixed percentage rates are specified by type of asset. The fixed percentage is multiplied by the tax basis of assets in service to determine the capital allowance deduction. The tax law or regulations of the country specifies these percentages. Capital allowance calculations may be based on the total set of assets, on sets or pools by year (vintage pools) or pools by classes of assets. Depreciation has got three methods only.

## Tax Lives and Methods

Some systems specify lives based on classes of property defined by the tax authority. Canada Revenue Agency specifies numerous classes based on the type of property and how it is used. Under the United States depreciation system, the Internal Revenue Service publishes a detailed guide which includes a table of asset lives and the applicable conventions. The table also incorporates specified lives for certain commonly used assets (e.g., office furniture, computers, automobiles) which override the business use lives. U.S. tax depreciation is computed under the double declining balance method switching to straight line or the straight line method, at the option of the taxpayer. IRS tables specify percentages to apply to the basis of an asset for each year in which it is in service. Depreciation first becomes deductible when an asset is placed in service.

## Additional Depreciation

Many systems allow an additional deduction for a portion of the cost of depreciable assets acquired in the current tax year. The UK system provides a first year capital allowance of £50,000. In the United States, two such deductions are available. A deduction for the full cost of depreciable tangible personal property is allowed up to $500,000 through 2013. This deduction is fully phased out for businesses acquiring over $2,000,000 of such property during the year. In addition, additional first year depreciation of 50% of the cost of most other depreciable tangible personal property is allowed as a deduction. Some other systems have similar first year or accelerated allowances.

## Real Property

Many tax systems prescribe longer depreciable lives for buildings and land improvements. Such lives may vary by type of use. Many such systems, including the United States and Canada, permit depreciation for real property using only the straight line method, or a small fixed percentage of cost. Generally, no depreciation tax deduction is allowed for bare land. In the United States, residential rental buildings are depreciable over a 27.5 year or 40 year life, other buildings over a 39 or 40 year life, and land improvements over a 15 or 20 year life, all using the straight line method.

## Averaging Conventions

Depreciation calculations require a lot of record-keeping if done for each asset a business owns, especially if assets are added to after they are acquired, or partially disposed of. However, many tax systems permit all assets of a similar type acquired in the same year to be combined in a "pool". Depreciation is then computed for all assets in the pool as a single calculation. These calculations must make assumptions about the date of acquisition. The United States system allows a taxpayer to use a half year convention for personal property or mid-month convention for real property. Under such a convention, all property of a particular type is considered to have been acquired at the midpoint of the acquisition period. One half of a full period's depreciation is allowed in the acquisition period (and also in the final depreciation period if the life of the assets is a whole number of years). United States rules require a mid-quarter convention for per property if more than 40% of the acquisitions for the year are in the final quarter.

## Economics

## Depreciation (Economics)

In economics, depreciation is the gradual decrease in the economic value of the capital stock of a firm, nation or other entity, either through physical depreciation, obsolescence or changes in the demand for the services of the capital in question. If the capital stock is $K_t$ in one period $t$, gross (total) investment spending on newly produced capital is $I_t$ and depreciation is $D_t$, the capital stock in the next period, $K_{t+1}$, is $K_t + I_t - D_t$. The net increment to the capital stock is the difference between gross investment and depreciation, and is called net investment.

## Models

In economics, the value of a capital asset may be modeled as the present value of the flow of services the asset will generate in future, appropriately adjusted for uncertainty. Economic depreciation over a given period is the reduction in the remaining value of future services.

Under certain circumstances, such as an unanticipated increase in the price of the services generated by an asset or a reduction in the discount rate, its value may increase rather than decline. Depreciation is then negative.

Depreciation can alternatively be measured as the change in the *market* value of capital over a given period: the market price of the capital at the beginning of the period minus its market price at the end of the period.

Such a method in calculating depreciation differs from other methods, such as straight-line depreciation in that it is included in the calculation of implicit cost, and thus economic profit.

Modeling depreciation of a durable as delivering the same services from purchase until failure, with zero scrap value (rather than slowing degrading and retaining residual value), is referred to as the light bulb model of depreciation, or more colorfully as the one-hoss shay model, after a poem by Oliver Wendell Holmes, Sr., about a carriage which worked perfectly for exactly one hundred years, then fell completely apart in an instant.

## National Accounts

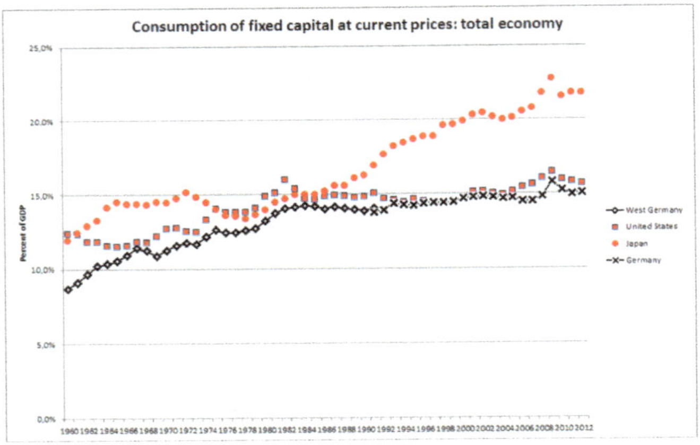


Consumption of fixed capital in percent of GDP, Germany, Japan, United States, computed from data of Ameco data base.

In national accounts the decline in the aggregate capital stock arising from the use of fixed assets in production is referred to as consumption of fixed capital (CFC). Hence, CFC is equal to the difference between aggregate gross fixed capital formation (gross investment) and net fixed capital formation (net investment) or between Gross National Product and Net National Product. Unlike depreciation in business accounting, CFC in national accounts is, in principle, not a method of allocating the costs of past expenditures on fixed assets over subsequent accounting periods. Rather, fixed assets at a given moment in time are valued according to the remaining benefits to be derived from their use.

## Wear and Tear

This neglected boot was ruined by a combination of wear and tear and extraordinary exposure to weather.

Wear and tear is damage that naturally and inevitably occurs as a result of normal wear or aging. It is used in a legal context for such areas as warranty contracts from manufacturers, which usually stipulate that damage from *wear and tear* will not be covered.

Wear and tear is a form of depreciation which is assumed to occur even when an item is used competently and with care and proper maintenance. For example, repeated impacts may cause stress to a hammer's head. This stress is impossible to prevent in the normal use of the tool for its designed task, and any attempt to avert it impedes its functionality. At the same time, it is expected that the normal use of a hammer will not break it beyond repair during a reasonable life cycle.

The phenomenon of wear and tear reflects the second law of thermodynamics, in which objects stray from their original form and function over time unless energy from an external force is used to maintain them. If restoration is impossible an object is regarded as consumable. Parts that are designed to wear inside a machine, like bearings and O-rings are intended to be replaced with new ones; consumables like paper, cardboard, fabrics, and product packaging are designed with a service life commensurate with their intended use. For example, grocery stores may issue customers a paper or plastic sack to carry out groceries, but it is intended that the sack will have a short lifespan before wear and tear would cause it to fail.

Durable goods (e.g. automobiles, heavy machinery, mainframe computers, musical instruments, handguns, water heaters) are designed with wear parts that are maintained generally by replacement of parts. One way to determine if a good is durable or not is whether a service technician or repairman would typically attempt repairs on it. A specialist may need to be consulted, such as an auto mechanic, a computer technician, a luthier, a gunsmith, or a plumber. An automobile's engine may be repairable with a simple adjustment or replacement of a single and inexpensive broken part. Similarly, an electric water heater element that fails from years of wear and tear may be replaced rather than the entire water heater.

Whereas an automobile needs consumable fuel and lubricants to operate, components such as tires, seats, and paint are subject to wear and tear and typically are not covered under any warranty when subjected to normal use.

## Accelerated Depreciation

Accelerated depreciation refers to any one of several methods by which a company, for 'financial accounting' or tax purposes, depreciates a fixed asset in such a way that the amount of depreciation taken each year is higher during the earlier years of an asset's life. For financial accounting purposes, accelerated depreciation is expected to be much more productive during its early years, so that depreciation expense will more accurately represent how much of an asset's usefulness is being used up each year. For tax purposes, accelerated depreciation provides a way of deferring corporate income taxes by reducing taxable income in current years, in exchange for increased taxable income in future years. This is a valuable tax incentive that encourages businesses to purchase new assets.

For financial reporting purposes, the two most popular methods of accelerated depreciation are the double declining balance method and the sum-of-the-years' digits method. For tax purposes, the allowable methods of accelerated depreciation depend on the tax law that the taxpayer is subject to. In the United States, the two currently allowable depreciation methods for tax purposes are both accelerated depreciation methods (ACRS and MACRS).

## Background

Companies in many countries pay taxes on profits: revenues minus expenses. There are various types of expenses, including salaries paid to workers, cost of inputs, and amortization and depreciation. Profits for tax purposes will, in most countries, differ from accounting profits or earnings.

Under both financial accounting and tax accounting, companies are not allowed to claim the entire cost of a capital asset (any asset which can be used for many years) as an expense immediately. They must amortize the cost of the asset over some period, usually an approximation of the useful life of the asset. The depreciation basis is the cost incurred by the company in acquiring the asset. The useful life of the asset is determined by looking at Section 168(e)(3) of the United States Tax Code, and is known as the class life of the property. An example would be that a railroad track has a useful life of 7 years. This is not the end of the analysis however, because then it becomes necessary to look at the applicable recovery period of the property. The applicable recovery period determines the number of years over which the property should be depreciated. Section 168(e)(1) provides a table for determining the applicable recovery period. Following our 7 year railroad track, the table states that property with a useful life of more than 4 years but less than 10 years will be treated as 5 year property. Finally, it is important to determine the applicable convention for depreciation. Section 168(d)(4) of the U.S. Tax Code gives three different types: half year convention, the mid-month convention, and the midquarter convention. Conventions determine how much of the depreciation deduction the taxpayer may take the first year. This prevents taxpayers from claiming a full year's deduction when the asset has only been in service for part of the year.

Governments generally provide opportunities to defer taxes where there are specific policy reasons to encourage an industry. For example, accelerated depreciation is used in some countries to encourage investment in renewable energy. Further, governments have increased accelerated depreciation methods in time of economic stress (in particular, the US government passed laws after 9-11 to further accelerate depreciation on capital assets).

### Example

As a simple example, a company buys a generator that costs $1,000 that is expected to last for 10 years. Under the most simple form of depreciation, the company might allocate $100 of the cost of the generator to its expenses every year, until the $1000 capital expense has been "used up." Under accelerated depreciation, the company may be allowed to allocate $200 of the cost of the generator for five years.

If the company has $200 in profits per year (before consideration of the cost of the generator or any effects of debt or other factors), and the tax rate is 20%:

(a) Normal depreciation: the company claims $100 in depreciation every year and has a tax profit of $100; it must pay tax of $20 on the $100 gain. Over ten years, $200 in taxes are paid.

(b) Accelerated depreciation: the company claims $200 in depreciation for the first five years, and nothing for the last five years. For the first five years, it has no taxable profit and pays no gains tax. For the last five years, the company has a gain of $200, and pays $40 per year in tax, for a total of $200.

To compare these two (simplified) cases, the company pays $200 in taxes in both instances. In the second case, it has deferred taxes to a much later period. The deferral of taxes to a later period is favorable according to the time value of money principle.

(This example has been simplified for a basic demonstration of how accelerated depreciation works. It does not factor in an accurate class life, recovery period or account for convention.)

## Diminished Value

Diminished value, Diminution in Value, or commonly referred to as "DV" are the terms generally used to describe the economic loss in a property's value as a result of having been damaged. Diminished Value (DV) is often associated with vehicles that have been damaged, however, it is applicable to other property of value including collectibles such as jewelry, artwork, etc. For the purposes herein, reference will involve the loss in value of a damaged automobile where the term is often applied.

Unlike "depreciation", which is an anticipated and predictable loss in value over time, 'Inherent Diminished Value' is a loss in value due to a specific, sudden and unexpected negative occurrence. Diminished value of an automobile following an accident may occur in one of three ways (or a combination thereof):

(1) repair-related diminished value;

(2) Immediate diminished value; and

(3) inherent diminished value.

Repair-related diminished value is the loss of value due to the inability to perfectly repair the vehicle, so it is worth less after repairs than it was before the wreck. Immediate Diminished Value – The difference in resale value of a vehicle immediately before damage has occurred and immediately after damage has occurred (prior to repair). As courts are rarely the chosen venue for recovery of property damage, the standard of "Immediate Diminished Value" is rarely employed in resolving Property Damage claims. This also refers to a loss of value caused by the insurer's direct involvement in the claim adjustment in which the insurer exerts control over the repairs and repairs are incomplete, insufficiently performed, or otherwise restore the vehicle to less than the standard condition.

Inherent Diminished Value - Assumes optimal repair quality has been achieved and is defined as the amount by which the resale value of a repaired vehicle has been reduced simply because the subject vehicle now has a significant damage history. This is the most widely recognized and accepted form of Diminished Value. It is also the basis upon which any supplemental form of Diminished Value would be added. A common "Supplemental" form of Diminished Value is "Repair Related Diminished Value".

Usually, a frame or structurally damaged vehicle cannot be re-sold as a "certified pre-owned vehicle."

The true measure of a damaged vehicle's inherent loss in value can be measured as the difference in the value of the vehicle before the loss to that after the loss, prior to or after repair. The standard rule as to establishing a value on late model vehicles would be: 20-25% behind book (Black Book, KBB, NADA) and utilize actual sales results, and not on advertised prices.

While some may claim Diminished Value (DV) is subjective and based upon perception or speculation, the old adage "perception becomes reality' applies and as such Diminution in Value is real simply because, for the most part, no reasonable and prudent person is willing to pay the same price for a vehicle with a history of damage as they would for one never having been damaged. Retailers often offer discounts for scratches and dents on appliances, electronics and dented canned goods; it is, therefore, reasonable that the value of a damaged motor vehicle will suffer a lessening in value.

Additional factors may be taken into consideration in evaluating the loss in value of a damaged and repaired vehicle and may include, but not be limited to: the vehicle itself (i.e. rare collectible, originality, market desirability etc.), the vehicle's pre-loss condition, severity of the sustained damages (i.e. frame damage, flood, fire etc.), the subject vehicle's history (i.e. one owner, prior damage/repair, death of occupants etc.), quality and thoroughness of the performed repairs, (i.e. quality of parts, materials, workmanship, etc.) and additional value considerations including, but not limited to values associated with pre-owned certification programs etc.

Auto insurance companies may not readily recognize or offer to pay for diminished value. Each state may have differing opinions of DV. Example; The state of Georgia allows the insured party (the first-party Policyholder) to make a claim for their remaining economic loss for DV from their own insurance company while the neighboring state of Florida does not. Most states, however, allow the victim of another's negligence (third-party) to make a DV claim from the at-fault party.

The length of time to collect Diminished Value will vary depending upon each state's statute of limitations for first party (contractual) claims and third-party (restatement of tort) claims.

## Diminished Value Appraisal

A diminished value appraisal evaluates the difference in value of a motor vehicle after a collision repair. Reports are usually compiled by an Auto Appraisal Expert experienced in the field of DV and who may provide expert testimony for Appraisals, Arbitration, Mediation or Litigation in a court of law. This Assessment report is used when filing or disputing a diminished value claim against another party and/or an insurance company. The report measures a damaged vehicle's inherent loss in value. The diminished value can be measured as the difference in the value of the vehicle before the loss to that after the loss, prior to or after repair. In most cases even if the repair was done expertly, the value of the automobile will still be considerably less after a loss. When consumers find that a vehicle has been in an accident, most consumers will never pay the same price for a repaired vehicle as compared to one with no loss history.

Some reports include an assessment of the damage done to a motor vehicle, the quality of the performed repair, the market value of the vehicle before and after the accident. There are no set rules for measuring diminished value, and since every vehicle loses value differently, a one size fits all formula would be fundamentally inaccurate.

## Regional

Recognition of concept of diminished value varies from country to country.

## United States

Some states' statutes acknowledge diminished value and provide the ability for consumers to collect first party claims of DV from their own insurance companies under their own policies. Most states allow the consumer to collect third party claims from the at-fault driver's insurance company. Some states recognize liability for third party claims but not first party claims.

## Georgia

In Georgia, vehicle owners can collect DV against their own policy.

## Florida

Diminished Value Case Law in Florida is based primarily on two cases.

- Siegle vs. Progressive Consumer's Insurance Company, 819 So.2d 732 (Florida 2002).

The ability to receive diminished value financial compensation from an at-fault driver for their negligence was decided by the Florida Supreme Court in the Siegle vs. Progressive Consumer's Insurance Company case.

- McHale vs. Farm Bureau Mutual Insurance Co. 409 So.2d 238 (1982)

The Florida Third District Court of Appeal, upheld that the correct measure of damages is the cost of repair plus any reduction in the value of the vehicle. The Court also directed that proving the reduction in value is the burden of the Plaintiff bringing the claim.

## Washington

On July 15, 2014, a policyholder in Washington state filed a proposed class action lawsuit in the Superior Court of Pierce County seeking diminished value insurance benefits under their automobile insurance policies. The insurance company filed a notice to remove the lawsuit to federal district court on August 20, 2014. The case is titled *Johnston v. United Services Automobile Ass'n.*

## Canada

The ability to recover damages for accelerated depreciation varies from Province to Province.

In British Columbia, law recognizes this loss as a recoverable damage and quantify the claim based on the diminished value at the time the collision occurs.

The Rules addressing the admissibility of depreciation reports in court vary by jurisdiction. For example, in British Columbia, Canada, the BC Supreme Court requires such reports to comply with Rule 11.

## Limits on Depreciation Deduction

Section 280F was enacted to limit certain deductions on depreciable assets. To put 280F in context a general understanding of 167(a) and 179 is useful.

Section 167(a) allows a depreciation deduction for property used in the trade or business of the taxpayer. If property is used partially for business and partially for personal use, the basis of the property must be allocated between those uses.

Under Section 179, a taxpayer may elect to expense (deduct) all or a portion of the cost of the depreciable property purchased during the taxable year if it was intended to have a business use, despite generally having to capitalize this property. However, Section 280F was enacted to limit these deductions on certain listed property.

Listed property includes luxury automobiles as well as the other assets listed in 280F(d)(4). For passenger automobiles, section 280F(a)(1)(A) limits the depreciation deduction by listing the amounts a taxpayer can deduct in the years following its purchase. These listed amounts are subject to an adjustment for inflation under 280F(d)(7).(a) The sum for 2007, after adjustment for inflation, is $12,800. These limits seem to reflect what the legislature means by using the term "luxury automobile."

Passenger automobiles fall within the definition of "listed property" as well. Other "listed property" is subjected to more limitations, under 168(g), if it is "not predominantly used in a qualified business." 280F(b)(1). If listed property is not used for a qualified business, the accelerated depreciation deductions will be recaptured under 280F(b)(2). Whether a listed property qualifies as being used predominantly for business is determined by section 280F(b)(3).

Under 280F(b)(3), if the business use is less than 50%, only straight-line depreciation may be used. Even if the taxpayer uses the automobile, or other listed property, exclusively for business use, the depreciation deductions are still limited by 280F(b)(3). There are some exceptions as seen in 280F(d)(5)(B) and 280F(d)(6)(C).

Section 280F is a policy that makes the Internal Revenue Code more accurate by allowing a taxpayer to report their business use on an asset they may also need for some personal reasons.

## Section 179 Depreciation Deduction

Section 179 allows a taxpayer to elect to deduct the cost of certain types of property on their income taxes as an expense, rather than requiring the cost of the property to be capitalized and depreciated. This property is generally limited to tangible, depreciable, personal property which is acquired by purchase for use in the active conduct of a trade or business. Buildings were not eligible for section 179 deductions prior to the passage of the Small Business Jobs Act of 2010; however, qualified real property may be deducted now.

Depreciable property that is not eligible for a section 179 deduction is still deductible over a number of years through MACRS depreciation according to sections 167 and 168. The 179 election is optional, and the eligible property may be depreciated according to sections 167 and 168 if preferable for tax reasons. Further, the 179 election may be made only for the year the equipment is placed in use and is waived if not taken for that year. However, if the election is made, it is irrevocable unless special permission is given.

For regular depreciation deductions in the United States.

### Limitations

The 179 election is subject to three important limitations.

First, there is a dollar limitation. Under section 179(b)(1), the maximum deduction a taxpayer may elect to take in a year is $500,000.

Second, if a taxpayer places more than $2,000,000 worth of section 179 property into service during a single taxable year, the 179 deduction is reduced, dollar for dollar, by the amount exceeding the $2,000,000 threshold.

The amounts after 2012 are to be adjusted for inflation by amounts that had not been released by mid-2012. Amounts for 2012 reflect the inflation adjustments.

Finally, 179(b)(3) provides that a taxpayer's 179 deduction for any taxable year may not exceed the taxpayer's aggregate income from the active conduct of trade or business by the taxpayer for that year. If, for example, the taxpayer's net trade or business income from active conduct of trade or business was $72,500 in 2006, then the taxpayer's 179 deduction cannot exceed $72,500 for 2006. However, the 179 deduction not allowed for any year because of this limitation can be carried over to the next year.

### Large Vehicles

Up to $25,000 of the cost of vehicles rated at more than 6,000 pounds gross vehicle weight and not more than 14,000 pounds gross vehicle weight (like RV) can be deducted using a section 179 deduction. This limitation on sport utility vehicles does not impact larger commercial vehicles, commuter vans, or buses.

## MACRS

The Modified Accelerated Cost Recovery System (MACRS) is the current tax depreciation system. Under this system, the capitalized cost (basis) of tangible property is recovered over a specified life by annual deductions for depreciation. The lives are specified broadly in the Internal Revenue Code. The Internal Revenue Service (IRS) publishes detailed tables of lives by classes of assets. The deduction for depreciation is computed under one of two methods (declining balance switching to straight line or straight line) at the election of the taxpayer, with limitations.

## History

Tax deductions for depreciation have been allowed in the U.S. since the inception of the income tax. Prior to 1971, these deductions could be computed in a variety of manners over a wide range of lives, under old Bulletin F. In 1971, Congress introduced the Class Life Asset Depreciation Range (ADR) system in an attempt to simplify calculations and provide some uniformity. Under ADR, the IRS prescribed lives for classes of assets based on the nature or use of the asset. Such classes included general classes (such as office equipment) and industry classes (such as assets used in the manufacture of rubber goods). Taxpayers could use their choice of several methods of depreciating assets, including straight line, declining balance, and sum of years digits. Asset costs and accumulated depreciation were tracked by “vintage accounts” consisting of all assets within a class acquired in a particular tax year. All vintage accounts for the same year were assumed placed in service in the middle of the year; however, a taxpayer could elect the modified half year convention with potentially favorable results.

In 1981, Congress again changed the depreciation system, providing generally for shorter lives for recovery of costs. Under the Accelerated Cost Recovery System (ACRS), broad groups of assets were assigned based on the old ADR lives (which the IRS has updated since). Taxpayers were permitted to calculate depreciation only under the declining balance method switching to straight line or the straight line method. Other changes applied as well.

The present MACRS system was adopted as part of the Tax Reform Act of 1986.

California is the only state which does not fully conform its depreciation schedule to MACRS.

## Depreciable Lives by Class

Under MACRS a taxpayer must compute tax deductions for depreciation of tangible property using specified lives and methods. Assets are divided into classes by type of asset or by business in which the asset is used. (See tables of classes below.) Where a general class based on the nature of the asset applies (00.xx classes below), that class takes precedence over the use class.

For each class, three lives are specified: one for regular depreciation (GDS in the tables below), one for the alternative depreciation system (ADS), and a class life. Taxpayers may be required to use ADS or otherwise may elect which of the three lives to use. Lives for personal property vary from 3 years to 20 years. Land improvements must be depreciated over 15 or 20 years. Other real property must be depreciated over 27.5 years for residential property, 39 years for business property, and 40 years under ADS.

In addition, shorter lives are provided for certain property, including computers and peripheral equipment, certain high technology equipment, special purpose agricultural structures, and certain other items. MACRS also excluded certain property in regulated industries, as well as films, video tapes, and sound recordings, and certain other items. Also, leasehold improvements to realty are generally treated as real property under MACRS.

## Depreciation Methods

Only the declining balance method and straight line method of computing depreciation are allowed under MACRS. Taxpayers using the declining balance change to the straight line method at the point at which depreciation deductions are optimized. See the tables below. All tangible personal property acquired during the year is considered placed in service in the middle of the tax year ("half-year convention"). Real property is considered placed in service in the middle of the month in which acquired ("mid-month convention"). Special rules apply for pro rating deductions for short tax years and for the first year of business, or where more than 40% of tangible personal property additions are in the final quarter of the year.

The method and life used in depreciating an asset is an accounting method, change of which requires IRS approval.

Taxpayers may track the basis and accumulated depreciation of assets individually or in vintage accounts, as in the old ADR system. Where assets are tracked in vintage accounts, a first-in-first-out convention is usually applied to determine basis of assets retired.

## Special Allowances and Bonus Depreciation

At various times, additional depreciation deductions have been allowed to encourage investment. These allowances generally have had limitations. For example, an additional deduction of 50% of the cost of qualifying property is allowed for certain property acquired after December 31, 2007 and before January 1, 2011 A nearly identical allowance was available for property acquired after September 10, 2001 and before 2005. The IRS recently issued guidance clarifying when taxpayers are eligible for 100 percent bonus depreciation. In addition, the guidance provides procedures for electing 100 percent bonus depreciation and 50 percent bonus depreciation for certain property. In addition to extending the availability of bonus depreciation in general, the Tax Relief Act provided for a new 100 percent depreciation deduction for qualified property that is acquired and placed into service by the taxpayer between

September 8, 2010, and January 1, 2014. Special rules have also apply for biofuel, recycling, and disaster assistance property.

*Decoupling modification* is a tax terminology resulting from the federal tax law enacted March 9, 2002, which created a new tax deduction for "bonus depreciation" that threatened to cost states very large amounts of revenue. Federal Bonus Depreciation, Section 168(k) of the Internal Revenue Code, allows the acceleration of depreciation on federal tax returns, for example, writing off a higher amount of depreciation for the first year an asset goes into service. States that refuse to accept this method of calculating depreciation for state taxes, for example, Iowa and Maryland, publish forms with instructions so stating.

## Alternative Depreciation System

Certain assets must be depreciated under the Alternative Depreciation System (ADS), using specified lives and the straight line method. It may be applied at the election of the taxpayer in lieu of regular depreciation, and it must be used for the following types of property:

- Listed property used 50% or less in a qualified business use.
- Any tangible property used predominantly outside the United States during the year (subject to certain exceptions).
- Any tax-exempt use property.
- Any tax-exempt bond-financed property.
- All property used predominantly in a farming business and placed in service in any tax year during which an election not to apply the uniform capitalization rules to certain farming costs is in effect.
- Any property imported from a foreign country for which an Executive Order is in effect because the country maintains trade restrictions or engages in other discriminatory acts.

In addition, the ADS must be used for computing depreciation deductions for the Alternative Minimum Tax. ADS lives are the same as regular depreciation lives for a few classes, but are generally somewhat longer than regular lives for most classes.

## Example

The following example is extracted from IRS Publication 946:

You bought office furniture (7-year property) for $10,000 and placed it in service on October 13, 2013. You use the furniture only for business.

| Part I | |
|---|---|
| 1. MACRS system (GDS or ADS) | GDS |
| 2. Property class | 7-year |
| 3. Date placed in service | 8/11/10 |
| 4. Recovery period | 7-Year |
| 5. Method and convention | 200%DB/Half-Year |
| 6. Depreciation rate (from tables) | .1429 |

| Part II | |
|---|---|
| 7. Cost or other basis* | $10,000 |
| 8. Business/investment use | 100% |
| 9. Multiply line 7 by line 8 | $10,000 |
| 10. Total claimed for section 179 deduction and other items | -0- |
| 11. Subtract line 10 from line 9. This is your tentative basis for depreciation | $10,000 |
| 12. Multiply line 11 by .50 if the 50% special depreciation allowance applies. Multiply line 11 by 1.00 if the 100% special depreciation allowance applies. This is your special depreciation allowance. Enter -0- if this is not the year you placed the property in service, the property is not qualified property, or you elected not to claim a special allowance | -0- |
| 13. Subtract line 12 from line 11. This is your basis for depreciation | $10,000 |
| 14. Depreciation rate (from line 6) | .1429 |
| 15. Multiply line 13 by line 14. This is your MACRS depreciation deduction | $1,429 |
| *If real estate, do not include cost (basis) of land. | |

## Multiple-asset Accounts

A taxpayer may group assets together into a general asset account. The grouped assets must have the same life, method of depreciation, convention, additional first year depreciation percentage, and year (or quarter or month) placed in service. Listed property or vehicles cannot be grouped with other assets. Depreciation for the account is computed as if the entire account were a single asset.

## Retirement of MACRS Assets

Gain or loss may be deferred or recognized on retirement of assets under MACRS, at the taxpayer's election. Under default rules, proceeds from disposing of a depreciable asset in a multiple asset account are recognized as ordinary income, and depreciation on the account is unaffected by the retirement. An optional method allows the asset to be removed from the account at the start of the year from retirement, in which case gain or loss is on the asset is subject to regular rules.

## MACRS Property Classes Table

From IRS Publication 946 Excerpt from Table B-1 (many asset classes omitted here)

| IRS Asset Classes | Asset Description | ADS Class Life | GDS Class Life |
|---|---|---|---|
| 00.11 | Office furniture, fixtures, and equipment | 10 | 7 |
| 00.12 | Information systems: computers/peripherals | 6 | 5 |
| 00.22 | Automobiles, taxis | 5 | 5 |
| 00.241 | Light general-purpose trucks | 4 | 5 |
| 00.25 | Railroad cars and locomotives | 15 | 7 |
| 00.40 | Industrial steam and electric distribution | 22 | 15 |
| 01.11 | Cotton gin assets | 12 | 7 |
| 01.21 | Cattle, breeding or dairy | 7 | 5 |
| 13.00 | Offshore drilling assets | 7.5 | 5 |
| 13.30 | Petroleum refining assets | 16 | 10 |
| 15.00 | Construction assets | 6 | 5 |
| 20.10 | Manufacture of grain and grain mill products | 17 | 10 |
| 20.20 | Manufacture of yarn, thread, and woven fabric | 11 | 7 |
| 24.10 | Cutting of timber | 6 | 5 |
| 32.20 | Manufacture of cement | 20 | 15 |
| 20.1 | Manufacture of motor vehicles | 12 | 7 |
| 48.10 | Telephone distribution plant | 24 | 15 |
| 48.2 | Radio and television broadcasting equipment | 6 | 5 |
| 49.12 | Electric utility nuclear production plant | 20 | 15 |
| 49.13 | Electric utility steam production plant | 28 | 20 |
| 49.23 | Natural gas production plant | 14 | 7 |
| 50.00 | Municipal waste water treatment plant | 24 | 15 |
| 57.0 | Distributive trades, and services | 9 | 5 |
| 80.00 | Theme and amusement park assets | 12.5 | 7 |

The depreciation deduction for automobiles is limited to $7660 (maximum) the first tax year, $4900 the second, $2950 the third year, and $1775 per year in subsequent years.

## MACRS GDS Property Classes Table

| Type | Property Class | Description |
|---|---|---|
| Personal class | 3-year property | Special handling devices for food and beverage manufacture.<br>Special tools for the manufacture of finished plastic products, fabricated metal products, and motor vehicles<br>Property with ADR class life of 4 years or less |
| | 5-year property | Information Systems; Computers / Peripherals<br>Aircraft and parts (of non-air-transport companies)<br>Computers<br>Petroleum drilling equipment<br>Property with ADR class life of more than 4 years and less than 10 years<br>Certain geothermal, solar, and wind energy properties. |
| | 7-year property | All other property not assigned to another class<br>Office furniture, fixtures, and equipment<br>Property with ADR class life of more than 10 years and less than 16 years |
| | 10-year property | Assets used in petroleum refining and certain food products<br>Vessels and water transportation equipment<br>Property with ADR class life of 16 years or more and less than 20 years |
| | 15-year property | Telephone distribution plants<br>Municipal sewage treatment plants<br>Property with ADR class life of 20 years or more and less than 25 years |
| | 20-year property | Municipal sewers<br>Property with ADR class life of 25 years or more |
| Real property | 27.5-year property | Residential rental property (does not include hotels and motels) |
| | 39-year property | Non-residential real property |

## MACRS Applicable Percentage for Property Class

From IRS Publication 946 Table A-1. Other tables are available for options different from those shown below.

| MACRS applicable percentage for property class | | | | | | |
|---|---|---|---|---|---|---|
| **Recovery Year** | **3-Year** | **5-Year** | **7-Year** | **10-Year** | **15-Year** | **20-Year** |
| 1 | 33.33 | 20.00 | 14.29 | 10.00 | 5.00 | 3.750 |
| 2 | 44.45 | 32.00 | 24.49 | 18.00 | 9.50 | 7.219 |
| 3 | 14.81 * | 19.20 | 17.49 | 14.40 | 8.55 | 6.677 |
| 4 | 7.41 | 11.52 * | 12.49 | 11.52 | 7.70 | 6.177 |
| 5 | | 11.52 | 8.93 * | 9.22 | 6.93 | 5.713 |
| 6 | | 5.76 | 8.92 | 7.37 | 6.23 | 5.285 |

| | | | | | | |
|---|---|---|---|---|---|---|
| 7 | | | 8.93 | 6.55 * | 5.90 * | 4.888 |
| 8 | | | 4.46 | 6.55 | 5.90 | 4.522 |
| 9 | | | | 6.56 | 5.91 | 4.462 * |
| 10 | | | | 6.55 | 5.90 | 4.461 |
| 11 | | | | 3.28 | 5.91 | 4.462 |
| 12 | | | | | 5.90 | 4.461 |
| 13 | | | | | 5.91 | 4.462 |
| 14 | | | | | 5.90 | 4.461 |
| 15 | | | | | 5.91 | 4.462 |
| 16 | | | | | 2.95 | 4.461 |
| 17 | | | | | | 4.462 |
| 18 | | | | | | 4.461 |
| 19 | | | | | | 4.462 |
| 20 | | | | | | 4.461 |
| 21 | | | | | | 2.231 |

- The 3-, 5-, 7-, and 10-year classes use 200% and the 15- and 20-year classes use 150% declining balance depreciation.
- All classes convert to straight-line depreciation in the optimal year, shown with an asterisk (*).
- A half-year depreciation is allowed in the first and last recovery years.
- If more than 40% of the year's MACRS property is placed in service in the last three months, then a mid-quarter convention must be used with depreciation tables that are not shown here.

## MACRS Percentage for Real Property Table

| Recovery Year | Month 1 | Month 2 | Month 3 | Month 4 | Month 5 | Month 6 |
|---|---|---|---|---|---|---|
| 1 | 2.461 | 2.247 | 2.033 | 1.819 | 1.605 | 1.391 |
| 2-39 | 2.564 | 2.564 | 2.564 | 2.564 | 2.564 | 2.564 |
| 40 | 0.107 | 0.321 | 0.535 | 0.749 | 0.963 | 1.177 |

| Recovery Year | Month 7 | Month 8 | Month 9 | Month 10 | Month 11 | Month 12 |
|---|---|---|---|---|---|---|
| 1 | 1.177 | 0.963 | 0.749 | 0.535 | 0.321 | 0.107 |
| 2-39 | 2.564 | 2.564 | 2.564 | 2.564 | 2.564 | 2.564 |
| 40 | 1.391 | 1.605 | 1.819 | 2.033 | 2.247 | 2.461 |

- The useful life is 39 years for nonresidential real property. Depreciation is straight line using the mid-month convention. Thus a property placed in service in January would be allowed 11½ months depreciation for recovery Year 1.

7

# Diverse Aspects of Asset Management

Turnkey asset management program is used to outsource the client's assets whereas mobile enterprise asset management is the maintenance of public assets, building and grounds. Mobile asset management and asset integrity management systems are other topics included in this section. The topics discussed in the chapter are of great importance to broaden the existing knowledge of asset management.

## Turnkey Asset Management Program

A turnkey asset management program (TAMP) allows independent financial advisors, typically fiduciaries, to outsource the management of some or all of their clients' assets. More recently, Certified public accountants, law firms and banks also are using them to enter the financial advice marketplace.

With a TAMP, financial advisors gain access to managed account services that allow them to offload time-consuming functions, such as research, portfolio construction, rebalancing, reconciliation, performance reporting, and tax optimization and reporting, which allows them to focus on clients' personal financial needs and concerns

TAMPs are a form of fee-account, which charge fees based on a percentage of the total assets managed in the program. TAMPs appeal to independent financial advisors who are building a fee-only business, because they can avoid the cost of building their own fee-accounts platform and can implement a TAMP in about 90 days, instead of the year or longer required to develop the same capabilities in-house.

TAMPs help independent advisors avoid employee hiring and payroll costs related to internal administration and research, which for a modest program requiring a staff of 8–10 employees can typically cost $1 million per year in ongoing overhead. Because TAMPs serve financial advisors, individual retail investors are not able to directly invest their assets in a TAMP.

### History

The foundation for fee-accounts was created in 1974 with the passage of the Employee Retirement Income Security Act (ERISA), which brought fiduciary law to the forefront, granted legal liability for trust officers and elevated consumer awareness of investing. Fixed commissions ended on May 1, 1975 when the legislation became law, which opened the door for the first discount brokerage firms such as the Charles Schwab Corporation, Scottrade and TD Ameritrade.

In the mid-1980s, the first TAMPs emerged. By 1986, $1 billion in assets was invested in a number of TAMPs, including PMC (absorbed by Envestnet, London Pacific Advisors, now SunGard Advisor Technology and Brinker Capital). By 1994, TAMP assets had increased to $4 billion, and over the next two years, the TAMP market grew to $16 billion in assets. This growth continued throughout the 1990s with the emergence of firms such as AdvisorPort, Asset Mark, Envestnet, Fund Quest and Lockwood. By 2001, the TAMP market was at $78 billion.

Since 1999, the TAMP market has experienced consolidation through acquisitions and mergers to one-in-three TAMPs each year. TAMP growth and consolidation has continued in the 21st century and by 2010, TAMP assets reached $255 billion with the ten largest firms accounting for nearly all assets under management. Those firms included PNC Managed Investments, Brinker Capital, Envestnet, Fund Quest, Assetmark, Lockwood, Prudential Financial, Russell, SEI Investments and SunGard.

The growth of the TAMP market (1000% since the market first emerged) remains small in comparison to the overall market for fee-accounts, which was measured by Tiburon at $1.5 trillion in assets at the beginning of 2010.

### TAMP Market Segments

TAMP providers vary widely in terms of investment philosophies and services, with some specializing in mutual funds, others offering separately managed accounts, or passive investing versus active investing – others offer a platform of multiple options. Market research indicates that two-thirds of TAMP assets are managed by mutual fund TAMPs.

In addition to asset management services, many TAMPs offer additional support and services for financial advisors, such as training programs for financial advisors with Genworth Wealth Management and Loring Ward recognized by Tiburon as offering "extensive" training and educational programs. Companies such as EBI Portfolios (a UK based TAMP), offer a variety of additional services such as automatic portfolio rebalancing, research requests, turnkey workbooks, risk profiling and repository access to evidence-based documents for their users.

## Mobile Enterprise Asset Management

Mobile enterprise asset management (or mobile EAM) refers to the mobile extension of work processes for maintenance, operations and repair of corporate or public-entity physical assets, equipment, buildings and grounds. It involves management of work orders (planned, break/fix or service requests) via communication between a mobilized workforce and computer systems to maintain an organization's facilities, structures and other assets.

The idea behind mobile EAM as a business practice is that it enables remote workers – employees who spend part or all of their time away from a central office – access to data from the organization's computer application software for enterprise asset management (commonly referred to as an enterprise system, EAM system or backend system), typically using a handheld or other mobile computer. This is to distinguish from the term mobile asset management, which refers more broadly to the actual tools, instruments and containers organizations use to track and secure equipment and other such assets frequently on the move.

In the mobile EAM process, the organization eliminates a need for paper forms or other data reporting and communication methods (push-to-talk and radio) to move work order information to and from the point where the work is being performed.

While enterprise asset management encompasses the management of an organization's entire asset portfolio across processes including equipment addition/ reduction, replacement, over-hauling, redundancy setup and maintenance budgets, mobile enterprise asset management is focused, by definition, strictly on the wireless automation of asset management data for such processes.

## Mobile EAM Technology

When viewed and used on a handheld device, mobile work order applications provide details such as location, stepwise job plans, safety alerts, lock-outs and prior work history on the asset, giving a maintenance technician or other remote worker more detailed asset information as well as the ability to transmit work data to the organization's enterprise system when completed – through a wireless network, docking station or other synchronization method.

Using computer software to achieve standard mobile EAM practices, organizations often report such advantages as an increase in timely, accurate data flow between their remote workers and central management such as planners and schedulers, which thereby improves capital and labor allocation decision processes (including an ability to schedule more planned/preventive maintenance work).

With the proliferation of smartphone and other mobile computing technologies, asset managers can expect an ever more tech-savvy workforce, lower costs in mobile devices and a higher propensity of feature-rich, workflow-specific mobile applications.

## Challenges

Nearly all challenges in mobile EAM practices can be traced to two factors: time and labor resources (including IT or information technology management) and investment costs.

Developing and implementing a mobile application architecture on the enterprise scale is not an easy undertaking by any means, as mobile applications are faced with a diversity of device operating systems, output media (voice and data) and connectivity methods, contrasting with a PC (personal computer) environment where in most cases software requires relatively few, if major, updates and lower upfront costs. Organizations looking to implement mobile EAM applications often seek the help of technology consulting firms and spend months researching, planning and selecting an implementation strategy.

## Industries using Mobile EAM

The use of mobile enterprise application platforms (MEAPs), designed around service-oriented architecture principles for multiple systems integration and custom modification, and other forms of wireless computing technology for mobile EAM solutions is growing rapidly, particularly in industries where physical assets form a significant cost proportion of organizations' total assets. These industries can include:

- Facilities management
- Utilities
- Life sciences
- Government organizations
- Manufacturing
- Oil and gas industry
- Transportation industry

In such high-value asset scenarios, the asset lifecycle improvements introduced by the increase in enterprise data flow of mobile EAM processes can bring significant savings, particularly when part of an enterprise-wide capital and labor management strategy that integrates multiple systems in an enterprise architecture (EAM system, mobile EAM application, labor dispatch/scheduling software, GIS, etc.).

## Market Growth

In a 2009 study, market analyst Gartner, Inc. forecasted, "for the MEAP and packaged mobile application market...we now expect market growth annually of 15 to 20% through 2013." Gartner attributes this anticipated growth to enterprises' increasing willingness (and ability) to extend decision-relevant information to employees, who are themselves increasingly mobile.

For EAM practices as a whole, this means that an increasing proportion of organizations in capital-intensive industry sectors (such as those above) are adopting mobile technology as an integral part of their enterprise asset management strategy – corresponding with an enterprise-wide emphasis on whole life planning, life cycle costing, planned and proactive maintenance and other industry best practices.

### Enterprise Systems Mobilized

The enterprise systems you will find most often mobilized are:

- Avantis EAM
- SAP
- Maximo
- Oracle
- TRIRIGA
- Datastream
- Ventyx

## Mobile Asset Management

Mobile asset management is managing availability and serviceability of assets used to move, store, secure, protect and control inventory within the enterprise and along the supply chain or in conjunction with service providing.

Mobile assets are e.g. of the classes of

- returnable, reusable containers used to transport raw materials, work-in-progress and finished goods through the supply chain.
- precious tools and apparatuses used in technical services and required for proper performing such services with fully valid certification
- any other objects of a value that justifies additional tagging for the purpose of managing the object and its availability
- any other objects with a certification that terminates after certain time which justifies the controlled return for next inspection
- persons under special threat on site of operation.
- Rental companies are increasingly turning to asset tracking for all larger pieces of equipment in order to manage theft, misuse of assets and to assist in the management of Preventive maintenance

## Tracking Mobile Assets

The business justification to invest in asset tracking capability is usually the risk of loss. This can be loss of the asset directly, or loss of the ability to render service to customers that is enabled by the asset. For example, the business may have a few critical tools, and the loss of just one of these tools would significantly degrade the ability to perform necessary work.

Thus, the assets being tracked may a) have specific quantifiable capital value or b) general aggregate operational value.

Examples for such assets include

- beer kegs,
- intermediate bulk containers (IBCs) used in the food and chemical industries,
- racks for glass and automotive parts,
- unit load devices (ULDs) used in the airline industry.
- Line-replaceable unit LRUs of in-field operational installations
- rolling cages,
- collapsible aluminum containers for raw materials,
- portable surgical instruments
- medical devices in hospitals and subject of repetitive certification.

## Non-Asset Mobile Tracking Applications

Persons may be tracked within a controlled geographical area; e.g. hospital patients, visitors in a secure facility, or workers in power plants, chemical plants, or tunnel construction sites. People can be actively tracked to locate them reliably and quickly in the unfortunate case of disaster. It should be noted that person-tracking is a highly specialized application that requires special-purpose technology, and is only workable within a specific, controlled environment. Tracking an individual person in an open, uncontrolled environment without special instrumentation is not realistically possible.

## Concerns with usage of Tracking Mobile Assets

These assets are often in the hands of third party entities (such as suppliers, customers, logistics providers and carriers) and out of sight and control of the owning entity. They usually represent a significant capital expenditure for companies and their management and maintenance is resource-intensive.

On average, businesses spend 5% of annual revenue on logistics assets, and almost one-fifth of respondents spend more than 10%. The annual costs include the replacement of lost or damaged special containers, where typically up to 30% of the containers are surplus in circulation just because nobody knows when and where.

## Outsourcing Mobile Asset Management

Mobile asset management providers manage asset operation within the supply chain, directing the activities of a client's third party logistics company as needed and ensure proper services are performed on the asset (handling, cleaning, maintenance, repair). These providers also study business processes within the supply chain and help optimize each process.

## Methods of Tracking

Different methods exist to track and manage mobile assets. Today, companies use labor-intensive manual processes to track assets between manufacturers and distributors, which can result in higher supply chain costs and processes that are less reliable due to natural human error. Specific identification of the container's origin and destination is virtually impossible under this method.

## Components of Mobile Asset Management

Mobile asset management solutions can include one or more of these parts:

- Server unit
- Database unit
- Wireless tags for the units
- Illumination bases for wireless communications (GSM)
- Locating receivers (GPS)

## Asset Tracking Technology

More sophisticated mobile asset management companies use the most advanced means of tracking assets available today, such as radio-frequency identification. RFID automatically captures data on each individual container and can indicate container contents without ever having to open the container. This technology is also combined with software applications that collect, maintain, track and analyze the data and provide customized reporting of the location, status, and audit and maintenance history of each asset. For example, Wayne Memorial hospital has saved $300,000 by tracking for infusion pumps with RFID technology that can piggyback on the Wi-Fi system already in place. That system is known as "Active" RFID because it uses tags that have batteries and constantly beacon. The most popular form of Asset Tracking using RFID is "passive" RFID using ISO Standard 18000-6c. The Financial Services Technology Consortium created a standard for tracking assets at bank locations. The company that performed the work for FSTC and most of the member banks is ODIN and they have a specialty RFID Asset Tracking Software.

### Flexible Pricing Options

Management providers typically offer flexible financing options, including pay-per-use, subscription or leasing models. Each financing option provides a predictable monthly asset-related expense.

### Benefits of Mobile Asset Management

The major benefits of mobile asset management include:

- Improve visibility of assets in the supply chain
- Meet compliance mandates of customers
- Improve asset tracking and inventory control across multiple facilities
- Reduce loss or damage of goods while in transit
- Streamline business processes having to do with assets
- Reduced labor cost and human error with automatic asset tracking technology
- Reductions in theft and improvements in rental utilization

## Asset Integrity Management Systems

Asset Integrity Management Systems (AIMS) outline the ability of an asset to perform its required function effectively and efficiently whilst protecting health, safety and the environment and the means of ensuring that the people, systems, processes, and resources that deliver integrity are in place, in use and will perform when required over the whole lifecycle of the asset.

An Integrity Management System should address the quality at every stage of the asset life cycle, from the design of new facilities to maintenance management to decommissioning. Inspections, auditing/assurance and overall quality processes are just some of the tools designed to make an integrity management system effective.

The AIMS should also endeavour to maintain the asset in a fit-for-service condition while extending its remaining life in the most reliable, safe, and cost-effective manner. The AIM programs (in the US) attempt to meet API-580, API-581, and PAS 55 requirements, as applicable. (However local legal requirements may differ, please refer to a competent, experienced local professional for advice).

The AIMS document will stipulate the requirements for subsequent Integrity Management Plans.

Asset Integrity management improves plant reliability and safety whilst reducing unplanned maintenance and repair costs.

But an asset integrity management system does not exist in isolation. In order to successfully implement an asset integrity management system in a dynamic operating environment, it is essential that all stakeholders have a consistent and a unified understanding of what the essentials of asset integrity are and how they can be applied in their day-to-day operations, yet this is often cited as among the most significant challenges in achieving an integrity culture within an organisation.

## References


- By Nela Ringquist and Dennis Clark, Forbes. "Tap Into The Right TAMP." March 12, 2010. Retrieved May 11, 2010
- By Max Alexander, Wall Street Journal. "PRACTICE MANAGEMENT: Weighing Third-Party Asset Management Services." March 23, 2009. Retrieved April 22, 2010
- By Deborah Nason, Investment News. "Turnkey asset management programs taking off." November 20, 2006. Retrieved April 22, 2010
- By Karla Paxton, Advisor Perspectives. "Freedom Though Independence: Outsourcing your Investment Research." Retrieved May 11, 2010
- By Christopher St. Laurent, Houston Business Journal. "Turnkey programs take load off investment advisers." October 2, 2002. Retrieved May 11, 2010
- "Tiburon Strategic Advisors, Separately Managed Accounts & Other Packaged Fee Account Programs: Recasting a Growing Industry." January 29, 2010. Retrieved May 11, 2010

# Maintenance of Fixed Asset

Assets need to be maintained in order to protect them from wear and tear. Effective maintenance involves systematic checking and assessment of fixed assets through scheduled maintenance and preventive maintenance. Asset management is best understood in confluence with the major topics listed in the following chapter.

## Maintenance, Repair and Operations

Mechanical repair

Maintenance, repair and operations (MRO) involves fixing any sort of mechanical, plumbing, or electrical device should it become out of order or broken (known as repair, unscheduled, casualty or corrective maintenance). In the aircraft maintenance market sector, maintenance, repair and overhaul (MRO) services also include inspection, rebuilding, alteration and the supply of spare parts, accessories, raw materials, adhesives, sealants, coatings and consumables for aircraft manufacturing and MRO.

In all sectors, effective MRO involves performing routine actions which keep devices, equipment, machinery, building infrastructure and supporting utilities in working order (known as scheduled maintenance) and prevent trouble from arising (preventive maintenance).

The marine transportation, offshore structures, industrial plant/equipment and commercial facilities market sectors depend on scheduled or preventive paint maintenance programmes to maintain and restore coatings applied to steel, and also concrete and masonry assets in environments subject to attack from erosion, corrosion and environmental pollution.

Field repair of aircraft engine (1915-1916 yy)

MRO can be categorised by whether the product remains the property of the customer (i.e. a service is being offered), or whether the product is bought by the reprocessing organisation and sold to any customer wishing to make the purchase (Guadette, 2002). In the former case it may be a backshop operation within a larger organization or smaller operation.

The former of these represents a closed loop supply chain and usually has the scope of maintenance, repair, or overhaul. The latter of the categorisations is an open loop supply chain and is typified by refurbishment and remanufacture. The main characteristic of the closed loop system is that the demand for a product is matched with the supply of a used product. Neglecting asset write-offs and exceptional activities the total population of the product between the customer and the service provider remains constant.

## Engineering

Road repair

In telecommunication, commercial real estate and engineering in general, the term maintenance has the following meanings:

- Any activity – such as tests, measurements, replacements, adjustments and repairs — intended to retain or restore a functional unit in or to a specified state in which the unit can perform its required functions.
- For material – all action taken to retain material in a serviceable condition or to restore it to serviceability. It includes inspection, testing, servicing, classification as to serviceability, repair, rebuilding, and reclamation.
- For material – all supply and repair action taken to keep a force in condition to carry out its mission.
- For material – the routine recurring work required to keep a facility (plant, building, structure, ground facility, utility system, or other real property) in such condition that it may be continuously used, at its original or designed capacity and efficiency for its intended purpose.

Manufacturers and industrial-supply companies often refer to MRO as opposed to original equipment manufacturer (OEM). OEM includes any activity related to the direct manufacture of goods, where MRO refers to any maintenance, repair or overhaul activity to keep a manufacturing plant or facility running. Maintenance is strictly connected to the stage of ideation, in which the concept of maintainability must be included. In this scenario, maintainability is considered as the ability of an item, under stated conditions of use, to be retained in or restored to a state in which it can perform its required functions, using prescribed procedures and resources. Overhaul extends to the concept of improving performance over and above original design specification.

## Maintenance Types

Generally speaking, there are two types of maintenance in use:

- Preventive or scheduled maintenance, where equipment or facilities are inspected, maintained and protected before break down or other problems occur.
- Corrective maintenance where equipment is repaired or replaced after wear, malfunction or break down.

Architectural conservation is another type of maintenance involving the preservation, rehabilitation, restoration or reconstruction of historical structures made from stone, brick, glass, metal, and wood with MRO materials which match the original constituent materials where possible, or with suitable polymer technologies.

## Preventive Maintenance

Preventive maintenance is maintenance performed with the intent of avoiding failures, safety violations, unnecessary production costs and losses, and to conserve original materials of fabrication. The effectiveness of a preventive maintenance schedule depends on the RCM analysis which it was based on, and the ground rules used for cost efficacy.

### Corrective Maintenance

Corrective maintenance of equipment after equipment break down or malfunction is often most expensive – not only can worn equipment damage other parts and cause multiple damage, but consequential repair/replacement costs and loss of revenues due to down time during overhaul can be significant. Rebuilding and resurfacing of equipment and infrastructure damaged by erosion and corrosion as part of corrective or preventive maintenance programmes involves conventional processes such as welding and metal flame-spraying, as well as engineered solutions with thermoset polymeric materials.

## Condition-based Maintenance

Condition-based maintenance (CBM), shortly described, is maintenance when need arises. This maintenance is performed after one or more indicators show that equipment is going to fail or that equipment performance is deteriorating.

This concept is applicable to mission critical systems that incorporate active redundancy and fault reporting. It is also applicable to non-mission critical systems that lack redundancy and fault reporting.

Condition-based maintenance was introduced to try to maintain the correct equipment at the right time. CBM is based on using real-time data to prioritize and optimize maintenance resources. Observing the state of the system is known as condition monitoring. Such a system will determine the equipment's health, and act only when maintenance is actually necessary. Developments in recent years have allowed extensive instrumentation of equipment, and together with better tools for analyzing condition data, the maintenance personnel of today are more than ever able to decide what is the right time to perform maintenance on some piece of equipment. Ideally condition-based maintenance will allow the maintenance personnel to do only the right things, minimizing spare parts cost, system downtime and time spent on maintenance.

### Challenges

Despite its usefulness, there are several challenges to the use of CBM. First and most important of all, the initial cost of CBM can be high. It requires improved instrumentation of the equipment. Often the cost of sufficient instruments can be quite large, especially on equipment that is already installed. Wireless systems have reduced the initial cost. Therefore, it is important for the installer to decide the importance of the investment before adding CBM to all equipment. A result of this cost is that the first generation of CBM in the oil and gas industry has only focused on vibration in heavy rotating equipment .

Secondly, introducing CBM will invoke a major change in how maintenance is performed, and potentially to the whole maintenance organization in a company. Organizational changes are in general difficult.

Also, the technical side of it is not always as simple. Even if some types of equipment can easily be observed by measuring simple values as vibration (displacement or acceleration), temperature or pressure, it is not trivial to turn this measured data into actionable knowledge about health of the equipment.

## Value Potential

As systems get more costly, and instrumentation and information systems tend to become cheaper and more reliable, CBM becomes an important tool for running a plant or factory in an optimal manner. Better operations will lead to lower production cost and lower use of resources. And lower use of resources may be one of the most important differentiators in a future where environmental issues become more important by the day.

A more down to earth scenario where value can be created is by monitoring the health of your car motor. Rather than changing parts at predefined intervals, the car itself can tell you when something needs to be changed based on cheap and simple instrumentation.

It is Department of Defense policy that condition-based maintenance (CBM) be *"implemented to improve maintenance agility and responsiveness, increase operational availability, and reduce life cycle total ownership costs"*.

## Advantages and Disadvantages

CBM has some advantages over planned maintenance:

- Improved system reliability
- Decreased maintenance costs
- Decreased number of maintenance operations causes a reduction of human error influences

Its disadvantages are:

- High installation costs, for minor equipment items often more than the value of the equipment

- Unpredictable maintenance periods cause costs to be divided unequally
- Increased number of parts (the CBM installation itself) that need maintenance and checking

Today, due to its costs, CBM is not used for less important parts of machinery despite obvious advantages. However it can be found everywhere where increased reliability and safety is required, and in future will be applied even more widely.

# Value-driven Maintenance

VDM - Value Driven Maintenance is a maintenance management methodology.

## History

VDM was developed by Mark Haarman and Guy Delahay. Both former chairmen of the Dutch Maintenance Association (NVDO) and authors of the book entitled "Value Driven Maintenance, New Faith in Maintenance".

## Value Drivers in Maintenance

What exactly is value? In financial literature; value (net present value) is defined as: Value = the sum of all free future cash flows, discounted to today.

A cash flow is the difference between income and expenditure. It is not the difference between turnover and costs, because this is easy to manipulate through accounting. There are companies that use highly creative lease, depreciation and reservation techniques to keep book profits artificially high or low; this does not always contribute to shareholder value. Recent stock market scandals are a painful but revealing illustration of what sometimes happens as a result of this. The second part of the definition concerns the knowledge that the value of a cash flow is time-related, given the term "present value". Future cash flows must be corrected or discounted to today. Managing by value necessitates maximizing future cash flows. Managing by value obliges companies constantly to search for new free cash flows. It's no longer enough for a company to go on doing what it is already doing. Today, it's all about creating *value*.

Now that we know what value is, we can translate the concept into maintenance. Within VDM, there are four axes along which maintenance can contribute to value creation within a company. The axes are also called the *4 value drivers* (see fig 1.).

## Asset Utilization

The first value driver is Asset Utilization. Asset Utilization seeks to increase the technical availability of a technical equipment. With higher technical availability, it is possible to produce and sell more products with the same invested capital, generating more income while the fixed costs remain the same. In other words, the free cash flows increase, which automatically means value creation. Maintenance can increase technical availability by preventing unwanted breakdowns, scheduling plant maintenance in a smarter way and performing repairs and inspections faster. A point to note is that higher technical availability produces value not only in growth markets. In markets where demand is stable or declining, greater availability can also create value. By making a plant more efficient, the number of shifts can be reduced or it may even be possible to close down sister plants. At corporate level, this does not generate more turnover, but it does significantly reduce costs, which is another way of creating value.

## Safety, Health & Environment

An increasingly important value driver for maintenance is Safety, Health & Environment, or SHE in VDM terminology. Compliance with legal directives covering SHE creates value in two ways. Firstly, it avoids the imposition of government penalties for breaches of legislation. Secondly, a good SHE policy has a positive effect on retention of the License to Operate. This is something else that has value, because it increases the likelihood of future cash flows actually materializing. Without a License to Operate, there will be no future cash flows and thus no value. Problem here is that it does not take the other error type into account (related to a lower false safety trip rate, but higher accident rate). It is very controversial to put a value on human life and therefore this VDM theory is just like the ALARP logic dangerous to use and might not be accepted by all legislation world-wide (specially in the US).

The importance of the SHE value driver becomes apparent when looking at the recent incident with the BP Oil Spill in the Gulf of Mexico; the Deepwater Horizon oil spill. Poor maintenance is believed to be the cause of one of the biggest oil spills in history, causing massive damage to the environment. Total accumulated consequence costs (both clean-up costs and loss of company value) are estimated on 12 billion.

## Cost Control

Even though maintenance is not a cost center in itself, it does gobble up a lot of money. The maintenance budget consists mainly of wage and training costs of technicians, managers and indirect personnel, the costs of spare parts and tools and the costs of contracted personnel and outsourced work. Savings on the maintenance budget automatically generate free cash flows in the future and, by consequence, value. The savings are achievable by having a smarter Preventive maintenance program, higher technician productivity, lower procurement prices for materials and services and the right ratio of the number of technicians, managers and indirect personnel. Controlling maintenance costs is called "Cost Control" in VDM.

## Resource Allocation

Finally, maintenance can create value through the smarter management of resources. This is called "Resource Allocation" in VDM. It is not about the consumption of resources, because that is already covered in the Cost Control value driver. Within VDM, a distinction is made between four types of resources: technicians, spare parts, contractors and knowledge. One need to think only of cash flows freed up as a result of smarter management or savings on warehouses, logistical employees, insurance and the avoidance of obsolete and surplus spare parts. In practise, it often turns out that the value potential of smart management of spare parts by far exceeds the value potential of the other resources.

As figure shows, a natural tension exists between the four value drivers. That is why today's maintenance manager is continually searching for the right balance between these value drivers. It is important to know how they square up to each other. Which are the dominant ones and which are the subordinate ones? One can determine this instinctively but many corporate managers require a financial validation because, for example, it will be a decisive factor in investment decisions or because stakeholders (e.g. financial manager, production manager) are not prepared to accept a judgement based on instinct. This is a situation where one should use the VDM formula.

## VDM Formula

The VDM formula is derived from the net present value formula and can be used to calculate the value of maintenance. The VDM formula is:

$$PV_{maintenance} = \sum \{F_{SHE,t} \text{ x } (CF_{AU,t} + CF_{CC,t} + CF_{RA,t} + CF_{SHE,t}) / (1+r)^t\}$$

where:

$PV_{maintenance}$ = present value potential of maintenance

$F_{SHE,t}$ = SHE factor in year t

$CF_{AU,t}$ = future free cash flow in year t from Asset Utilization

$CF_{CC,t}$ = future free cash flow in year t from Cost Control

$CF_{RA,t}$ = future free cash flow in year t from Resource Allocation

$CF_{SHE,t}$ = future free cash flow in year t from Safety, Health & Environment

r = Discount rate

SHE stands out prominently in the formula. This factor shows how great the probability is that the License to Operate will be retained in the coming years and that the expected cash flows from all four value drivers will actually be attainable in the future.

Consequently, the SHE factor is a probability factor with a value of 0 to 1. A SHE factor of 0 means 0% probability of retention of the License to Operate, for example in a fictitious case where a company decides to stop performing all maintenance for cost reasons. The free cash flow that this creates on Cost Control will be enormous. But because the company fails to satisfy SHE laws and this loses its License to Operate, this cash flow will not create any value. The VDM model can be simplified in certain situations. Assume that we work with Perpetuity. This means there will be indefinitely be a free cash flow that is the same year after year and the SHE factor is constant; the VDM formula thus becomes:

$$PV_{maintenance} = F_{SHE,t} \text{ x } (CF_{AU,t} + CF_{CC,t} + CF_{RA,t} + CF_{SHE,t}) / r$$

# Predictive Maintenance

Predictive maintenance (PdM) techniques are designed to help determine the condition of in-service equipment in order to predict when maintenance should be performed. This approach promises cost savings over routine or time-based preventive maintenance, because tasks are performed only when warranted.

The main promise of predictive maintenance is to allow convenient scheduling of corrective maintenance, and to prevent unexpected equipment failures. The key is "the right information in the right time". By knowing which equipment needs maintenance, maintenance work can be better planned (spare parts, people, etc.) and what would have been "unplanned stops" are transformed to shorter and fewer "planned stops", thus increasing plant availability. Other potential advantages include increased equipment lifetime, increased plant safety, fewer accidents with negative impact on environment, and optimized spare parts handling.

Predictive maintenance differs from its cousin preventive maintenance because it relies on the actual condition of equipment, rather than average or expected life statistics, to predict when maintenance will be required.

## Overview

PdM evaluates the condition of equipment by performing periodic or continuous (online) equipment condition monitoring. The ultimate goal of PdM is to perform maintenance at a scheduled point in time when the maintenance activity is most cost-effective and before the equipment loses performance within a threshold. This is in contrast to time- and/or operation count-based maintenance, where a piece of equipment gets maintained whether it needs it or not. Time-based maintenance is labor-intensive, ineffective in identifying problems that develop between scheduled inspections, and is not cost-effective.

The "predictive" component of predictive maintenance stems from the goal of predicting the future trend of the equipment's condition. This approach uses principles of statistical process control to determine at what point in the future maintenance activities will be appropriate.

Most PdM inspections are performed while equipment is in service, thereby minimizing disruption of normal system operations. Adoption of PdM can result in substantial cost savings and higher system reliability.

Reliability-centered maintenance, or RCM, emphasizes the use of predictive maintenance (PdM) techniques in addition to traditional preventive measures. When properly implemented, RCM provides companies with a tool for achieving lowest asset Net Present Costs (NPC) for a given level of performance and risk.

One area that many times is overlooked is how to, in an efficient way, transfer the PdM data to a computerized maintenance management system (CMMS) so that the equipment condition data is sent to the right equipment object in the CMMS system in order to trigger maintenance planning, execution and reporting. Unless this is achieved, the PdM solution is of limited value, at least if the PdM solution is implemented on a medium to large size plant with tens of thousands pieces of equipment. In 2010, the mining company Boliden, as a first, implemented a combined Distributed Control System (DCS) and Pdm solution integrated with the plant CMMS system on an object to object level, transferring equipment data using protocols like Highway Addressable Remote Transducer Protocol (HART), IEC61850 and OLE for process control (OPC).

## Technologies

To evaluate equipment condition, predictive maintenance utilizes nondestructive testing technologies such as infrared, acoustic (partial discharge and airborne ultrasonic), corona detection, vibration analysis, sound level measurements, oil analysis, and other specific online tests. A new approach in this area is to utilize measurements on the actual equipment in combination with measurement of process performance, measured by other devices, to trigger equipment maintenance. This is primarily available in collaborative process automation systems (CPAS). Site measurements are often supported by wireless sensor networks to reduce the wiring cost.

Vibration analysis is most productive on high-speed rotating equipment and can be the most expensive component of a PdM program to get up and running. Vibration analysis, when properly done, allows the user to evaluate the condition of equipment and avoid failures. The latest generation of vibration analyzers comprises more capabilities and automated functions than its predecessors. Many units display the full vibration spectrum of three axes simultaneously, providing a snapshot of what is going on with a particular machine. But despite such capabilities, not even the most sophisticated equipment successfully predicts developing problems unless the operator understands and applies the basics of vibration analysis.

Remote visual inspection is the first non destructive testing. It provides a cost-efficient primary assessment. Essential information and defaults can be deduced from the external appearance of the piece, such as folds, breaks, cracks and corrosion.The remote visual inspection has to be carried out in good conditions with a sufficient lighting (350 LUX at least). When the part of the piece to be controlled is not directly accessible, an instrument made of mirrors and lenses called endoscope is used. Hidden defects with external irregularities may indicate a more serious defect inside.

Acoustical analysis can be done on a sonic or ultrasonic level. New ultrasonic techniques for condition monitoring make it possible to "hear" friction and stress in rotating machinery, which can predict deterioration earlier than conventional techniques. Ultrasonic technology is sensitive to high-frequency sounds that are inaudible to the human ear and distinguishes them from lower-frequency sounds and mechanical vibration. Machine friction and stress waves produce distinctive sounds in the upper ultrasonic range. Changes in these friction and stress waves can suggest deteriorating conditions much earlier than technologies such as vibration or oil analysis. With proper ultrasonic measurement and analysis, it's possible to differentiate normal wear from abnormal wear, physical damage, imbalance conditions, and lubrication problems based on a direct relationship between asset and operating conditions.

Sonic monitoring equipment is less expensive, but it also has fewer uses than ultrasonic technologies. Sonic technology is useful only on mechanical equipment, while ultrasonic equipment can detect electrical problems and is more flexible and reliable in detecting mechanical problems.

Infrared monitoring and analysis has the widest range of application (from high- to low-speed equipment), and it can be effective for spotting both mechanical and electrical failures; some consider it to currently be the most cost-effective technology. Oil analysis is a long-term program that, where relevant, can eventually be more predictive than any of the other technologies. It can take years for a plant's oil program to reach this level of sophistication and effectiveness. Analytical techniques performed on oil samples can be classified in two categories: used oil analysis and wear particle analysis. Used oil analysis determines the condition of the lubricant itself, determines the quality of the lubricant, and checks its suitability for continued use. Wear particle analysis determines the mechanical condition of machine components that are lubricated. Through wear particle analysis, you can identify the composition of the solid material present and evaluate particle type, size, concentration, distribution, and morphology.

The use of Model Based Condition Monitoring for predictive maintenance programs is becoming increasingly popular over time. This method involves spectral analysis on the motor's current and voltage signals and then compares the measured parameters to a known and learned model of the motor to diagnose various electrical and mechanical anomalies. This process of "model based" condition monitoring was originally designed and used on NASA's space shuttle to monitor and detect developing faults in the space shuttle's main engine. It allows for the automation of data collection and analysis tasks, providing round the clock condition monitoring and warnings about faults as they develop. This method has been uniquely adapted into a tool called "Artesis MCM" for industrial motors, generators and driven equipment by the Turkish company Artesis. In an agreement with General Electric the product was rebranded "AnomAlert". Artesis has received the "Editor's Choice Award" for the 40 best products of 2000 by control Engineering USA and the "Technology Innovation Award 2007" for simplifying predictive maintenance by the Institution of Engineering in the UK for their work on the AnomAlert Motor Anomaly Detector.

### Applications (by industry)

#### Railway

- Detect problems before they cause downtime for linear, fixed and mobile assets.
- Improving safety and track void detection through a new vehicle cab-based monitoring system
- Siemens Tracksure track monitoring system is able to identify voids underneath track from the acceleration measured in the vehicle cab.
- Can also identify the type of track asset that the void is located under and provide an indication of the severity of the void

## Planned Maintenance

Planned preventive maintenance (PPM), more commonly referred to as simply planned maintenance (PM) or scheduled maintenance, is any variety of scheduled maintenance to an object or item of equipment. Specifically, planned maintenance is a scheduled service visit carried out by a competent and suitable agent, to ensure that an item of equipment is operating correctly and to therefore avoid any unscheduled breakdown and downtime.

Along with condition-based maintenance, planned maintenance comprises preventive maintenance, in which the maintenance event is preplanned, and all future maintenance is preprogrammed. Planned maintenance is created for every item separately according to manufacturers recommendation or legislation. Plans can be date-based, based on equipment running hours, or on the distance travelled by the vehicle. A good example of a planned maintenance program is car maintenance, where time and distance determine fluid change requirements. A good example of condition-based maintenance is the oil pressure warning light that provides notification that you should stop the vehicle because engine lubrication has stopped and failure will occur.

Planned maintenance has some advantages over condition-based maintenance (CBM), such as:

- easier planning of maintenance and ordering spares,
- costs are distributed more evenly,
- no initial costs for instruments used for supervision of equipment.

Disadvantages are:

- less reliable than equipment with fault reporting associated with CBM
- more expensive due to more frequent parts change
- requires training investment and ongoing labor costs

Parts that have scheduled maintenance at fixed intervals, usually due to wearout or a fixed shelf life, are sometimes known as time-change interval, or TCI items.

## References


- Marine Painting Manual Paperback (softcover reprint of original 1st ed. 1989 edition), A. M. Berendsen, Springer, 2013, ISBN 978-90-481-8244-2
- Liu, Jie; Wang, Golnaraghi (2010). "An enhanced diagnostic scheme for bearing condition monitoring". IEEE Transactions on Instrumentation and Measurement. 59 (2): 309–321. doi:10.1109/tim.2009.2023814
- A. Duyar and W. C. Merrill, "Fault Diagnosis for the Space Shuttle Main Engine", AIAA Journal of Guidance, Control and Dynamics, vol. 15, no. 2, pp. 384-389, 1992
- "Commercial Electrical Contractor and Domestic Electrician Leeds". 247 Electrical Services Leeds. Retrieved 2017-01-26
- Materials for Conservation: Organic Consolidants, Adhesives and Coatings by C.V. Horie, Butterworth-Heinemann, 2nd ed., 2010, ISBN 978-0-75-066905-4
- Gopalakrishna Palem (2013), Condition-Based Maintenance using Sensor Arrays and Telematics, International Journal of Mobile Network Communications & Telematics, Vol 3, No 3, pp. 19-28
- Pagnamenta, Robin (2010-05-26). "Lloyd's syndicates launch legal action over BP insurance claim". The Times. UK. Retrieved 2010-05-26
- Jardine, A.K.S.; Lin, Banjevic (2006). "A review on machinery diagnostics and prognostics implementing condition-based maintenance". Mechanical Systems and Signal Processing. 20 (7): 1483–1510. doi:10.1016/j.ymssp.2005.09.012
- Industrial Polymer Applications: Essential Chemistry and Technology, Royal Society of Chemistry, UK, 1st edition, 2016, ISBN 978-1782628149

9

# Software used in Asset Management

The software used in asset management are software asset management, asset recovery software, ManageEngine AssetExplorer, AMS device manager, rational asset manager and computerized maintenance management system. Software asset management is the practice of managing the maintenance and deployment of the software application of any institution. The major software used in asset management are discussed in this chapter.

## Software Asset Management

Software asset management (SAM) is a business practice that involves managing and optimizing the purchase, deployment, maintenance, utilization, and disposal of software applications within an organization. According to the Information Technology Infrastructure Library (ITIL), SAM is defined as "all of the infrastructure and processes necessary for the effective management, control and protection of the software assets...throughout all stages of their lifecycle." Fundamentally intended to be part of an organization's information technology business strategy, the goals of SAM are to reduce information technology (IT) costs and limit business and legal risk related to the ownership and use of software, while maximizing IT responsiveness and end-user productivity. SAM is particularly important for large corporations in regard to redistribution of licenses and managing legal risks associated with software ownership and expiration. SAM technologies track license expiration, thus allowing the company to function ethically and within software compliance regulations. This can be important for both eliminating legal costs associated with license agreement violations and as part of a company's reputation management strategy. Both are important forms of risk management and are critical for large corporations' long-term business strategies.

SAM is one facet of a broader business discipline known as IT asset management, which includes overseeing both software and hardware that comprise an organization's computers and network.

### Role within Organizations

SAM can serve many different functions within organizations, depending on their software portfolios, IT infrastructures, resource availability, and business goals.

For many organizations, the goal of implementing a SAM program is very tactical in nature, focused specifically on balancing the number of software licenses purchased with the number of actual licenses consumed or used. In addition to balancing the number of licenses purchased with the amount of consumption, an effective SAM program must also ensure that the usage of all installed software is in keeping with the terms and conditions of the specific vendor license agreement. In doing so, organizations can minimize liabilities associated with software piracy in the event of an audit by a software vendor or a third party such as the Business Software Alliance (BSA). SAM, according to this interpretation, involves conducting detailed software inventories on a periodic basis to determine the exact number of software consumption, comparing this information with the number of licenses purchased, reviewing how the software is being used in respect to the terms and conditions and establishing controls to ensure that proper licensing practices are maintained on an ongoing basis. This can be accomplished through a combination of IT processes, purchasing policies and procedures, and technology solutions such as software inventory tools.

Counting installations is the most common means of measuring license consumption but some software is licensed by number of users, capital, processors or CPU Cores.

More broadly defined, the strategic goals of SAM often include (but are not limited to) the following:

- Reduce software and support costs by negotiating volume contract agreements and eliminating or reallocating underutilized software licenses
- Enforce compliance with corporate security policies and desktop/server/mobile standards
- Improve worker productivity by deploying the right kinds of technology more quickly and reliably
- Limit overhead associated with managing and supporting software by streamlining and/or automating IT processes (such as inventory tracking, software deployment, issue tracking, and patch management)
- Establish ongoing policies and procedures surrounding the acquisition, documentation, deployment, usage and retirement of software in an effort to recognize long-term benefits of SAM

## SAM Technology

A number of technologies are available to support key SAM processes:

- Software inventory tools intelligently "discover" software installed across the computer network, and collect software file information such as title, product ID, size, date, path, and version.
- License manager solutions provide an intelligent repository for license entitlements which can then be reconciled against data provided by Software invento-

ry tools to provide the organization with an 'Effective License Position' or view of where the organization is under-licensed (at risk of a compliance audit) or over-licensed (wasting money on unnecessary software purchases).

- Software metering tools monitor the utilization of software applications across a network. They can also provide real-time enforcement of compliance for applications licensed based on usage.
- Application control tools restrict what and by whom particular software can be run on a computer as a means of avoiding security and other risks.
- Software deployment tools automate and regulate the deployment of new software.
- Patch management tools automate the deployment of software patches to ensure that computers are up-to-date and meet applicable security and efficiency standards.
- Request management tools allow employees to place requests for software products using a centralized form and process specifically designed to capture and assess specific license requirements as well as to manage and track the procurement and deployment process.
- Product catalog tools capture product specific information such as name, edition, version and license agreement types as well as other key top level information for products used within the business. This information normalizes product naming conventions with the organization and allows mapping between other technologies tools used in the composite SAM solution.

## International Organization for Standardization (ISO)

The latest version of the SAM standard from ISO is 19770-1:2012. This revised standard is designed to allow the implementation of SAM processes to be "accomplished in multiple staged increments or tiers." Part 1 of the standard details SAM processes including control environment, planning and implementation, inventory, verification and compliance, operations management and life cycle. In 2003, the International Organization for Standardization (ISO) and the International Electrotechnical Commission (IEC) began working with the SAM industry to develop a standard of best practices for software asset management programs. Standard ISO/IEC 19770-1:2006, Information technology – software asset management – Part 1, was published by the ISO and IEC in May 2006.

ISO/IEC 19770-2:2015: Software identification tag; establishes specifications for tagging software to optimize its identification and management. The current version was published in 2015 and is a revision to the 2009 original Software ID Tag standard. Using software identification tags or SWID tags makes discovery a simpler and more accurate process that can be verified by software vendors if they audit an organisations entire estate. SWID tags are implemented and supported by many vendors including IBM, Microsoft and Adobe.

ISO/IEC 19770-3: Entitlement Management Schema outlines a technical schema which can be used to encapsulate license details including contract information, entitlements, rights, limitations and details about invoice, PO numbers, etc. This is currently at FDIS (Final Draft International Standard) stage and is due to be published in 2016.

ISO 55000:2014 is the new international standard for asset management and was ratified in January 2014. It provides an overview of asset management, its principles and terminology, and the expected benefits from adopting a comprehensive asset management strategy. This standardisation is driving increased interest in the whole asset management market, including asset management software, and is particularly interesting to asset-intensive organisations including Utilities, Chemical and Transport companies. 19770-1 is aligned with this standard.

ISO 55000:2014 can be applied to all types of assets and by all types and sizes of organization. It is intended to be used for managing physical assets in particular, but it can also be applied to other asset types. By itself it does not cover many of the requirements for IT and Software Asset Management, such as licensing, and the additional controls which are needed in general for software (e.g. for access and integrity), and for complex control situations such as SaaS and BYOD. These additional requirements are being incorporated in edition 3 of ISO/IEC 19770-1 which is based on ISO 55000:2014. Publication is not likely until 2017.

### Issues with Scalability

An example of issues faced when scaling up discovery tools is with Microsoft's System Centre Configuration Manager (SCCM). Using SCCM Metering Rules to monitor software usage across a small estate or a small number of applications is relatively easy and reliable given the total number of unique executables (.exe files) and the number of instances of each executable. Turning on Metering Rules for every packaged application and every executable in a large estate quickly makes the volume of data generated unmanageable and expensive to maintain. Most SAM tools which consume SCCM data rely on these Metering Rules to understand usage.

## Asset Recovery Software

Asset Recovery Software is a business term that refers to a set of software tools or modules used in executing asset recovery transactions, managing buyer relationships, and controlling associated business processes. The key purpose of these tools is to help companies effectively identify, reuse, and divest idle assets.

Although the functionality included in these systems can vary, it commonly includes one or more of the following:

1. Idle asset identification
2. Internal asset redeployment
3. Divestment management
4. Idle asset tracking
5. User management
6. Order management
7. Asset promotion

## Web Accessibility

Asset recovery software can include anything ranging from a small desktop application to an application that resides on a server that can be accessed by many people across diverse geographic locations. The current trend in larger asset recovery departments is toward increased collaboration and web applications. The introduction of cloud technology and the rise Software-as-a-service model led to many new offerings focusing on different aspects of asset recovery. Firms can choose between solutions focusing on internal asset redeployment (e.g. AssetGlobe) or alternatives developed by online auction, asset trading and recycling providers.

## Potential Benefits

Organizations that adopt asset recovery software generally expect to realize several benefits. These can be monetary or process improvement benefits. Some of these benefits include:

1. Process standardization
2. Higher asset sale prices
3. Increased collaboration
4. More redeployments
5. Better identification of idle assets
6. Effective buyer management
7. Better audit preparation
8. Transparent divestment process
9. Increased visibility

# AMS Device Manager

AMS Device Manager is plant asset management software from Asset Optimization (a business unit of Emerson Process Management). It provides a single application for predictive diagnostics, documentation, calibration management, and device configuration for managing field instruments and digital valve controllers.

AMS Device Manager is based on open communication standards, and is a core component of the PlantWeb digital plant architecture.

## Common Uses

AMS Device Manager is used in chemical, food & beverage, life sciences, LNG, pulp & paper, refining, and water & wastewater companies. It is used to increase quality, throughput, and availability, while reducing costs around operations & maintenance, safety, health & environment, In addition, AMS Device Manager facilitates plants and mills to startup faster and deliver a significant return on investment.

## Communication

AMS Device Manager supports digital instrument inputs and outputs; FOUNDATION fieldbus, HART, PROFIBUS DP, PROFIBUS PA, and WirelessHART.

# ManageEngine AssetExplorer

ManageEngine AssetExplorer is asset management software which manages IT assets. It was developed by ManageEngine from ZOHO Corporation. It scans and audits workstations across a network (connected by LAN, WAN and VPN) available in each of the workstations. It requires an initial license fee and annual maintenance fees based on the number of assets and nodes. The free edition has fully functional features but is restricted to 20 nodes.

## Features

ManageEngine AssetExplorer scans all Windows and Linux workstations, and other network devices such as printers, routers, and switches. The scan provides details about installed hardware and software. It uses focused asset groups for better management and control, which allows asset ownership details to be tracked (to get a clear picture of who owns what).

AssetExplorer also manages group licensed software and tracks total number of actual installations versus purchased software licenses.

ManageEngine AssetExplorer provides a single interface to track and view all your assets, audit hardware/ software & track asset ownership with integrated purchase and contract management. Its features also includes software license compliance and usage tracking, Asset tracking, IT asset scanning, asset ownership tracking, hardware & software inventory, maintain audit history, software asset management, software license management, maintain software compliance, software usage tracking, PO & contracts, maintain asset contracts and PO with approvals.

## Rational Asset Manager

Rational Asset Manager (RAM) is a collaborative software development asset management solution that supports the Reusable Asset Specification (RAS) and enables organizations to identify, manage and govern the design, development and consumption of software assets, including services as part of a service-oriented architecture (SOA) initiative.

### Overview

Rational Asset Manager is a development asset management repository that uses the Reusable Asset Specification (RAS) to define, create and modify assets. It provides asset type specific search & governance, and measures asset reuse in development.

Rational Asset Manager handles any kind of asset, such as applications, components, patterns, software that runs systems and products, services, frameworks, templates, etc. Rational Asset Manager includes the following functionality:

Asset upload, download, update, packaging

- Support for asset types, asset categorization, attributes and asset relationships.

Security and access control

- Asset permissions based on groups, roles, users and asset types

Search

- Search using categories/facets/keywords
- File contents search, text, word, powerpoint, ear, war, zip files

Workflow & Review Boards

- Basic review/approval flow built in with configuration possible through integration with Rational ClearQuest

Metrics and reporting

- Record usage, feedback
- Export delimited file

Collaboration

- Discussions, Email and RSS feeds

User interface

- Eclipse v3.2 client
- Web Client

Process guidance

- Asset-based development guidance in Rational Method Composer

Create and update asset versions

- Support for Rational ClearCase, Rational ClearQuest and WebSphere Service Registry and Repository

## Benefits

Rational Asset Manager provides several benefits for development organizations.

- Supports asset based development, warehousing and asset management
- Allows disparate teams to communicate securely and eliminate rework with asset traceability, categorization and utilization monitoring
- Implement compliant standards related to your intellectual property, providing the right level of access to countries, and/or teams.
- Mitigation of risks and lower costs of meeting compliance mandates by securing Intellectual property
- Straightforward discovery, storage and deployment of services in a service-oriented architecture
- Store information that is useful for collaborating on software development of Assets.
- Provides tools for defining, creating, reviewing and retrieving assets.
- Uses the Reusable Asset Specification to describe and classify assets
- Supports any kind of asset - source code, DLLs, documentation, presentations, patterns, process flows, etc.

- Enables you to implement asset based development to and succeed with reuse strategies, cutting development costs.
- Flexible access to assets via an Eclipse or Web client.
- Integrates with other Rational Software and IBM tools, such as Rational System Architect, Rational ClearCase, Rational ClearQuest or WebSphere Service Registry and Repository.

## Computerized Maintenance Management System

Computerized maintenance management system (CMMS), also known as computerized maintenance management information system (CMMIS), is a software package that maintains a computer database of information about an organization's maintenance operations. This information is intended to help maintenance workers do their jobs more effectively (for example, determining which machines require maintenance and which storerooms contain the spare parts they need) and to help management make informed decisions (for example, calculating the cost of machine breakdown repair versus preventive maintenance for each machine, possibly leading to better allocation of resources). CMMS data may also be used to verify regulatory compliance.

CMMS packages may be used by any organization that must perform maintenance on equipment, assets and property. Some CMMS products focus on particular industry sectors (e.g. the maintenance of vehicle fleets or health care facilities). Other products aim to be more general.

CMMS packages can produce status reports and documents giving details or summaries of maintenance activities. The more sophisticated the package, the more analysis facilities are available.

Many CMMS packages can be either web-based, meaning they are hosted by the company selling the product on an outside server, or LAN based, meaning that the company buying the software hosts the product on its own server.

# Permissions

All chapters in this book are published with permission under the Creative Commons Attribution Share Alike License or equivalent. Every chapter published in this book has been scrutinized by our experts. Their significance has been extensively debated. The topics covered herein carry significant information for a comprehensive understanding. They may even be implemented as practical applications or may be referred to as a beginning point for further studies.

We would like to thank the editorial team for lending their expertise to make the book truly unique. They have played a crucial role in the development of this book. Without their invaluable contributions this book wouldn't have been possible. They have made vital efforts to compile up to date information on the varied aspects of this subject to make this book a valuable addition to the collection of many professionals and students.

This book was conceptualized with the vision of imparting up-to-date and integrated information in this field. To ensure the same, a matchless editorial board was set up. Every individual on the board went through rigorous rounds of assessment to prove their worth. After which they invested a large part of their time researching and compiling the most relevant data for our readers.

The editorial board has been involved in producing this book since its inception. They have spent rigorous hours researching and exploring the diverse topics which have resulted in the successful publishing of this book. They have passed on their knowledge of decades through this book. To expedite this challenging task, the publisher supported the team at every step. A small team of assistant editors was also appointed to further simplify the editing procedure and attain best results for the readers.

Apart from the editorial board, the designing team has also invested a significant amount of their time in understanding the subject and creating the most relevant covers. They scrutinized every image to scout for the most suitable representation of the subject and create an appropriate cover for the book.

The publishing team has been an ardent support to the editorial, designing and production team. Their endless efforts to recruit the best for this project, has resulted in the accomplishment of this book. They are a veteran in the field of academics and their pool of knowledge is as vast as their experience in printing. Their expertise and guidance has proved useful at every step. Their uncompromising quality standards have made this book an exceptional effort. Their encouragement from time to time has been an inspiration for everyone.

The publisher and the editorial board hope that this book will prove to be a valuable piece of knowledge for students, practitioners and scholars across the globe.

# Index